MODERNISING SOCIAL WORK
Critical considerations

Edited by John Harris and Vicky White

HAVERING COLLEGE

LEARNING RESOURCES CENTRE

This edition published in Great Britain in 2009 by

The Policy Press
University of Bristol
Fourth Floor
Beacon House
Queen's Road
Bristol BS8 1QU
UK

Tel +44 (0)117 331 4054
Fax +44 (0)117 331 4093
e-mail tpp-info@bristol.ac.uk
www.policypress.org.uk

North American office:
The Policy Press
c/o International Specialized Books Services
920 NE 58th Avenue, Suite 300
Portland,
OR 97213-3786, USA
Tel +1 503 287 3093
Fax +1 503 280 8832
e-mail info@isbs.com

British Library Cataloguing in Publication Data
A catalogue record for this book is available from the British Library.

Library of Congress Cataloging-in-Publication Data
A catalog record for this book has been requested.

ISBN 978 1 84742 005 3 paperback
ISBN 978 1 84742 006 0 hardcover

Cover design by Robin Hawes
Front cover: image kindly supplied by www.jupiterimages.com
Printed and bound in Great Britain by the MPG Books Group

Contents

List of figures

Notes on contributors

(All of the contributors are members of the Modernisation, Managerialism and Social Services Group, School of Health and Social Studies, University of Warwick.)

Katrin Bain (Diplom–Pädagogin) is a PhD student in the School of Health and Social Studies at the University of Warwick. She is a qualified social worker and has worked in Germany and Britain in the fields of children and family social services, youth work and training. Her current research interests include: modernisation of social services, citizenship and service user participation. She is the author (with Simon Lapierre) of 'Parental responsibility and partnership: citizenship and gender in British children and families social services', in E.H. Oleksy, A. Petö and B. Waaldijk (eds), *Gender and Citizenship in a Multicultural Context*, Peter Lang, 2008, pp 77-92.

Nigel Coleman is a Senior Lecturer in Social Work in the School of Health and Social Care at the University of Teesside and a PhD student in the School of Health and Social Studies at the University of Warwick. He is a qualified social worker who has worked in the learning disability and mental health fields both as a practitioner and as a manager. Prior to training as a social worker, he qualified and worked as a nurse with people with learning disabilities. He is the author (with John Harris) of 'Calling social work', *British Journal of Social Work*, 2008, vol 38, no 3, pp 580–99.

Tony Evans is an Associate Professor in the School of Health and Social Studies at the University of Warwick. He is a qualified social worker who has worked in mental health, community care and forensic social work. Before training as a social worker, he worked in policy development and service user representation in social services and the health service. His research and teaching interests focus on: practising policy, community care and mental health and practice research. His forthcoming publications include *Regimes of Discretion in Modern Social Services*, Ashgate, and *Evidence and Knowledge for Practice* (with Mark Hardy), Polity Press.

John Harris is a Professor in the School of Health and Social Studies at the University of Warwick. Before moving into social work education he worked for several years as a social worker and a manager in social services. His teaching and research interests include: managerialism, citizenship and the history of social work. He has written a range of articles and books on these and other topics, including *The Social Work Business*, Routledge, 2003.

Denise Tanner is a Lecturer in the Institute of Applied Social Studies at the University of Birmingham. She worked for many years as a social worker, initially in the voluntary sector, but primarily in adult services in the statutory sector. Her current teaching and research interests include: older people and preventive services; social perspectives on mental distress; and service user involvement in social work education. She has published work in these areas, including: 'Starting with lives: supporting older people's strategies and ways of coping', *Journal of Social Work*, 2007, vol 7, no 1, pp 7–30, and *Working with Older People* (with John Harris), Routledge, 2008.

Peter Unwin is a Senior Lecturer in Health and Social Care at the University of Worcester and a PhD student in the School of Health and Social Studies at the University of Warwick. He is a qualified social worker who has worked at senior levels in managerial and inspectorial positions across the mixed economy of care, as well as having run his own domiciliary care business. He has been involved in a series of consultancies concerning modernisation issues in both children's and adults' services and is particularly committed to working with service users. He is the author of *Health and Social Care Theory and Practice: An Introduction to the Principles and Practice of Care*, Reflect Press, forthcoming.

Vicky White is an Associate Professor in the School of Health and Social Studies at the University of Warwick. In addition to substantial experience in social work education at qualifying and post-qualifying levels, she has worked as a social worker in the statutory sector in a range of services in field and residential settings. Her publications include: *Developing Good Practice in Children's Services* (edited with John Harris), Jessica Kingsley, 2004, and *The State of Feminist Social Work*, Routledge, 2006.

Modernising social work

John Harris and Vicky White

Over the last decade, New Labour's modernisation agenda for social work has produced a barrage of changes, the pace and scale of which have, at times, seemed to pose formidable challenges for everyone involved in social work, whether as service users, practitioners or managers. Those changes have been part of a much wider reform project across the economy and society, driven by how New Labour sees the place of the UK in the contemporary world. The focus of New Labour's sweeping vision of change has been predominantly future-directed; its appeal, or sometimes – more accurately – coercion, to get on board with the changes it has proposed has been pitched around portrayals of desirable destinations to be reached. At the same time, change (obviously) has also involved movement away from somewhere, usually denigrated by New Labour as the redundant past that had nothing very much to commend it. This means that amidst the much-trumpeted processes of reform, there have also been processes of destabilisation. One of these destabilising processes has shattered a view of public services (long held during the period of the post-war social democratic welfare state) as being essentially administrative.

From administering ...

Within the welfare state, a distinction was made between state *administration* of public services, including social work, and *management* of private businesses. This distinction assumed that the ethos of public services was very different from that of private business and that public services had to be grounded in a sympathetic appreciation of their specific purposes, conditions and tasks (White and Harris, 1999). The administrative approach to the welfare state's public services was founded in part on respect for professionalism – its knowledge base and its identification of what was considered to be professionally correct practice. Administration and professionalism coexisted, in the case of social work within local government, through structures that had a measure of bureaucratic hierarchy and that embodied rules and procedures within and through which professionalism operated. By such means, an administrative system was conducive to professional staff, such as social workers, being accorded considerable areas of discretion within their practice and their 'clients' were assumed to benefit from the deployment of their expertise (Harris, 2003, ch 2).

... to managing social work

Movement away from the *administration* of public services and towards their *management* began with the coming to power, from 1979 onwards, of Conservative governments influenced by neo-liberal ideas. The neo-liberal belief that the market was superior to the state in every way undermined the position accorded to public sector professionals, such as social workers, who were seen as cosseted by the administrative systems of the social democratic welfare state. Such ideas also urged a rethinking of the view of service users as passive recipients of professional expertise. The Conservatives saw welfare state professionals as needing to be immersed in 'the bracing competitive stimulus of market forces ... Professions were seen as very much secondary to management as an instrument of effective social policy' (Foster and Wilding, 2000, p 146). They contended that public services such as social work needed to become more like businesses and managed in ways that were drawn from the private sector, functioning in a context that was as market-like as possible (Harris, 2003, ch 3). The advocacy of quasi-markets and the extended role and increased power envisaged for managers (including their perceived ability to speak on behalf of service users against the alleged entrenched self-interest of professionals) undermined the administrative system that had provided the habitat within which welfare state professionalism had thrived.

In this period, the Labour Party echoed the key themes of the Conservative governments' shift from administration to management in public services (Taylor-Gooby and Lawson, 1993, p 2; Butcher, 1995, p 161). Commentators concluded that regardless of which political party was in power in the future, a neo-liberal orientation towards public services was likely to endure (Wilding, 1992, p 204; Pierson, 1994, p 109).

New Labour, neo-liberalism and globalisation

When New Labour came into office in 1997, it inherited public services, including social work, in which aspects of neo-liberalism had become firmly entrenched over 18 years of Conservative government. During the transition, it became clear that there were substantial areas of overlap between the Conservative governments and New Labour. With regard to neo-liberalism, New Labour had much in common with the Conservatives, stressing: the primacy of economic competitiveness; the subordination of social policy to the needs of a competitive national economy; the limited or reduced scope envisaged for government intervention or direction; and a central concern with control over public expenditure (Clarke et al, 2000a, p 13). In this reading of New Labour, it represents a *readjustment* of neo-liberalism,[1] rather than its replacement:

> New Labour ... has embraced most of the neoliberal legacy of Thatcherism and has extended it into new areas. It has also taken the first steps on the road to a routinization of neoliberalism. Thus more

emphasis has been given to securing the operation of the emerging neoliberal regime through normal politics, to developing supporting policies across a wide range of policy fields and to providing flanking mechanisms to compensate for its negative economic, political and social consequences. (Jessop, 2002, p 266)

Within this neo-liberal paradigm, New Labour has laid stress on the significance of globalisation and the need to change 'UK Ltd' so that it is equipped to compete within the modern world that globalisation represents. Globalisation, and the need for national competitiveness in order to respond to its demands, is the macro-context within which New Labour sees its welfare regime, including social work, as operating. This macro-context is defined by the increased openness of national economies to trade and financial flows (Mishra, 1999, ix) and the ensuing 'mobility of capital, investment, production processes and the new forms of technology (particularly information technology)' (Clarke, 2000, p 203). Thus, New Labour's denigration of administrative approaches to public services, such as social work, and its insistence on their managerial transformation, is an aspect of a much wider political rationale concerned with the pressure on nation states to reform their public services in response to the demands for competitiveness in the global economy. At the point New Labour came to power, it became widely accepted that international markets and the global economy exert pressures on the directions social welfare policy takes in particular societies (see, for example, Deacon et al, 1997; George, 1998; Barns et al, 1999). From the position of acceptance of adaptation to globalisation as an uncontrollable phenomenon (Hall, 1998), New Labour consolidated the Conservatives' reforms and pushed beyond them, ensuring that public services, such as social work, were drawn deeper into managerial, market oriented ways of thinking and practising. As in many other countries, what began as a national project under neo-conservative governments became generalised as part of the economic agenda of globalisation (Mishra, 1999, p 51).

For New Labour, as an enthusiastic proponent of globalisation, the phenomenon has not been seen as simply a 'fact of life', although this aspect has often been reiterated. It has also been a source of legitimation for the restructuring of public services: '... globalization is not simply a market-driven economic phenomenon. It is also – and very much – a political and ideological phenomenon ... Thus globalization must also be understood as the transnational ideology of neoliberalism which seeks to establish its ascendancy world-wide' (Mishra, 1999, p 7). So far as social work is concerned, the most relevant dimensions of neo-liberalism have been: first, its emphasis on contracting out service delivery from the public sector to the private and voluntary sectors; second, applying ideas to public services that are drawn from private business management and that focus on securing more economic, efficient and effective services; and third, the privileging of managers, rather than professionals, insisting on managers' brief to improve performance and bring about change, with 'a high degree of prominence placed upon the achievement of targets, the attainment of pre-ordained service levels and a high degree of emphasis placed upon efficiency' (Milner and Joyce, 2005, p 49).

Modernisation

If globalisation has been New Labour's justification for change, the buzzword it has used to capture the changes globalisation requires has been 'modernisation'. Globalisation is the touchstone of New Labour's view of the modern world and modernisation is the process of bringing public services into alignment with that world. In the quest to stamp the rationale of modernisation on the culture of public services, the programme of 'Best Value' played a prominent role soon after New Labour came to power (Department of the Environment, Transport and the Regions,1998; see Harris and Unwin, this volume, Chapter One, for a more detailed consideration). The neo-liberal ethos of Best Value seemed to place 'everything up for grabs'. Best Value was a potent symbol that New Labour was indeed 'new' – different from Labour governments that had been associated with the public services provided by the welfare state. Best Value announced to public services that the mantra of 'economy, efficiency and effectiveness' was not synonymous with Conservative government but represented the kind of ideological consensus discussed earlier.

Under 'Best Value', therefore, the neo-liberal drive for efficiency, which had begun under the Conservatives, continued and was intensified by forcing services such as social work into a 'business performance' mould, with an emphasis on achieving managerial results defined by central government's performance targets (Waine, 2000, p 247). By this means, private sector-style entrepreneurialism and modern commercial practices were harnessed as core components in challenging and transforming the shape and role of public sector services like social work (Newman, 2000). While New Labour accepted the Conservatives' neo-liberal legacy and incorporated it into its modernisation agenda, it gave it twists of its own, intensifying the use of performance measures, emphasising partnership and the use of new concepts derived from 'modern business practice' such as 'stakeholders' (Newman, 2005). Just as significant, however, was New Labour's concern to distance itself from its 'Old Left' past. It did so by depicting itself as 'the Third Way' (Blair, 1998), presenting New Labour as pragmatic, business-like, ideologically neutral and able to find a position on the 'middle ground' in response to any issues it faced (Hall, 1998; Powell, M., 2008a). For example, in *Modernising Social Services*, a key White Paper so far as social work was concerned (Department of Health,1998; discussed at a number of points elsewhere in this volume), difficulties were acknowledged in relation to eligibility and equity in market-based social services, but New Labour was at pains to emphasise that it did not take an 'ideological approach' to service provision (Department of Health, 1998, ch 7).

Modernising Social Services (Department of Health, 1998) signalled that as well as bringing social work within the general ambit of the 'Best Value' regime, New

Labour was setting in train more specific changes. The *Quality Strategy for Social Care* (Department of Health, 2000a) amplified the vision set out in *Modernising Social Services* and emphasised New Labour's desire to see local government delivering the modernisation agenda for social work: 'Delivering high-quality social care services is essentially a local responsibility. The Quality Strategy will set a national framework to help raise local standards, but this will only be achieved through local policy and implementation' (Department of Health, 2000a, para 18). Elements of the design of New Labour's quality system were set out in the *Quality Strategy* and included national service frameworks, national standards, service models and local performance measures against which progress within an agreed timescale would be monitored (Department of Health, 2000a, para 26).

New Labour's early attachment of itself to a discourse of the modernisation of social work (through Best Value, *Modernising Social Services* and the *Quality Strategy*), within the macro-context of globalisation, has continued in the years that have followed. This book picks up on significant strands in New Labour's modernisation agenda for social work during the succeeding years, organising them around three main subject areas.

Part One is concerned with *modernisation and managerialism*. As we have seen, modernisation has been intertwined with neo-liberal managerialism and the contributors to Part One explore three key areas in which this intertwining is evident. Chapter One identifies performance management as the core element in New Labour's vision of the modernisation of social work because it has been the means by which strong central government control of the agenda to be implemented has been maintained. Part of that agenda has been New Labour's embrace and promotion of the use of information and communications technology, which underpins the subject of Chapter Two. In a development that has to date been subject to surprisingly little comment, call (or 'contact') centres are now in widespread use by local authorities as a means of accessing social work. Chapter Two explores the impact of this development. Another largely unremarked but far-reaching development has been the expansion of the employment of agency social workers, which is considered in Chapter Three. The chapter identifies the growth of a 'contract culture' in modernised social work that has brought with it a growth in private sector employment agencies supplying social workers to local authority teams. It considers the ramifications of this form of social work.

Part Two turns to *modernisation and service users*. Chapter Four identifies the problems in squaring New Labour's depiction of those who use modernised social work as independent, choice-seeking consumers with social work's day-to-day involvement with people who are negotiating issues of independence, dependence and interdependence, often in fraught and/or risky situations, or who are subject to controlling interventions in their lives. The limitations encountered in seeking to construct consumerism as a key aspect of modernised social work point to the need to examine the nature of social work's engagement with service users in specific services and this is considered further in Chapters Five and Six. In services for children and families, the relationship between the state and parents is supposedly shaped by the rhetoric of partnership found in New Labour's modernisation policy documents. Chapter Five unravels the concept of partnership by examining how parents are constructed in policy and practice. Chapter Six identifies a growing affinity between research evidence about what adult service users want from social work services and the messages conveyed in modernisation policy documents, but argues that a variety of conflicts and constraints continue to operate at the level of practice and that these can obstruct the delivery of services that meet the requirements and preferences of service users.

Part Three focuses on *modernisation and professional practice* and explores the ways in which professional discretion survives within the intensified culture of scrutiny and control brought about by New Labour's modernisation agenda. Contrary to the arguments of much of the existing literature, Chapter Seven suggests that professional discretion continues to play a role in practice within modernised social work and that social workers use it, in the form of 'quiet challenges', to resist managerial expectations that they consider are not in the interests of service users. In a similar vein, Chapter Eight considers that the widespread characterisation of the relationship between social workers and their managers as fundamentally antagonistic within modernised social work has obscured the extent to which some local managers resist its prevailing 'business culture' through the ways in which they interpret policy and cooperate with practitioners in the structuring of day-to-day practice.

Note

[1] Of course, New Labour is not just a readjustment of neo-liberalism. It also invokes social democratic ideas in order to buttress its arguments. The position taken here follows Hall in seeing neo-liberal ideas as in the 'leading position' in New Labour's agenda (see Hall, 2003).

Part One
Modernisation and managerialism

ONE

Performance management in modernised social work

John Harris and Peter Unwin

Introduction

This discussion of the rise and consolidation of performance management and its impact on social work begins by considering the era from 1945 to 1979, during which faith was placed in professionals as guarantors of the performance of welfare state services, including social work. The New Right's erosion of professionals' responsibility for safeguarding performance standards and its introduction of managerialist approaches to performance management (1979–97) are reviewed, followed by an account of the intensification of such approaches under New Labour (1997 onwards). Issues and implications raised by the current performance management regime are explored and the day-to-day realities of using measures that are primarily quantitative in a work environment that continues to be viewed by much of its workforce as being essentially qualitative are highlighted. After identifying the key features of the performance management regime, the chapter concludes that performance issues will continue to be seen by many as an instrument of control unless their political, ethical, cultural and moral implications are open to debates in which the range of stakeholders with interests in social work can participate.

Performance and bureau-professional social work (1945–79)

In services provided by the post-war welfare state, the individual words 'performance' and 'management' were rarely heard and the concept of 'performance management' had not yet surfaced in that context. Terms such as 'management' and 'performance' were associated with the business world, with 'performance management' originally understood as a company-wide human resources approach to getting the best out of individuals through leadership, coaching, mentoring and appraisal systems. (For more recent contributions based on this understanding of performance management see, for example, Dransfield, 2000, ch 6; Forster, 2005). In contrast to the organisational forms and preoccupations of the business world, the welfare state's services were provided in the main through bureau-professional regimes, such as that of social work in social services departments, established following the Seebohm Report (1968).[1] In these bureau-professional regimes, the 'bureau' element was seen as ensuring impartiality through 'administration', characterised by rules and procedures; administration was 'the process whereby public officials, employed by state agencies, implement[ed] and execute[ed] governmental policies determined by the political authorities, within a framework of law' (Farnham and Horton, 1993, p 27). Within this overarching legal and administrative framework, the provision of services that were seen as not being amenable to the straightforward application of rules, such as social work, were assigned to professional staff, who were given areas of considerable discretion within which to operate (Parry and Parry, 1979, pp 42–3). Any concern with performance, even though not labelled as such, was delegated to this professional element in bureau-professional regimes because professionals were regarded as possessing knowledge and skills that enabled them to define the goals of their work and what constituted acceptable practice in pursuit of those goals. The primacy accorded to professional self-management of performance is captured here in comments by front-line managers responsible for social workers in this era:

> "My intervention would only be through consultation and discussion in the supervisory process. I try to get the individual to develop professionally. I cannot see me dropping into a situation and saying 'I'm not happy about this, this is what I want you to do'. There is a continual dialogue on cases from which decisions come."

> "I see social workers as autonomous. They should accept the responsibilities they have and supervision should be sharing those situations that they feel they need to talk over ... You have to allow social workers their autonomy."

> "Supervision is about giving people a large degree of autonomy about what they do and how they get on with their work. I can't think of an example of a worker going so obviously wrong that I've had to intervene against their wishes."

> "If I was a social worker I would like to think that I was the person who knew better than my supervisor what was happening in a family situation. I would want to be the person to say which people had the visits. Therefore if I were to be allowed to develop in a professional way, my assessment of the situation would have to have bearing on what happens. So I don't interfere as a supervisor. I don't interfere in people's decisions because I don't find the need to."

> (Harris, 1998a, pp 99–100, quoting earlier research by Harris)

The idea that welfare state services comprised bureau-professional regimes that located responsibility for managing performance in the domain of professionals themselves, as reflected in the quotations above, was supported by all parliamentary political parties from 1945 until the late 1970s – that is, until the rise of New Right ideas in the Conservative governments that came to power from 1979 onwards.

Performance and the New Right (1979–97)

The shift to a managerialist approach to performance by Conservative governments was intertwined with their wider commitment to managerialism (Carter et al, 1992). The key ideas underpinning the introduction of managerialism were:

- 'management' is a separate and distinct organisational function;
- progress is seen in terms of increasing productivity;
- increased productivity will come from the application of information and organisational technologies;
- there must be a shift from a focus on inputs and processes to outputs and outcomes;
- measurement and quantification needs to increase;
- markets or market-type mechanisms should be used to deliver services;
- contractual relationships should be introduced;
- customer orientation should be central;
- the boundaries between the public, private and voluntary sectors should be blurred. (Adapted from Pollitt, 1993, pp 2–3, and Pollitt, 2003, pp 27–8)

These specific features of managerialism were welded together by the embrace of managerial power, usually formulated as managers having the 'right to manage'. The manager's role was seen as central to changing the bureau-professional approach to the performance of services by limiting the discretion of professionals. With regard to the latter, public sector services in bureau-professional regimes were depicted as dominated by 'producer interests' (King, 1987; Pollitt, 1993; Cutler and Waine, 1994; Harris, this volume, Chapter Four), particularly those of the professionals who provided them. The spotlight of this critique was turned on local government through the introduction of performance management, which resulted from the interplay of a number of factors: pressure from central government, particularly via the Audit Commission; the promotion of consumerism in public services; the introduction of compulsory competitive tendering; and seeking to change local management cultures (Ghobadian and Ashworth, 1994). As a consequence, services came under pressure to become more efficient so as to reduce their demands on taxpayers, or at least not increase them, while maintaining the volume and quality of services provided to the public (Brignall and Modell, 2002). Thus, Conservative governments' concern with the importance of managing the performance of professionals in local government was located in the rejection of bureau-professionalism and its replacement by an emphasis on performance measured by results (Loughlin, 1994), as the central responsibility of managers, for the purposes of compliance and control (Kloot and Martin, 2000).

Conservative governments pursued the emphasis on performance management in general through the Audit Commission and, specifically in the case of social work, through the Social Services Inspectorate, as well as through the combination of the two bodies in the activities of the Joint Reviews Team (Humphrey, 2002; 2003a; 2003b). The Audit Commission originally located performance management in an approach that stressed the generic expertise and capacity of accountancy-based management as a basis for questioning professional practice (Cochrane, 1994). Subsequently, the Audit Commission developed performance management from this narrower, accountancy-based activity to broader evaluations of performance in resource use, captured by the extent to which performance was giving 'value for money'. 'Value for money' was underpinned by the Audit Commission's advocacy of the three 'e's as a means of judging performance:

> *Economy* means ensuring that the assets of the authority, and the services purchased, are procured and maintained at the lowest possible cost consistent with a specified quality and quantity.

> *Efficiency* means providing a specified volume and quality of services with the lowest level of resources capable of meeting that specification.

> *Effectiveness* means providing the right services to enable the local authority to implement its policies and objectives. (Audit Commission, 1983, p 8)

In parallel to the work of the Audit Commission, the Social Services Inspectorate took on the role of implementing central government's policies in relation to social work (Day and Klein, 1990), as part of an overall shift in the balance of power between central and local government through which central government was able to promulgate its values, methods and language by managing local performance (Burns et al, 1994). In social work at the local level, it became increasingly difficult to adopt policies and priorities that differed from those of central government.

In the context of this developing performance management culture, performance indicators were adopted in a widespread fashion, first in relation to the Citizen's Charter[2] initiative (Audit Commission, 1992; Stewart and Walsh, 1992; Harris, this volume, Chapter Four). Subsequently, the Local Government Act (1992) set the tone for the role performance indicators have played in performance management ever since, by requiring the Audit Commission to produce standardised performance indicators for local authorities so that people would know how their local authorities were doing when measured against the indicators and in order to encourage competition between local authorities (Sanderson, 1992). Performance indicators had first been developed for social services, in a more limited way, a few years before by the Social Services Inspectorate (Warburton, 1988) and subsequently the Social Services Inspectorate was used increasingly not just to regulate the public sector but also to provide public confidence in the performance of the growing independent sector of service providers. Further sets of performance indicators, amended each year, provided comparative data and included benchmarking against similar local authorities, on the assumption that all local authorities would want to attain the levels set by the 'best performers'. In the era of the Conservative governments, reporting on and managing performance as a form of accountability to central government were key aspects of the reconstruction of bureau-professional approaches to performance, discussed earlier. These aspects were to have an enduring impact, way beyond the confines of the Conservative governments, and they continued to exert an influence after the Conservatives lost power.

Performance and New Labour (1997 onwards)

Given that the origins of performance management lay in the agenda of the Conservative governments from 1979 onwards, when New Labour came into office in 1997 it inherited social services, and a public sector generally, in which managerialist approaches to measuring performance had been well established over a period of 18 years. New Labour shared a key assumption of the previous Conservative governments that predisposed it to retain such approaches:

> New Labour is sceptical of the claim that welfare professionals, motivated by a public service ethic, can be relied upon to develop high quality, cost efficient services without external monitoring. From this perspective, a modern welfare state will only operate effectively if central government sets rigorous targets and establishes audit and inspection regimes. (Page, 2007, pp 109–10)

Under New Labour, the Audit Commission reiterated the Conservatives' previous twin rationales for the use of performance management systems: to *improve public services*, through economy, efficiency and effectiveness and to *reinforce accountability*, holding public sector services to account for the resources deployed and the outcomes achieved (Audit Commission, 1999; 2000). In addition, New Labour not only took over the terminology and activities of performance management, such as the setting of explicit targets for services and monitoring performance against them, but also extended performance management, with more measures and greater attention to using performance management in pursuit of its policy goals (Newman, 2005). This intensification of central government's performance management regime has given rise to detailed definition at national level of social work's objectives, the setting of targets to be met locally and central monitoring of the results. In so doing, New Labour has generated a strong performance culture, with local politicians and managers expected to concentrate on achieving

New Labour's targets and ensuring that its programmes are delivered by social workers. These expectations have been reinforced by the production of 'naming and shaming' reports, star rankings and league tables. Exposing performance in this way has been assumed to stimulate continuous improvement.

The most significant initiative early in the life of the first Labour government was the requirement placed on local authorities that they should meet the demands of 'Best Value'. This was a much more extensive, challenging and comprehensive performance regime than anything that had been attempted by the Conservative governments. As part of New Labour's wider modernisation agenda, the White Paper *Modern Local Government: In Touch with the People* (Department of the Environment, Transport and the Regions, 1998) stipulated that constant improvement in both quality and cost would be expected from local government, with 'Best Value' becoming a statutory duty from 1 April 2000. In the process, the three 'e's (mentioned earlier) were resurrected: '[Best Value] is a statutory duty to deliver services taking into account quality and cost by the most effective, economic and efficient means possible' (1999 Local Government Act, Annex A). Over a five-year period, all local authority services were subjected to Best Value Reviews, and Best Value Performance Plans were drawn up. Not only was social work included in this far-reaching evaluative activity, it was also linked specifically to Best Value through requirements to deliver services to clear standards, paying attention to quality and cost and demonstrating a commitment to continuous improvement in the efficiency and effectiveness of its performance (Department of Health, 1998). Thus, the 'modernisation' of social work was rooted in the Best Value regime and was routed through the implementation of national performance standards and targets.

At the core of the Best Value regime were four principles:

- *Challenge* (why and how a service is provided)
- *Compare* (with others' performance, including the use of performance indicators in benchmarking exercises)
- *Consult* (local taxpayers, service users and the business community in setting performance targets)
- *Compete* (as the means to efficient and effective services). (Department of the Environment, Transport and the Regions, 1998)

These four principles gave the performance imperative new urgency: there was no assumption that a particular local authority service should continue, there were no assumptions that services that did continue had to be provided in the same way as previously and there was a constant pressure to save money, which was exacerbated by local authorities having to soak up the cost of the 'baseline assessment' and review processes integral to the Best Value regime, as well as by the expectation that the process would result in efficiency savings (Community Care, 2000, pp 20–1). Overall, as Sanderson commented:

BestValue can be seen as representing a strengthening of the framework of performance management for local government, with a more elaborate structure of performance standards and improvement targets with strengthened central definition, a tighter regime of external audit and inspection, and a more rigorous approach to sanction and intervention by central government in the event of designated performance 'failures'. Moreover, the requirement to subject all services and activities to 'fundamental' review which poses an effective challenge to the 'status quo' represents a more rigorous test of performance than authorities have faced in the past. (Sanderson, 2001, p 307)

BestValue specifically, and the intensification of performance management more generally, have been key dimensions of modernisation: 'The governance of public services is increasingly focused on questions of "performance". The management, measurement, evaluation and improvement of performance have become the dominant concern of an interlocking array of organizations, relationships and practices of governing' (Clarke, 2004, p 126). This 'interlocking array' has been seen as necessary by New Labour in order to meet the requirements of the modern world and find business-based solutions for the operation of public sector services. Business principles and methods have been seen as core components in challenging and transforming the shape and role of the whole of the public sector (Newman, 2000), including social work (Harris, 2003, ch 6). Within this approach, one particular initiative was the establishment of the Public Services Productivity Panel in 2000, which brought together business and public sector leaders in a quest for greater productivity and efficiency in public services and a drive to improve their performance. This was to be achieved in part through the introduction of Public Service Agreements between central and local government, with SMART (specific, measurable, achievable, relevant, timed) targets to fine-tune the attainment of central government priorities at the local level, later measured through Comprehensive Performance Assessments of local councils in England and Wales, devised by the Audit Commission (Page, 2007, p 119).[3]

In relation to social work, performance elements were set out in the *Quality Strategy for Social Care* and included national service frameworks, national standards, service models and local performance measures against which progress within an agreed timescale would be monitored (Department of Health, 2000a, para 26). The *Strategy* gave the Social Services Inspectorate the responsibility for setting and monitoring standards for each local authority's social services functions. These were specific to each inspection and were intended for use by local authorities in their own audit and review processes (Department of Health, 2000a, para 27), keying the *Strategy* into the surrounding performance regime in its support for the implementation of BestValue (Department of Health 2000a, para 31).

The *Quality Strategy for Social Care* reflected New Labour's overall concern to modernise government through performance management and to place the modernisation of social services within that concern (Department of Health, 1998) through its typically top–down approach within a competitive ethos (Hood, 1998). Following the *Strategy*, a Performance Assessment Framework was developed and a system of star ratings became the way of 'badging' a local authority's social services performance as follows:

- three stars – excellent
- two stars – good
- one star – adequate
- zero stars – inadequate.

The awards are based on meetings with councils and inspections of council social care services, looking at council statistics and how well councils had met their own plans for improving their services (Commission for Social Care Inspection, 2008a).

Although social services in local councils have since divided according to whether they cater for adults or children and families, the performance indicators that were initially developed in the generic Performance Assessment Framework live on in the work of the Commission for Social Care Inspection's performance management activities in relation to services for adults.[4] Here is one example of a performance indicator against which local authority performance is assessed:

Indicator	**AO/B12 Cost of intensive social care for adults and older people**
Definition	Average gross weekly expenditure per person on supporting adults and older people in residential and nursing care and providing intensive home care.
The numerator	Gross total cost for residential and nursing care and home help/care for all adult client groups and older people during the year. *Source: PSS EX1 sheet Incl SSMSS column I (Gross total cost (Current expenditure including capital charges): Total (including joint arrangements)) lines (C2 + C3 + C6 + D2 + D3 + D6 + E2 + E3 + E6 + F2 + F3 + F6) (nursing care placements, residential care placements and home care for older people (aged 65 or over) including older mentally ill, adults aged under 65 with a physical disability or sensory impairment, adults aged under 65 with learning disabilities and adults aged under 65 with mental health needs)*
The denominator	The total number of weeks all adult client groups and older people were supported in residential and nursing care during the year (including both permanent and temporary residents) plus the total number of weeks that full cost paying residents spent in local authority care homes or, if

the fees are included in the expenditure for the numerator, in other residential care or nursing care placements.
Source: PSS EX1.

Plus 52 times   The number of households receiving intensive home care (More than 10 contact hours and 6 or more visits during the week) during the sample week.
Source: HH1 Table 3B (collected on PSS EX1).

(Department of Health, 2007a)

This single example serves to illustrate the impenetrability of the performance indicators as a whole. While it is widely accepted within social work that care at home is the preferred choice of the vast majority of older or disabled people, and hence it would be appropriate that any performance regime looked at, say, comparative levels of intensive home care and residential/nursing home provision, there are many complex qualitative considerations that are obscured by such performance indicators. Similarly, such quantitative indicators of performance do not allow for professional judgement or discretion by social workers once a certain financial threshold is reached, as the example below, from the working week of a social worker in an acute hospital, illustrates:

"Mr 'X' was an elderly man with very complex physical and mental health problems whose supportive family wanted to play a part in a discharge plan coordinated by the social worker which involved intensive home care. However, the cost of this care package was more than the net cost of a residential home placement. Mr 'X' was informed that unless either he or his family could pay the difference between the costs of the cheaper provision (the residential home) and his preferred care at home package, then he would have to go into a residential home. The financial situation of Mr 'X' and his family meant that the additional 'top-up' fee that such an arrangement would have entailed made the residential home in effect the only choice – cheaper and 'efficient' in managerial terms but totally against core social work values of empowerment and participation in service delivery." (Unpublished interview conducted by Peter Unwin)

Banks' reflection on this kind of situation suggests:

While social workers may work towards empowering individuals to take control over parts of their personal lives, unless the policies and practices in the state welfare system and in society generally that oppress certain individuals and groups are changed, then social work can only go so far towards putting these principles into action. (Banks, 2006, p 122)

We now turn to the wider issues and implications that are raised by the embedding of social work in performance management systems.

Performance management – issues and implications

Sanderson et al (1998) identify seven limitations in the adoption of performance management within local authority services:

- Performance measurements tend to be 'top down' in nature, reflecting the perspectives and values of senior management and neglecting the positions of other stakeholder groups.
- The emphasis on quantifiable measures of performance means there is a danger that aspects of service quality that are particularly valuable to service users will be underplayed.
- There is difficulty in capturing broader effects and impacts which may be of particular concern to local communities.
- There are limits to the degree to which equity considerations can be captured through quantitative indicators.
- Performance measurement has particular limits in the context of multi-agency partnership working where it may be difficult to ascribe outcomes to individual agency effort.
- There are limits to which factors that have contributed to processes in organisational performance can be captured quantitatively.
- Performance measurement systems provide a partial picture of what is happening; they do not provide an understanding of why it is happening and, therefore, contribute little to a culture of learning.

In Smith's (1995) consideration of the use of performance indicators, he argues that the dominant philosophy informing their use is 'managerial cybernetics':

> In its crudest form this envisages the managerial process as follows. Organizational objectives are identified. Performance indicators are developed to reflect these objectives. Targets are set in terms of the performance indicators. Management then chooses action and effort to achieve the targets. Progress towards targets is monitored using the PIs and – if there is a divergence from targets – new targets are set and appropriate remedial action is taken. So the process continues. Thus central to the cybernetic model is the notion of *feedback* as serviced by the system of PIs. (Smith, 1995, pp 279–80, original emphasis)[5]

However, in an account that is otherwise supportive of performance management, Smith nevertheless suggests that the use of the cybernetic model of performance management will have unintended consequences for the internal management of public sector organisations because the people involved can anticipate the actions of the controller, the performance management system. He identifies eight unintended consequences:

tunnel vision – an emphasis by management on phenomena that are quantified in the performance management system at the expense of unquantified aspects of performance;

suboptimisation – the pursuit of narrow local objectives at the expense of overall objectives;

myopia – the pursuit of short-term targets at the expense of legitimate long-term objectives. Kloot and Martin similarly suggest that 'performance management in local government is ... largely grounded in operational concepts of efficiency ... much of the pressure for improved performance in the short-term may militate against strategic planning and strategic performance management' (2000, pp 233–5);

measure fixation – despite a measure not fully capturing all of the dimensions of an associated objective, the pursuit of the reported measure rather than furthering the associated objective. For example, managers may be concerned to meet performance measures rather than being interested in the quality of social workers' practice as the associated objective (and see Hunt and Campbell, 1998);

misrepresentation – the deliberate manipulation of data;

misinterpretation – the controller (the performance management system) misinterpreting the data provided;

gaming – minimising the apparent scope for performance improvement to avoid increased expectations and higher targets in the future;

ossification – organisational paralysis brought about by an excessively rigid performance evaluation system.

Such dysfunctional consequences of performance management are frequently the source of jokes and anecdotes in behind-the-scenes conversations with managers but are massaged out of official accounts. This is a scenario reminiscent of Eastern European countries during Communist Party government. Then, officials would convey privately the 'reality' of what was happening, for example in relation to their responsibility for meeting some aspect of a five-year plan, often through stories and jokes that pointed to the absurdity of the system and their role within it, only to return to poker-faced seriousness and apparent deep commitment to that system when in meetings. This is uncannily like organisational experiences in 'modernised' social work.

Other aspects of those organisational experiences are that: performance management is essentially concerned with quantitative data, with contemporary social work ever more focused on forms of case management in which budgetary considerations predominate; the environment in which social workers operate is becoming increasingly complex and resource-constrained; and social work practice is subject to myriad local and national reorganisations and new legislation. Yet the core of everyday social work interactions and decisions remains essentially qualitative and small-scale in nature (Thompson, 2005; Watson and West, 2006). Given this tension between the qualitative nature of everyday social work and its surrounding quantitative performance management environment, it is perhaps not surprising that the experience of the hospital social worker mentioned earlier (in the case of Mr 'X') and that of the children's team manager, to be considered shortly, indicates a level of commitment to the culture of performance management that views it, at best, as 'interesting' and, at worst, as 'another stick to beat us with'.

Performance management in practice

A team manager for children's services in an inner city receives a 'Monthly Performance Management Report' that contains over 1,600 individual pieces of data against 22 identified targets. The performance indicators include measures such as 'number of referrals processed within 24 hours', 'number of initial assessments processed in 7 days' and 'percentage of children in need without a named worker'. The team manager reports that, at best, such measures are 'interesting' but take no account of the socio-economic make-up of the team's community, nor do they reflect vacancy levels and sickness levels. (There is a column for sickness and vacancy levels in the midst of this data, but this column is apparently always blank.) The data contain other measures such as 'average days to complete child protection enquiries', suggesting (although not actually stating) that there is an objective empirical measure for such activities. There is a further section of the Monthly Performance Management Report concerned with 'Looked After Children' that identifies educational and health targets, reflecting needs that have been neglected historically in the population of Looked After Children. However, the stark statistic showing that the teams across the authority do not even reach 50% attainment of the set targets in this area makes it unsurprising that the team manager sees such numbers as "another stick to beat us with – it's not that we don't want Looked After Children to have education and dental plans, it's their prioritisation against a flood of child protection plans and high vacancy levels that we cannot manage at our level".

The team manager goes on to report that his first reaction on receiving the monthly information is to establish where his team is in the comparative rankings with other teams, not wanting to be the best or the worst, stating that the best position to occupy is somewhere in the middle. If his team is the 'best' performing, then the perceived risk is that the team will be held up by management as an example of excellence to be emulated and visited and would be criticised should it lose this position in the rankings. The worst position is seen as being at the bottom of the rankings, as this is seen as likely to attract great attention from management, directed towards a 'problem' team that is letting down the corporate performance, ostensibly for no good reason. Performance management reasoning seems to be that if other teams can achieve the targets, then any team can do so, regardless of issues such as vacancy and sickness levels and without reference to a team's socio-economic context, which may vary significantly from that of others in terms of age stratification, income, wealth, employment and cultural mix. These factors compound recruitment difficulties; it is harder to find social workers for teams that operate in stressful socio-economic environments, many social workers preferring to work in the more attractive parts of a local authority. There is little room on the performance management agenda, however, for the consideration of such factors and the senior managers and politicians in any authority are presented with the 'facts' rather than with any contextualised analysis of those 'facts'. It could be argued, therefore, that rather than being a driver for excellence, performance management is a driver for mediocrity, team managers being concerned primarily to be 'somewhere in the middle' and hence out of the spotlight in terms of senior management attention. This team manager's experience points to the power of the 'unintended consequences' of the managerial cybernetics model of performance management, mentioned earlier (Smith, 1995). The account highlights 'ossification' within the system, 'tunnel vision' (in the concentration on certain aspects of social work) and subsequent 'gaming' as a response by the team manager and his peers.

This example begins to suggest that the issue of performance management within local authority social work teams is contentious and characterised by a range of professional–managerial–political tensions. The position of the increasing numbers of social workers who work in settings outside local authorities is even more complex in terms of accountability, value base and the extra performance measures that might be brought to bear on the social work task. For example, many social workers in acute hospital settings have now been incorporated into 'integrated discharge teams', this change of name in itself indicating that an instrumental, managerial role is expected of social workers in their work alongside health professionals. The traditional tensions inherent in being a hospital social worker have been greatly exacerbated since the advent of the 2003 Community Care (Delayed Discharges etc.) Act, which introduced a performance policy for social work of reimbursements being payable to a health authority if a patient were assessed as being fit for discharge but the local authority was unable to effect discharge plans within a set period. Such measures, while consistent with performance management in being designed to increase efficiency and effectiveness, take little consideration of the personal, familial, social and cultural components of a hospital discharge, particularly where older people are concerned (Henwood, 2006; Taylor, 2007). Such a policy is also difficult to reconcile with the wealth of government (Department of Health, 2001a; 2006) and best practice advice (Taylor, 2005; Sharkey, 2007) regarding the key role of high-quality, multi-dimensional models of assessment.

Thus, social workers in health settings have to work in environments with two lines of managerial accountability and with performance indicators that do not sit easily with core social work values. The NHS White Paper (Department of Health, 1997) emphasised the need for performance management across the

NHS and led to the 1999 Health Act, which imposed systems of targets, league tables and payment by results incentives aimed at motivating the NHS to be more efficient. As we have seen, subsequent legislation, such as the 2003 Community Care (Delayed Discharges etc.) Act, has amplified the controlling nature of such policies by introducing financial sanctions on local authorities if patients who are ready for discharge are not processed within a set period. Such strategies might be seen to sit uneasily with the mantra of 'partnership' that underpinned the *NHS Improvement Plan* (Department of Health, 2000b) and certainly they serve to heighten the tensions and conflicts around performance management for social work staff based within hospital settings.

The tensions in the hospital social work role created by this heightened performance-management culture are described by the hospital social worker mentioned earlier:

> "When working as part of a hospital discharge team, the pace of work is fast. The social worker glimpses and is privy to a brief snap-shot of the patient's long life. The pressures of reimbursement dictate that assessments are completed within a very short time frame. The social worker will encounter families where there may have been many years of complicated dysfunctional relationships. Different family members may have their own agendas; their relative's property/finances may be viewed differently by different family members. My line manager's not a social worker by profession and his favourite phrase is 'quick and dirty assessment'."

The social worker's reservations about performance in relation to hospital discharge are in part supported by the Commission for Social Care Inspection, whose report analysed seven local authorities' performance in this area of work and found that 'Reimbursement seems to have speeded up hospital discharge but its impact, in terms of the quality of older people's post hospital support is much more mixed ... in some cases disempowering individuals and undermining their potential for improvement and rehabilitation' (Commission for Social Care Inspection, 2004a, p 4). There was no outcry at this indictment of a performance management system, despite the same report's also finding that emergency admissions of older people to hospital were continuing to rise, with a particular rise in readmissions, following the introduction of reimbursement under the 2003 Community Care (Delayed Discharges etc.) Act. However, as Henwood comments, all the readmission data in this report failed to reveal anything of 'the qualitative experience of people who may have been discharged too soon or with inadequate support and who somehow cope, but whose quality of life could have been considerably enhanced given more effective discharge planning and adequate post-discharge support arrangements' (Henwood, 2006, p 400).

Financial penalties for failing to meet performance targets were also part of the experience of the hospital social worker mentioned earlier, when working as part of an accident and emergency team, given that the Department of Health had set a performance management target, with associated financial incentives for providers, that 98% of patients should be processed through accident and emergency departments in hospitals within four hours. Accordingly, if financial penalties for breaching this target are to be avoided, multi-disciplinary screening of patients within a maximum four-hour time span is the performance standard that has to be achieved. The different ways in which hospital patients are viewed in the light of performance management imperatives are illustrated by the hospital social worker:

> "My own experience of working in A&E as part of such a team is that, in reality, there are relatively few patients who fit the criteria of being a social admission. The danger can be seen that medical staff, under pressure of patients breaching[6] and also under pressure of no bed availability, will declare a patient as having a social need when there are underlying medical issues that have not yet been explored. From my own experience it is not unusual to have a patient referred when they have been in A&E for over 3 hours. Once received, the Rapid Response Team (usually a nurse/therapist and a social worker) has a set timescale to respond. Very often the patient is elderly, has fallen and cannot mobilise. However, often the X-ray results are not available and the patient may not have been given any pain relief. The Rapid Response Team cannot therefore assess and the patient may consequently breach. The A&E department would seem to have been responding to the pressure of the penalty rather than thinking and acting in the best interest of the patient."

In hospital settings, then, the social worker is faced with additional and conflicting demands of performance management from different disciplines. A&E has a four-hour target to move patients on from its department, the hospital as a whole has targets to meet in terms of reducing waiting lists and there are payment-by-results and reimbursement fines to consider. These pressures easily run into conflict with social work values, and even when a social worker has agreed a discharge plan with the patient, carer(s) and health personnel there may then be a funding panel for the hospital social worker to attend, where financial help with domiciliary care costs is considered by a panel of managers. The social worker has to complete the assessment and care plan and then send it electronically to be considered by a panel of managers. These managers are from different areas of social care: there is a representative from the hospital, who will be mindful of reimbursement, and a representative from Intermediate Care, who will be mindful of performance indicators and the 'best' type of referral to accept. There is also a home-care manager, who will be mindful of her own service's pressures. The patient/service user and the social worker are far removed from this layer of managing performance.

Limitations of performance management

The two examples we have considered from social work practice would seem to support the view of Sanderson et al (1998), whose research across local authorities found a general failure to promote a shared culture of learning and understanding about performance management strategies to staff at the grass roots. Hence performance management was perceived by front-line staff largely as an instrument of control. Davis et al (2001) express similar reservations in an examination of the impact of inspectorate regimes across a number of local authorities and state that, while strong a priori reasons for inspection exist, there is a need to balance local flexibility with national prescription if a sense of ownership by front-line staff is to stand any chance of being achieved. Davis et al (2001) also draw attention to the costs of such forms of performance management, estimating that the cost of the range of external local government inspectorates in the UK was then around £600 million. Additional costs of this form of performance management were also identified in the study, including compliance costs, opportunity costs, the stifling of innovation, the skewing of priorities and damage to staff morale. The dominance of inspection as the preferred mode of performance monitoring in many areas was seen to derive from a lack of trust in the alternatives, rather than in the proven nature of inspection as a way to improve performance. Sanderson et al (1998), Sanderson (2001) and Davis et al (2001) found that public sector performance management was experienced as a top-down instrumental managerial imposition, with a dominant concern for enhancing control and securing accountability upwards and the emphasis being placed on 'the right to manage'.

Whereas early incarnations of managerialism were concerned with establishing the legitimacy of the right to manage, contemporary performance management seeks to secure the right to manage *anything and everything*, to bear down on workers and work processes in pursuit of the required performance targets. In this sense, the emphasis on performance 'sustains managerialism, emphasising the value, authority and autonomy of managers' (Clarke, 2004, p 31). The managerial language reflects this, with managers referring to 'driving down', 'drilling down', 'tying down'; the phrases always seem to express forceful intentions and those intentions are always travelling downwards in pursuit of performance indicators, in much the same way that performance measures in the private sector exert a downward pressure in pursuit of profits.

That is not the only sense in which performance management in the public sector simulates features of the private sector and of the business world in which the private sector operates. There are two other respects in which comparisons can be made. First, the publication of performance indicators mimics the operation of the market. Moriarty and Kennedy (2002) highlight the use of performance measurement as a substitute for market pressures, and Johnsen stresses:

> The potential [*sic*] important functions that PIs can have in political competition analogous to how prices function in market competition

... PIs may effectively function as carriers of information, functioning as 'prices' in political markets, in much the same way as prices do in ... product markets. (Johnsen, 2005, p 14)

Another dominant image of the public in performance management is that of the taxpayer, anxious to see her/his interests met through the revelation of efficient, cost-effective services with business-like practices (Clarke et al, 2000a, p 260). Drawing on this imagery, performance indicators create a public sector version of the stock market, with the taxpayer as investor, scrutinising league tables to see whether her/his stock at the local school or hospital or social work agency has risen or fallen and how the performance of these local services compares with those of similar organisations elsewhere. This public aspect of performance management, represented in league tables and a flow of naming and shaming reports, creates mistrust, the very opposite to the declared intention of the performance management system. Mistrust is also a feature of some of the dysfunctions of performance management identified by Smith (1995) and set out earlier. The adaptation to the process of performance management on the part of those subjected to it is fertile ground for the development of mistrust. If organisations are to render accounts of their performance in a form that is manageable, they have to produce and shape the information on which performance management relies. They have to construct what counts as performance.

Even if there were none of these dysfunctions in the process of constructing what counts as performance, the measures of performance would only help those receiving a service. Performance management focuses overwhelming attention on *current* service users and neglects those refused a service (Tanner, 2001a; 2001b), because it zooms in on efficiency in delivering 'core business' (Newman, 2000, p 54). From this perspective, social work is reduced to a series of service transactions, translated into categories for judgement, for the purposes of performance management. In the process, social work is represented as a neutral machine for the production of services, divorced from wider questions of equity and social justice. Questions in relation to the latter are compartmentalised in vague policy aspirations about social inclusion and in the 'value base' of the people providing the service:

> The panoply of performance monitoring and management systems ... has provided a means of separating workers from the lived experience of users. The detailed documentation of virtually everything that is done for clients ... which is now embodied in care ... planning documents, assessments and reviews ... monitoring reports etc. is fast becoming a vast simulacrum, a deceptive substitute, for real contact. The point is that such documentation is not designed to promote emotional contact, dialogue and learning but to enable the organisation to look *as if* it is doing these things. Appearance has become inextricably confused with reality or, semiotically speaking, the system of signification (the

documentation) has become a thing in itself, masking rather than revealing actual social relations of welfare. (Hoggett, 2000, pp 151–2, original emphasis)

Similarly, Clarke et al (2000b, p 257) describe how performance management within local authorities has led to a situation in which 'the single-minded pursuit of "success" is now understood to have both unanticipated consequences and perverse effects'. For example, organisations try to promote good news stories, despite their dwindling resources, because they must promote themselves as successful in the climate of competition.

Having considered some of the issues, implications and limitations of performance management in social work, we turn finally to aspects of the functioning of the performance management regime itself.

The performance management regime

In principle, a distinction should be made between performance measurement and performance management. The former entails the surveillance of performance, whereas the latter is concerned with what is to be done in response to the results of performance measurement (Radnor and McGuire, 2004). In most social work organisations, this clear analytical distinction is no longer valid. Performance is managed *in advance*, in anticipation of and in preparation for performance measurement. As a consequence, there are contractual relationships at every level of the organisation (Newman, 2005, pp 101–2), based on the criteria against which performance measurement will occur in the future, and constructed in terms of principal–agent transactions (Alford, 2004):

> These roles, (that is of principal and agent) operate in a cascading chain of relationships from politicians to department heads down through the hierarchy all the way to the team leader and the social worker. A principal is she who sets the task; an agent is he who implements it … Through [the use of performance measurement and performance indicators] control is exerted all the way down from the centre of government to the street-level of service delivery … Performance measurement 'creates' social work practice in that it determines which specific forms of practice are drawn into the framework of accountability (and are therefore authorised) … In this way, the design principles of a reformed state become the driving force for the reconstitution of professional practice. (McDonald, C., 2006, p 71)

Seen in this light, performance management is shorthand for a whole range of changes at different levels in the delivery of social work, some of which can be tentatively sketched out.

Central government (principal) – local government (agent)

The New Labour vision of how social work should be 'modernised' emanates from strong central government control and direction of the modernisation agenda that has to be implemented. Acting like a corporate headquarters, New Labour defines social work's objectives at national level, sets targets to be achieved locally and measures the results. Local government, as central government's agent, is expected to exhibit local leadership, entrepreneurialism and a strong performance culture with regard to the achievement of the targets set by central government (Waine, 2000). This smacks of a public sector model of (quasi-)franchising – 'franchise holders, although legally independent, must conform to detailed standards of operation designed and enforced by the parent company' (Dicke, quoted in Ritzer, 2000, p 36) – with central government requiring local government to carry out its policies according to its requirements. The *Quality Strategy for Social Care* (Department of Health, 2000a), considered earlier, exemplified this understanding of the principal–agent relationship as involving the local delivery of central government's agenda: 'Delivering high-quality social care services is essentially a local responsibility. The Quality Strategy will set a national framework to help raise local standards, but this will only be achieved through local policy and implementation' (Department of Health, 2000a, para 18). Central government designs the framework and local (authority) franchisees deliver, thus ensuring the primacy of central government in determining what is seen as significant, in performance terms, in social work.

Councillors/senior managers (principals) – local managers/social workers (agents)

Performance management has strengthened the power of senior managers in their pursuit of the numbers that will stack up to a satisfactory assessment of performance for local councillors vis-à-vis their positioning in relation to central government. As we noted earlier, senior managers' language is increasingly characterised by top-down expressions. This bearing down through the organisation sometimes results in overbearing, frantic activity, particularly as a day of reckoning on performance looms, in a way that is reminiscent of the pursuit of targets in the five-year plans of Stalinist Russia. Figes' account of the latter has echoes of the atmosphere in local authority social work agencies as an inspection looms and the pressure is on to chase information, fill in forms etc. as ends in themselves: 'It made sense to "storm" production, to work for a brief and frenzied spell to reach the goal' (Figes, 2007, p 187).

Social workers (principals) – service users (agents)

Social workers experience performance management as control and, sometimes, the arbitrary pursuit of a particular performance indicator.[7] One aspect of control is social workers' sense of having decisions taken away from them, for example, through the gatekeeping exercised by resource panels, as discussed above, and of not being valued other than in their role of feeding the demand for performance measurement information. There is little in performance management that intrinsically values or encourages social workers to improve the detailed content of their practice and there is a lack of meaning and fit between quantitative performance measures and what is valued by social workers in the qualitative content of their day-to-day work, as they do the best they can for service users. Accordingly, social workers are increasingly having to resist the robotic tendencies of care management or the inflexibility of the expectations placed on parents (Bain, this volume, Chapter Five), as service users are seen as potential statistics to be measured for the performance management system.

Conclusion

What has become clear is that performance management presents measures of performance, and identification of the extent to which they have been met, as readily identifiable through the use of what is portrayed as a technical, objective, neutral approach to which all can subscribe and in which all can be actively involved; this ideal typifies New Labour's overarching search for ways in which total inclusion in a perfect consensus can be achieved (O'Sullivan, 2000). In contrast, we might point to 'the ineliminable place of conflict' (Mouffe, 2000) in the constitution of anything so politically, ethically and morally charged as social work. There are many interests and many goals at play when its performance is considered. Schaarschuch and Schnurr (2004) make this clear in their consideration of the determination of the quality of social work services, which they see as a 'field of conflict'; they argue that the quality of services is always a relative and relational concept (as is 'performance').[8] For example:

> **The state** has an interest in intervening in the way of life of service users and in doing so economically, efficiently and effectively.
> **Social workers** have an interest in maintaining a level of discretion within which they can define what counts as a high standard of performance (i.e. what they see as 'good work').
> **Service users** have an interest in being provided with a service that connects with the difficulties they are experiencing and respects their autonomy.

> (Adapted from Schaarschuch and Schnurr, 2004)

Even this initial identification of some of the interests that may be at stake suggests that there will be a struggle over what counts as performance and how performance should be managed (and by whom). Performance is, at least potentially, contentious and contested. It is simply that the domination of political and managerial interests in the current performance management system obscures this complexity and forces it below the surface. One example of this is the way in which performance management systems are represented as being centrally concerned with the 'customer' and moulding services to their needs: 'Evaluative agencies have been constructed as representatives (if not champions) of the public as consumers. They construe themselves as at least potentially adversarial to "producer interests" in the role of representatives of users/consumers' (Clarke et al, 2000b, p 261). If the range of interests with a stake in the performance of social work were surfaced, rather than subsumed within political and managerial interests, there would need to be processes through which dialogue could take place, leading to (temporary and renegotiable) agreements and compromises about what counted as performance that recognised the power relations of different participants, as well as their different interests in and perspectives on performance.

The challenges in trying to shake off many social workers' perception of issues of performance as anything other than a form of control are clearly formidable. It may be that any embedding of such issues will only come about when social workers, their local managers, service users and communities are able to have an input into the process and the type of data collected and are given access to meaningful fora in which the political, ethical, cultural and moral implications and interpretations of such data can be openly debated and contextualised.

Notes

[1] This refers to developments in England and Wales. There were variations in the other two UK jurisdictions (Haubrich and McLean, 2006).

[2] John Major's *Citizen's Charter* set out the means by which services were supposed to be made more responsive to their users (Prime Minister, 1991), particularly through the more specific charters that were developed, such as the Community Care Charter. By 1996 there were 42 charters for public services, accompanied by over 100,000 local charters (May, 2001, p 288).

[3] One impact of devolution has been that Wales and Scotland have developed performance assessment frameworks that are less prescriptive and less intrusive, relying to a greater extent on self-assessment, than those still in use in England (see Haubrich and McLean, 2006), although, at the time of writing, changes are being contemplated for the English system from 2009.

[4] Children's services are monitored by OFSTED through Joint Area Reviews (OFSTED, 2007).

[5] The then Chief Inspector at the Commission for Social Care Inspection provided an account of the role of regulation that is entirely consistent with this cybernetic model: 'Modern inspection should contribute to improvement but does it? Yes – but we are not an improvement agency. It is those who deliver services and

purchasers or commissioners that implement improvement. Through inspection the Commission assesses whether a particular service needs to improve. Through our dialogue with the people who own or manage a service, we agree what should improve. Later on we assess whether the service has indeed improved' (Behan, 2006, p 17).

[6] 'Breaching' refers to occasions when the four-hour target is breached (not met).

[7] As, for example, when a team of social workers told us about being pressured to 'come up with a child' that could be adopted so that a target would be met in time.

[8] The discourse on quality management is, in effect, about performance.

TWO

This is the modern world! Working in a social services contact centre[1]

Nigel Coleman

Introduction

> Information Technology is a powerful enabler but the starting point should always be to identify what the customer wants and then look to how we use IT to achieve this. The public sector must embrace new ways of thinking, new ways of doing business, new alliances and new technology. This is vital in order to give people the services they want, when they want them and with the minimum cost and bureaucracy. Electronic access to government services will become increasingly important to citizens and by 2005 we plan to have all of our services available in this way. (Cabinet Office, 2000a)

New Labour's modernisation agenda is epitomised by e-government, which sees the use of information and communications technology (ICT) as the principal means of achieving modern 'joined-up' public sector services. The use of ICT in social services is consistent with this general concern and the use of call centre technology (in 'contact centres'[2]) is the latest development in this direction. E-government has been presented as a way of increasing citizen participation and access to both central and local government services. As the opening quotation makes clear, the target set for all services was that they should be e-accessible by 2005 (brought forward from the original target of 2008). This target put pressure on local authorities for their services to be 'open all hours' and encouraged them to set up contact centres to achieve this. The readiness to employ ICT can be seen as consistent with managerialism in public sector services and as a visible manifestation of a commitment to one of its central features – consumerism (Harris, this volume, Chapter Four). An example of this is the contact centres now in widespread use in local authorities as a means of accessing a diverse range of services, including social care services (Coleman and Harris, 2008). This development has resulted in social workers being employed in a different environment and having to work in new ways. Despite this far-reaching development, and its implications for social work staff and service users, there has been a distinct lack of research in this area and studies of public sector contact centres have 'barely registered on the academic radar' (Bain et al, 2005, p 4).

This chapter analyses the relationship between New Labour's modernisation agenda, managerialism and ICT and then moves on to look at the relationship between ICT and social work in a contact centre. The principal focus is on the experience of working in a contact centre as a social worker and the role and identity of social workers in this context is examined. The contact centre employs not only qualified social workers but also unqualified 'first contact officers'[3] and is used to resolve callers' problems, redirect callers to other sources of help or refer them to specific social work teams. The chapter provides insights into how the contact centre environment positions social workers in relation to service users and how the use of ICT affects work processes. It also considers what motivates social workers to work in this environment, their perceptions of occupational stress in this setting and the effect that this model of service delivery has on their social work skills. Finally, it examines research in the public and private sectors to see what it has to offer in relation to the social services context, before reflecting on the implications for social work in the future.

New Labour: using ICT to modernise social work

Since 1997, New Labour governments have actively promoted the use of ICT as a key feature of their modernisation of the public sector and as a way of addressing what have been characterised as its failings (this volume, Chapters One [Harris and Unwin] and Four [Harris]). A key feature of the modernisation agenda has been the facilitation of 'electronic government' (e-government). This is intended to provide public access via computer and telephone to information about the services offered by both central and local government agencies, as well as offering the ability to engage with these services (Coleman and Harris, 2008, p 582). The use of contact centres, and the technology associated with them, appeared to be one way (within already over-stretched budgets) that they could meet the requirement to make their services e-accessible and operational outside normal office hours (National Audit Office, 2002). The development of contact centres to facilitate the delivery of social services can be seen, therefore, as an example of the government's eagerness to promote technological systems and approaches as part of more consumer-oriented e-government.

Previously, public sector services (in contrast to the private sector) were portrayed as ineffective, inefficient, inflexible and unresponsive to the demands of the modern 'consumer' (Langan, 2000; Newman, 2002). Managerialist approaches were underpinned by a belief that the public sector could learn from the private sector, which was seen as being more attuned to the needs of its consumers (Harris, this volume, Chapter Four) and New Labour actively supported this notion, with the business discourse assuming even greater significance in the public sector than it had under the previous Conservative administrations (Harris, 2003, ch 6). As part of this general approach, the exposure of the public sector to private sector practices was seen as crucial in shaping and facilitating the e-government agenda (Bloomfield and Hayes, 2004, pp 3–5). As part of that agenda, technology-based solutions and 'joined-up' working are presented as a modern (and therefore better) alternative to the 'old' systems of central and local government organisation (Cabinet Office, 1999) and as a way of breaking down the 'silo culture' of departmentalism associated with traditional organisational forms (Coleman and Harris, 2008, p 582). In this regard, e-government can be seen as the ultimate demonstration by the government of faith in technological solutions; as part of the 'radical transformation of our society ... the application of e-business methods throughout the public sector challenges all public sector organisations to innovate' (Cabinet Office, 2000b, p 1). The discourse of e-government is clearly a powerful one, as it is intended to affect 'every aspect of how an organisation delivers services to the public. It is not just technology; it is not just business processes; it is not just human resources. It is all of these areas combined [and] at the centre of it is the customer' (Silcock, 2001, p 88). The use of contact centres has also been portrayed as a way of increasing community participation and citizenship, facilitating 'e-government' for 'e-citizens' (Richter et al, 2005) and positioning them 'at the heart' of 'e-democracy' (Office of the Deputy Prime Minister, 2002, p 2).

The centrality of ICT and New Labour's belief in the transformational potential of e-government (Cabinet Office, 2005) signifies the continued evolution of managerialism and the emergence of a hybrid form that can be characterised as 'e-managerialism'. E-managerialism incorporates new features and technologies and is underpinned by, and mediated through, ICT. This form has evolved in tandem with, and as a result of, the reinvention of government as 'e-government' (Silcock, 2001) and elevates ICT beyond the status of an ancillary tool to something that is now embedded in the day-to-day operation of work processes (most obviously in contact centres). It offers the potential for a particular form of 'technical control' (Callaghan and Thompson, 2001). The use of ICT as an aspect of managerialism is not 'neutral'; it is a reflection of the economic trends, cultural influences and power relations in which it exists (Harlow, 2003, p 17). Its adoption occurred in a context in which managerialism had already fundamentally changed the way in which the public sector was organised and managed, through the introduction of private sector management practices. In parallel in this context, consumerism was represented as empowering citizens as 'customers' (Harris, this volume, Chapter Four). Thus, the employment of ICT can be seen as a visible manifestation of a commitment to consumerism and the continuing development of managerialism, as well as involving the deployment of e-government and providing evidence of local authorities embracing 'leading edge' systems of delivery for their social services. This association with state-of-the-art solutions was also a way of disassociating New Labour from 'Old Labour', which was caricatured as supportive of 'centralized, bureaucratic, hierarchical – and inefficient – modes of service delivery' (Langan, 2000, p 154), as well as distancing

New Labour from the 'old' public sector's image of 'paternalism, protectionism and parochialism' (Newman, 2002, p 79).

In the late 1990s, social work was seen as typical of the malaise affecting local government, being portrayed as inherently bureaucratic and wasteful and implicated in 'an apparently endless series of scandals' that served to focus 'public attention on the deficits of social services' (Langan, 2000, p 153). The government concluded that 'social services often fail[ed] to provide the support that people should expect' (Department of Health, 1998, p 5). In this sense, social work was seen as symbolic of the failure of the old welfare systems and representative of a service-led approach that did not respond adequately to the demands of its 'customers' and which was, therefore, a prime candidate for modernisation. Modernisation occurred in the context of a series of previous New Right reforms that had resulted in the imposition of private sector working practices and 'quasi-markets' (Le Grand and Bartlett, 1993) as the route to efficiency, effectiveness and economy and as a means of increasing the choice of services available via competition and by separating the purchaser and provider functions within local authorities (Harris, 2003, pp 43–5). In this 'market', users of welfare services were characterised as rational 'customers' who had choices, rather than being supplicants or 'clients' (Harris, this volume, Chapter Four). Modernisation added to this consumerist approach the notion that the citizen would be technologically equipped and able (Moss and O'Loughlin, 2005) and required 'modern public services to be adaptive, responsive, flexible and diverse' (Clarke et al, 2000b, p 261). These dimensions of managerialism are represented as being embodied in contact centres, which, ostensibly, had previously been introduced in the private sector to increase responsiveness, accessibility (particularly out of office hours) and flexibility for customers. Flexibility for customers is one aspect of a form of consumerism that has placed increasing emphasis on the notion of 'customer care', with public sector organisations seeking to promote 'the enchanting myth of customer sovereignty' (Korczynski, 2002, p 64; and see Bolton and Houlihan, 2005). This is how public sector contact centres are represented, with the depiction of social services 'customers' as being no different from other consumers and needing to be treated in much the same way as users of call centres in the private sector.

Given the omnipresence of ICT and its enthusiastic endorsement by New Labour, its increased use within social services appears to have been inevitable as part of the government's modernisation agenda. The greater prominence of ICT in social work generally has been covered elsewhere (see for example, Harlow and Webb, 2003) and may be seen as an indication that social services are now fully integrated into the 'information society' (Steyaert and Gould, 1999). ICT has affected social work practice and management in a number of ways beyond the more obvious use of computers for recording, data storage and communication. It has been used to delimit social workers' autonomy and discretion, restrict service options and encourage managers to engage in the surveillance of their teams (Harris, 1998b, pp 856–8). Social workers now engage with ICT on a daily basis and are routinely subject to direction by on-screen prompts and electronic pro formas, a feature of the 'screen-level bureaucracy' (Bovens and Zouridis, 2002) that regulates social work as a result of New Labour's modernisation agenda. As ICT has become more sophisticated the potential for further control has increased and has led to questioning whether social work faces the prospect of working in a 'wired wonderland or hypertext hell?' (Harlow, 2003, p 7). These issues are explored further by drawing on a case study of a contact centre.

Case study

'Northshire Care Direct' (NCD) is a contact centre that was developed over a three-year period by 'Northshire County Council' and went 'live' in 2003. At the time of the study it had been in operation for approximately two and a half years. Since commencing operation, NCD has attracted a considerable amount of attention and press coverage and has been held up as a model of good practice, attracting visits from other local authorities wishing to set up similar centres. A review of NCD commissioned by Northshire County Council from the Improvement Development Agency (IDeA) and the Employers' Association in 2004 supports this exemplar view, concluding: 'As a result of our research and observational work, we can categorically state that [NCD] has succeeded in achieve [*sic*] what it set out to do in the original Business/Service Plan. [NCD] is a unique operation for Social Services both at (Northshire) County Council and nationally' (IDeA, 2004, p 3)

NCD was developed as a result of pressure from the government to use electronic media to improve the services for its citizens and the target for e-accessibility as part of the e-government strategy, discussed earlier. In addition, a White Paper had clearly spelt out what local authorities were expected to do in order to modernise their social services in relation to accessibility, efficiency and access to information (Department of Health, 1998). The need to improve accessibility and extend opening hours was further emphasised by the findings of the 'People's Panel' (Cabinet Office, 2000b; 2000c). This detailed the results of research that surveyed both users and non-users of social services, finding that over half wanted out-of-hours access, with 31% wanting to be able to resolve problems, 21% wanting access to information and 91% preferring to resolve problems and obtain information by telephone (Cabinet Office, 2000b, p 67). The results of a 'stakeholder consultation', as part of Northshire's Best Value Review of care management in 2000, also supported making mainstream social services available outside the usual Monday-to-Friday office hours availability and providing a 'more customer focused service' (Director of Social Services, 2000, p 3).

The e-government strategy (Cabinet Office, 1999; 2000a) was explicit, stating that 'all services which can be electronically delivered, should be', and called for personal contact to be 'better supported by new technology'. Northshire County Council also noted the need to comply with Best Value Performance Indicator 157 (Cabinet Office, 1999), which measured telephone contact as an electronic service but only if the 'transaction carried out is electronically abled, i.e. the officer receiving the call can access electronic information or update records on line there and then' (Northshire Social Services, 2001, p 1). Northshire concluded that its 'response to the government legislation and the Best Value Review was to consider the development of a Centralised Contact Centre as a means of improving contact with the public and providing a more efficient and effective service' (Northshire Social Services, 2001, p 1).

Northshire's Social Services Department was also conscious of the need to avoid the negative connotations normally associated with call centres in a region where there was already a high concentration of them in the private sector and the name 'Northshire Care Direct' (NCD) was eventually adopted (the original working name was Northshire Connect) to suggest something new and different while retaining the association with social services (interview with independent consultant employed on the project, 2007). Contact centres have been depicted as differing from call centres in having greater integration of different electronic media to communicate with their customers alongside telephone contact, particularly using the internet (Suomi and Tähkäpää, 2003, p 2). The integration of different technologies and methods of access is clearly evident at NCD, where service users can use a variety of methods to contact the centre, including e-mail and SMS text messaging (the use of mobile phones was also recommended in the government's e-government strategy), the latter being seen as one way of helping to facilitate contact with younger service users.

NCD serves the whole of Northshire, which is a large county with an urban and rural population of approximately 500,000 people in 12 main population centres. NCD operates via a single, county-wide access telephone number for all agencies involved in social and health care and for potential service users through self-referral. This is in keeping with the government's direction to make 'one-stop shops' the norm for social care (Department of Health, 1998), in recognition that people may present with a range of problems that span social, health, legal, housing or other issues. NCD employs 24 staff, of whom 19 are full time and 5 part time. As stated at the outset, the aims of the contact centre are to 'resolve, redirect or refer' enquiries. This involves resolving callers' problems at first contact (for example, by offering advice or information), redirecting callers to the appropriate source of help for their problems or referring callers to social work teams, health professionals or other agencies. The 'referral' response initiates the formal assessment process. The contact centre staff is a mix of unqualified 'first contact officers' (FCOs) and qualified social workers with varying degrees of post-qualifying experience, ranging from 2 to 33 years. At the beginning of the research, seven of these staff were qualified social workers, with two being employed as assistant managers. (This changed mid-way through the study, with one assistant manager leaving, whereupon the second assistant manager post was replaced by two part-time social workers.)

The contact centre receives on average 350 telephone calls a day and this is supplemented by other technology such as minicom,[4] e-mail, fax and mobile phone text messages. It uses standard call centre technology, such as automatic call distribution (ACD) and 'calls waiting' display boards. The technology employed, including the customer resource management (CRM) system, is largely bespoke to the county, apart from telephony and voice recording systems.

The data were obtained over a period of eight months, using a variety of research methods including non-participant observation, spontaneous informal discussion following calls, and taped semi-structured interviews with the majority of the contact centre staff, senior managers within the department and the independent consultant employed to research and commission the service. This included all of the qualified social workers, who were also observed in practice. This observation was carried out either 'remotely' (listening to only one side of the conversation) or by listening to the whole conversation with the caller (after consent had been given) via a headset. Extensive documentary analysis was also used and detailed contemporaneous field notes were taken.

Social work practice in the contact centre environment will now be examined, using the voices of NCD staff to offer some insight into how this radical change of environment and the use of call centre technology affects their work and relationships with callers. Their motivation to work at NCD will also be examined, along with their perception of the levels of stress in the centre.

"Like working blindfolded": social work in a contact centre

We might speculate that the idea of social work practice that does not involve face-to-face contact would be anathema to most social workers and, therefore, being asked to adapt to this form of work probably offers a challenge on a number of levels, including a revision of social workers' sense of their professional identity. The obvious difference for a social worker who is used to 'field' social work is the absence of the usual visual and olfactory aids to assessment. One social worker, when asked to explain how his practice differed in the contact centre, said that he had been forced to sharpen his listening skills in order to compensate for the missing sensory input. He also offered an insight into what is sometimes a difficult relationship with the teams with which NCD has to deal when making referrals:

> "I think the best way that a social worker could understand it is if we blindfolded [them].... I know that I have developed different skills now in listening to people on the telephone and trying to interpret what they are saying ... you cannot see their body language, you can't experience the smells, and you can't see their eyes, which I think ... is the window of the soul ... it is almost like being blind because you have got to interpret what is being said, and I think a lot of our colleagues who are in the field when we pass the referrals to them forget that, they go out and they might see an entirely different scenario

to what has been described to us, but we can only work with what people tell us."

The occasional brush between NCD and field social work teams, alluded to above, might be partly the result of the initial hostility of Northshire's field social workers to the replacement of the traditional role of 'duty social worker' based in 'assessment and information' (A&I) teams. This resulted in some workers losing their jobs in this setting and being redeployed elsewhere. This antipathy was summed up by one of the qualified social work staff, who said that when the A&I teams were summoned to an initial briefing to discuss the idea of a contact centre she was appalled, thinking, "oh my God, what is happening to the department?, and I think about 99% of the people there were against it". The idea of a contact centre was evidently not a popular one with social workers, and the staff at NCD were aware of this and in some cases had equal misgivings. This sense of the contact centre having been imposed, and doubts as to the wisdom of using such a system, were widespread. One of the assistant managers, who had previously worked in an A&I setting, was recruited to the working group that had been established to research and commission the project and was able to offer a practitioner's perspective that served to counterbalance the technophiles' and senior managers' views as to what was desirable or achievable in the setting. She was also given the role of roving ambassador in order to help to sell the concept to her former colleagues. She was in no doubt as to the necessity of her role, as she explained:

> "I always said I was the bit of rough on the team because I was the practitioner and they were the IT experts, and they had some fabulous ideas but I was there to say 'No, no, no, that won't work. Nobody rings you up and says "This is my problem, these are my needs".'"

Despite the unambiguous 'motto' of NCD (Resolve, Redirect or Refer), there appeared to be some initial confusion as to the role of NCD in relation to assessment, although the assistant manager was very clear that what NCD does is not, and never should be, part of an assessment. As she explained:

> "I think it's dangerous to make it part of the assessment ... because I don't think you can actually do the assessment on the phone. We've been asked to do that and I'd said to them clearly, no way. When they brought out the FACS criteria[5] we were asked to actually take all the details and say to somebody, 'no you don't meet the criteria', and to me that's doing an assessment over the phone and I said no way are we doing that."

This might be seen as a defence of the professional role in assessment, but it is debatable whether it can remain as an exclusively 'face-to-face' activity, given the development of increasingly sophisticated 'expert software' that is able to replicate some diagnostic functions (Greatbatch et al, 2005) and is already in use in other professional settings, as discussed later. The increased use of web-based systems as a result of the e-accessibility initiative has also seen the emergence of online self-assessment to determine eligibility in some areas, which, after completing an online form, gives 'an instant response informing if you or the person you are completing the assessment for are eligible for services' (Kent County Council On-Line, 2008).

A non-social work trained manager was appointed to head the contact centre. This is consistent with managerialist perspectives on the need for professional expertise to be subordinated to the ability to manage (Pollitt, 1993; Clarke et al, 2000a). From this viewpoint, specialist knowledge or experience of an operational area is not essential and may be seen as an obstacle to 'business-like' management. In recent years this has become a familiar phenomenon in social services with the advent of care management, the integration of health and social care teams as a result of the 1999 Health Act and the wholesale adoption of managerialism within the public sector. As a result, managers have been recruited at both strategic and team level without any social work training or background. This was an issue at NCD, where a social work practitioner (later to become assistant manager at NCD) had her misgivings about recruitment of a manager from outside social work and concerns about the centre becoming a *call centre* rather than a contact centre as a result. These doubts had been raised with senior management as part of the planning process but had been overruled and the need for a social work background was not one of the essential criteria used in the recruitment process. When asked whether the fact that a non-social work manager was eventually appointed had surprised her, she replied, "Yes, very, very surprised ... and it did concern me, you know, even before [the manager] was appointed because I did feel like is this going to be a call centre rather than a contact centre?"

In the event, the manager appointed was a communications expert with over 30 years' experience in the armed forces. This gave a clear signal that the centre was to be run as a 'business', making a clear break from the old systems that had been in place prior to NCD's inception. This was a mutual culture shock for both the workforce and the manager, as he readily admitted, saying that "what wasn't there obviously, when I came to this job, was any knowledge whatsoever of social care". The manager was aware of the doubts about the appointment of someone from his background, saying that he was able to "sense it in some quarters" and that he knew that some people "didn't think [that] anyone could manage such an organisation without a background in social services. But I suppose you could say that was indicative of them not thinking outside of the box either."

Although managerialism positions the consumers of social services as the same as any other customers, there are clearly significant differences, as illustrated in a conversation that an assistant manager recalled having had with the contact centre manager: "You know, this is not where people are phoning up to complain about their mobile phone bill, or to ask for a change of mobile phone ... I said nobody contacts social services because they want to. It is always people who are in some kind of crisis in their life." This undermines the principle that underpins the consumerism of the government's modernisation agenda, which sees the customer of the contact centre as making a conscious choice to engage with social services rather than the action (as is more likely) being the result of desperation (Coleman and Harris, 2008, p 591). Very few studies have examined the role and characteristics of call/contact centre customers and only one study describes them as the 'many-faceted, complex and sophisticated social actors' (Bolton and Houlihan, 2005, p 685) that they undoubtedly are in the context of a social care contact centre.

One facet of this complexity is the centre being contacted by people who may not be willing or able to express their needs. The ability to work with such people has long been a staple ingredient of social work practice, requiring the practitioner to exercise interpersonal skills and sensitivity to both verbal and non-verbal communication. As we have already seen, this is complicated in social work practice in a contact centre because of the removal of visual and other clues and the reliance on technological mediation in order to inform an initial assessment of the situation. ICT is the principal means of obtaining and using information in a contact centre, so how does this affect the social work process?

ICT and social work in the contact centre

As we have seen, managerialism and its affinity with technological solutions has progressively affected social work practice, having produced

> increasing bureaucratic control, together with a reduction in resources [which] furnish the ideological and material spaces within which social workers are expected to practice ... [and] the role of the social worker who engages with her client in a supportive, nurturing encounter appears, at least officially, to be dying. (Davies and Leonard, 2004, p x)

The future of social work in this context is, Davies and Leonard argue, unavoidably 'tied to "mastering" scientific knowledge and new technical skills, the latest and most glamorous forms of expertise that provide the grounds on which, in a world of uncertainty and occupational competition, social work can stake its claim to professional competence' (2004, p x).

The new technical skills to which they refer encompass the need to be conversant with and competent in the use of ICT, as this is seen as an essential social work skill. This is demonstrated in the requirement for student social workers to be able to evidence their competence through the European Computer Driving Licence (or equivalent) in order to qualify (Department of Health, 2002a). As we have seen, the incursion of ICT into social work practice has been recognised for some time (Postle, 2002; Harlow and Webb, 2003) and contact centres can be seen as another example of this. Their use offers further opportunities for the deployment of sophisticated ICT systems to mediate and possibly replace some aspects of social work skills. The development of so-called 'expert' software systems has already made this a possibility in areas of professional practice that until recently would have been regarded as immune to incursions, such as medicine or nursing (Greatbatch et al, 2005). Programmes are now available in general practice that can offer online diagnosis or screening options; in NHS Direct a computerised clinical assessment system is used to provide expert clinical reasoning; and 'senior management make no secret of the fact that they are attempting to limit the extent to which conduct and outcomes of nurse triage depends on the professional judgement of individual nurses' (Gann, quoted in Greatbatch et al, 2005, p 803). There is no reason to believe that social work will have any greater claim to the sanctity of individual practice than medicine or nursing; indeed it may be that, given the difficulty in precisely defining social work expertise, which has long been an issue, it may be more vulnerable. ICT's ability to shape and to some extent control work processes is well documented (Callaghan and Thompson, 2001) and social work contact centres may be as susceptible to technological manipulation and control as commercial call centres.

In this regard, Callaghan and Thompson (2001) describe the direct control of employee tasks via technology such as ACD, but also the subtler controls of the 'call queue'. This was in evidence at NCD. A first contact officer stated that even when he was on 'wrap-up' (time 'out of the loop' when written recording and other tasks can be done), he was still very conscious of the beep in the headset, which made it 'very stressful':

> "If you are in wrap-up it bleeps at you, telling you that there are calls waiting and when everybody is answering fast and furiously … there is a lot of noise because everybody is on the phones, it just feels like the pressure is being racked up, because the technology is telling you get a move on there are more calls to answer, rather than, relax and just concentrate on [what] you are doing."

The fact that the worker referred to this as 'stressful' was, as we shall see, atypical, and it is significant that the stress was engendered more by the technology than by the work itself. The ability of technology to control and frustrate was also a feature of the only research thus far into a comparable social work setting by van den Broek (2003), which looked at Childline, a contact centre in Australia that employed qualified social workers. As with NCD, van den Broek found that worker 'discretion over workflows was shaped as much by call centre technology as by occupational status, and by managerial policies and practices embedded in public sector reforms' (van den Broek, 2003, p 238).

The ability of technology to regulate and exercise 'perfect control' over the workforce (Fernie and Metcalf, 1999) is, though, a notion that has been overplayed, assuming as it does that the technology is sufficiently elaborate and reliable to accomplish this degree of control. It also does not acknowledge that staff can potentially undermine or sabotage this process. A similar point is made by Fisher's (2004) study of the introduction of contact centres in the civil service, which, like that of Mason et al (2002), highlights the unreliability of the technology and the limits that this lack of reliability imposes on management's ability to control the workforce and their "realization of a Taylorist decomposition of call handling tasks" (Fisher, 2004, p 157). Mason et al's (2002) depiction of technology as inherently flawed and prone to breakdown was nearer to the experience of the equipment employed at NCD, where, as in their study, 'considerable collective energy was expended in actually making the technology work, rather than in circumnavigating its supposed negative effects' (Mason et al, 2002, p 144).

During my time at NCD I witnessed technological problems on an almost daily basis, sometimes happening many times during the working day to either one member of staff, several staff members or the entire staff group. This varied from the (sometimes intensely) annoying to the potentially dangerous, as numerous entries in my field notes illustrate: two of these are reproduced below and illustrate the technological fallibility to which Mason et al (2002) refer:

> **12.35:** Computers down 20 minutes (for the second time today). Social worker says "I don't know why we put up with this. It happens every bloody day", saying it is "a bloody stupid American idea and we should get rid of the bloody lot". Asked him to clarify whether he was referring to computers or contact centres. He said "the whole bloody lot!" Frustration was clearly evident in the room as the calls mounted up. (Field notes, 22 June 2005)

> **15.25:** Technical problem. FCO suddenly shouts, "I'm going to kill this computer!" When I ask what the problem is she says that the PC won't allow her to record her outcomes. I speak to her about how frustrating this must be and she says that it happens nearly every day – "it's crazy". It eventually allows the entry after what I thought was three or four attempts. She corrects me though, saying, "more like ten!". (Field notes, 24 June 2005)

In addition to the propensity of ICT to frustrate, there is also a more serious implication of work being impeded and/or risks to service users being increased. In one such instance, an FCO's computer screen 'froze' so that she had to summon help from the ICT help desk, which was located in County Hall. The problem took over 20 minutes to rectify and was further compounded by a simultaneous problem in the office from which she was receiving a referral:

> **11.16:** Computer finally back on. She tells me that a hospital discharge has taken her more than 20 minutes as a result of the computer problem. She had [then] rung the duty officer in the other area office when she had received the discharge notice and found that all of the

computers were down in that area also! The duty officer asked the FCO to email everyone to tell them to ring [the area office] as all computers were down. (Field notes, 29 June 2005)

The FCO's awareness of the potentially damaging effect on the service user is clearly illustrated by her subsequent comment that "it could have meant that someone was waiting in a corridor; they weren't as it happens, but they could have been".

The potential of ICT to manipulate social work in this context is illustrated by the control that the use of on-screen processes offers when information is being entered into the database. The procedure ensures that certain protocols are followed, as failing to do so will result in the computer not allowing a referral to proceed. This may relate to categorising the care need, or entering data relating to the caller's religion or ethnicity, for example. However, the ability of staff to undermine such controls was clearly demonstrated while I was observing a social worker making a referral where they had what they felt was a 'deserving' caller who clearly was in need of help but who did not fit into any of the categories on the system. This was a situation that had occurred before and usually applied to a vulnerable adult, a category that (surprisingly) did not exist on the system. When this happened, it initiated an ad hoc solution by the staff that necessitated allocating the caller a classification that did not correspond to their presenting needs in order to get them a service, as the entry below illustrates:

> **16.15:** Discussion with SW about data entry problems, regarding adults that don't fall into a specific specialism category but just need help of some kind. She says that if they are under 65 they have to be recorded as 'disabled' or if over 65 as 'older person' – interestingly she says that she thinks "it may be that the government limit the categories that can be recorded". (Field notes, 31 August 2005)

If this type of manipulation is occurring elsewhere, it has implications for the accuracy of national data being recorded in relation to presenting needs.

The geographical location of NCD, in common with centres in the private sector, was not seen as significant, as the use of ICT makes it possible to network with and cover any area, as private sector call centres 'outsourcing' to India and other countries has demonstrated (see, for example, Taylor and Bain, 2005). This represents a very different method of service delivery for social services, which have traditionally been located within the community that they serve (Coleman and Harris, 2008, pp 590–1). As van den Broek noted, a location that was selected on the grounds that it offered 'economic advantages' rather than being coterminous with the population it served actually impeded the workers, who were unable to build up helpful local knowledge (van den Broek, 2003, p 248). The ability to be aware of and use local networks and resources is a factor that has traditionally been important in social work practice and was an issue that was commented upon by several staff. One of the assistant managers gave this as one of the reasons why she was initially against a centralised facility: "[One of] the reasons that I felt at that time of why we shouldn't go centralised was losing all the local knowledge, you know, the regional things that you all know about your own area and you don't know about anywhere else."

Given the negative image of this type of setting, the difficulty in using traditional social work skills and the frustrations arising directly or indirectly from the technology employed, why would a social worker want to work at NCD?

Contact centre social work as convalescence?

The image of the private sector call centre environment as inherently oppressive, stressful and damaging for its employees' well-being has been described in great detail in a number of studies (Taylor and Bain, 1999; Bain et al, 2002; Batt and Moynihan, 2002; Holman, 2004). There has been a notable lack of corresponding research in public sector contact centres, with only a handful of studies (see for example Collin-Jacques, 2004; Fisher, 2004; Bain et al, 2005; Collin-Jacques and Smith, 2005) that offer some insight into the potential differences between private sector and public sector centres and only one (van den Broek, 2003) that is directly comparable to NCD. Despite the lack of research, it has been suggested that a public sector setting is no different from the commercial sector and that the same levels of stress and ill-health are evident here as in any other setting (Bain et al, 2005). These conclusions were drawn from a study of a police control room, where it was anticipated that a higher degree of discretion, coupled with less surveillance, would be afforded to its workers, given that they were in the public sector and provided a 'professional' service, as some authors had suggested (Batt and Moynihan, 2002; Glucksmann, 2004). In the event, it was found to resemble private sector call centres, where the aim is to 'maximise volume and minimise costs' (Batt and Moynihan, 2002, p 15). The problem here is that, as has been noted elsewhere, most research 'has treated all call centres as the same' (Kinnie et al, 2000, p 983). The police control room study falls into this trap by suggesting that this setting is typical of the public sector as a whole. Bain et al suggest that the 'life and death' calls that the police control room dealt with may account for the high levels of stress and staff turnover observed, but this was the case at NCD also. Here the social workers dealt with serious and often life-threatening issues routinely, covering anything from keeping an overdose victim talking in order to keep them alive, to serious cases of child abuse or complications associated with mental illness. Even though there were similar work pressures, the levels of stress in NCD did not tally with Bain et al's findings. This suggests that the implication that it is possible to see police control rooms as typical and representative of public sector contact centres does not stand up to scrutiny.

Despite the negative image of call centres and their representation as stressful and unhealthy work environments, I encountered social workers in the contact centre who had made a conscious decision to work there in order to escape what they saw as the eminently more stressful environment of field social work. This was also true of the unqualified staff who had previously worked in commercial call centres such as banking or on consumer helplines. None of the social workers saw working in NCD as being remotely comparable in terms of stress to the type of social work that they had been engaged in previously. (The range of experience of social work within the practitioner group covered both adult and child care team settings.) The social workers saw their employment in the contact centre either as a way of taking a break from stress in order to re-evaluate their career path, to take them up to retirement or as a way to earn supplementary income in retirement. The response below (in reply to why had they applied for the job) was typical of the first motivation:

> "I just found [the] Children in Need [team] very stressful and I just felt like I needed time away and I just needed to ... not to have a big case load and [be] writing reports and arranging meetings and that sort of thing, and this seemed like a good place to do that, just to clear my head of everything, [and to ask] where am I going to go and what am I going to do?"

The apparent lack of pressure and stress was not always seen as positive by all. One social worker was very vocal about the type of work he was doing and bemoaned the lack of intensity. He was worried about being deskilled by working at NCD (a view that was echoed by others, see below) and he described the different pace of work he had encountered at the contact centre:

> "I have been sat on my backside for 8 weeks. I've come from what I would term 100 miles an hour working environments, from the first minute you walk in the door to the minute you walk out of the door and beyond, constantly thinking, on the go, adrenaline pumping, using your initiative, seeking resolutions as quickly as possible or dealing with situations to the best of your ability hoping that things won't develop too much to a crisis point over a period of time; that being when you're asleep. I feel now that I've come in to a work environment where there just isn't that same level of intensity that you function at. I've gone from 100 mph to the zones of 30 mph, 40 and 50 mph and occasionally 60 mph but I don't think I'll reach 70."

This worker, however, had also made a conscious choice to move to NCD in order to escape the pressures that he was now apparently missing and was able to explain the positive effects that this had had on his home life: "When you go out the door that's it. Your mind's not thinking, 'oh God, what have I got to do tomorrow? I'm going to have to sit up tonight and write myself a to-do list and take work home'. I haven't got that [any more]."

This recognition of the benefits to be gained from the reduction in intensity of work in comparison with field social work was a feature of the interviews conducted with the qualified social work staff. There was, however, an enduring concern in relation to the possibility of losing some of their professional skills: "I felt really deskilled by doing this job coming from writing reports, going to court, going out assessing people and I do miss the client contact. I didn't realise I would miss it as much but the benefits I've got in my own personal life outweigh all that." This supports the view of the contact centre experience as quasi-therapeutic and contrasts sharply with the universal view (born out of research in the private sector) of the call/contact centre as being a highly pressured and damaging work environment. In this context, the contact centre is perceived as benign and beneficial and an environment that could be helpful in restoring a work/life balance for social workers. This view is in stark contrast to the way that local authority field social workers now work, in environments structured by managerialist forms of care management, the business culture and the ascendancy of performance management measures (see, for example, Harris, 1998b; Lymbery, 2001; Postle, 2002; Harris, 2003; Harris and Unwin, this volume, Chapter One).

The potential for contact centre work to be used to alleviate work-based stress was recognised by one of the assistant managers, who had discussed this with the centre manager:

> "I've said this to [the manager], especially for people in child care teams who are often talking about burn-out, would this not be an ideal place for someone to come for a year to 18 months to recharge their batteries, get away from caseloads and then go back into it?"

One area that did coincide with commercial sector call centre studies was that of a relatively high staff turnover, although at NCD this was not as a result of stress and burn-out or the enervating effects of electronic surveillance – the reasons most frequently cited in other studies (see, for example, Deery et al, 2002; Taylor et al. 2003). In both the private and public sectors there is a consensus that there is a 'shelf-life' for this type of work, with people only being able to remain productive for a limited period (see, for example, Callaghan and Thompson, 2001; van den Broek, 2003). When asked about whether she thought that this was the case at NCD, an assistant manager (who was about to leave, having worked there for two and a half years) explained that she thought time in this environment should be limited: "I think [it] should be and I think for social workers [it] definitely should be … I think I've done longer than I should have done really."

In the commercial sector the prime concern is maintaining worker productivity and this is usually seen as only being possible for a maximum of two years. Callaghan and Thompson (2001) cite an Australian study (Wallace, 1999) in which a call centre manager sums up the pragmatic and rather brutal attitude regarded as typical of this sector: "I don't want an agent working for me longer than eighteen months. By that time they are burnt out and not effective" (Callaghan and Thompson, 2001, p 33). For social workers, the potential for deskilling was a more important consideration. One social worker had decided that she would leave sooner than she had anticipated because of this: "Well I actually thought I would probably look at staying here a couple of years, but I don't think I will be … I think it is quite deskilling for the social workers."

As we have seen, the apparent lack of stress experienced at NCD was not due to the fact that the social workers (and the FCOs) did not deal with difficult cases. NCD staff all described their 'regulars' with mental health problems who rang at night and who had to be handled in a particularly sensitive manner. One unqualified FCO described two incidents where she had been directly involved in saving someone's life, as the extracts below illustrate:

> "One guy who rings a lot and he said he didn't want to go on any more, saying he'd rather be dead. I kept him talking while a colleague – the social worker – rang EDT [Emergency Duty Team] who knew him well to see whether it was likely that he would [commit suicide] and then I kept him talking while she rang the police to go around."

She goes on to describe another call where decisive action was clearly necessary and was literally a case of life or death:

> "I had another lad who took an overdose and I asked for help and [the assistant manager] rang the police – well an ambulance actually as he wouldn't [agree to] have the police, and I kept him talking. It went on for about 40 minutes until the ambulance arrived, but it felt like forever. My hands were really shaking as I took that one."

All of the employees, whether social workers or FCOs, were able to describe callers who were challenging, upsetting or memorable for some reason. This varied from callers being aggressive or hostile to having to deal with people suffering from terminal illness, or their carers and relatives. This aspect of the work most closely resembles field social work, although in the absence of face-to-face contact the intensity is inevitably lower.

How does the contact centre compare with private sector call centres?

There have been a number of attempts to describe and analyse the organisational models employed in call centres (Frenkel et al, 1998; Batt and Moynihan, 2002; Deery and Kinnie, 2002; Houlihan, 2002; Glucksmann, 2004) and these have been considered elsewhere (Coleman, 2007; Coleman and Harris, 2008). The case study suggests that these models cannot adequately describe or encapsulate what happens in a setting such as NCD and that further specific research is required. The enchanting myth of 'customer sovereignty' that Korczynski (2002) identifies as dictating practice within a 'customer-oriented bureaucracy' (Frenkel et al, 1998) does not describe the situation at NCD or similar centres. Social work 'customers' do not possess consumer power (Harris, this volume, Chapter 4) and do not ordinarily choose to engage with social workers, but do so as a result of statutory requirements or dire need.

In relation to the employee experience, the suggestion by some (Bain et al, 2005) that a contact centre's being situated in the public sector does not make any significant difference to the negative experience of workers in relation to high stress levels or the potential for surveillance cannot be supported. The case study challenges this view and the 'one size fits all' characterisation of call centres that Kinnie et al (2000) have criticised. For social workers, the fear of becoming deskilled by a lack of face-to-face contact with service users appears to be the prime reason for their electing to leave what appears to be a relatively stress-free environment and this gives some support to the shelf-life notion held in the private sector. The assumption that the models and analyses applied to the private sector can be used to understand organisational behaviours in a public sector setting appears to be presumptuous and gives some support to Glucksmann's (2004) plea to take the research on call centres in a different direction, as well as highlighting the need for more research into this rapidly expanding area of social services.

Conclusion

As we have seen, New Labour's discourse of modernisation has changed the way that social work is managed and delivered. Where previously people who sought help from social services were designated as 'clients' of the professionals, modernising managerialism depicts them as 'customers' (Harris, this volume, Chapter 4). In this guise they are seen as willing and able to make their own choices about accessing services. The social work professional in this relationship becomes a 'partner', who guides rather than directs. The discourse of modernisation supports this notion by purportedly redesigning services around the customer and updating the apparatus used to deliver them. The process of modernisation, therefore, has completely changed this aspect of the public sector's working environment and culture. The use of ICT in this context has had a profound effect on work practices, and social workers, like other public sector workers, can never again be sure how, or indeed where, they will be working.

This chapter has reflected on how contact centres have emerged as a result of New Labour's modernisation agenda and how they are now viewed as the way for consumers to gain access to social services in the modern world. Contact centres signify a convergence of managerialism and modernisation and represent a fundamental change in the relationship that ICT has had with the public sector. Where previously ICT had been incorporated as a tool within a social work environment, contact centres see social work being relocated into an ICT domain. The view of this type of work environment as being oppressive or damaging to its employees has been challenged, suggesting that for some the choice (as long as it remains a choice) of working in a contact centre is a positive one.

It is inevitable that social work practice will continue to be influenced and changed by ICT as its knowledge base moves from the 'social to the informational' (Parton, 2008), and any hope that it will be somehow able to resist this is unfounded. As the technology becomes more sophisticated, particularly in relation to expert software, the likelihood of increased rationalisation of social work processes and the substitution of people with non-human technology (Ritzer, 2000) will increase. The improving capabilities of ICT systems may yet threaten to realise Fernie and Metcalf's (1999) nightmare vision of 'perfect control' by technology, given that managerialism is 'dead' according to some authors and we are now subject to 'digital-era governance' (Dunleavy et al, 2006). With ICT assuming ever more significance in controlling public sector functions, it may be a moot point as to whether the social services contact centre will remain a benign setting that retains the high degree of professional discretion (and potential for subversion) currently enjoyed by its employees or whether those employees will continue to be able to exercise a choice about whether to work there. The research (although thus far on a limited scale) suggests that the public sector experience is distinct from that of the private sector. The models that have been used to define the characteristics of private sector call centres do not fully encapsulate the experience of a social worker practising in this way. As contact centres are increasingly used by local authorities, the likelihood is that they will become the standard way of accessing social services in the UK. It remains to be seen what the implications are for social work in the long term.

Notes

[1] Parts of this chapter appeared in a conference paper ('Resolve, redirect or refer: a case study of a social care contact centre') delivered at the 24th International Labour Process Conference at Birkbeck College, University of London, April 2006.

[2] The term 'contact centre' rather than call centre has been in use in the public sector since 1996 (Employers' Organisation and Improvement Development Agency, 2001) and may be seen as a way of disassociating such centres from the private sector, where 'call centre' has generally had a negative connotation in the public mind. This term is used throughout when referring to public sector facilities.

[3] First contact officers are unqualified workers who take all incoming calls and normally deal with them. They can, however, redirect calls to social workers if child protection, mental health or other complex issues are evident.

[4] This is an aid used for people with a hearing impairment that allows text communication via a telephone line. There is a single minicom number which, like the telephone number, covers all of Northshire.

[5] *Fair Access to Care Services* (Department of Health, 2003d), the national framework for eligibility criteria.

THREE

Modernisation and the role of agency social workers

Peter Unwin

Since the 1980s, social work in the UK has been increasingly subject to scrutiny and managerial control, a considerable body of literature having charted the shifts within state social work as it has changed from being a 'bureau-profession', a hybrid model accommodating both professional and bureaucratic ideologies (Parry and Parry, 1979), to being a profession operating in the context of 'new managerialism' (Pollitt, 1990; Harris, 1998b; 2003; Clarke et al, 2000a) and being subject more recently to 'modernisation'. Clarke et al state that 'a central issue in the managerialization of public services has been the concerted effort to displace or subordinate the claims of professionalization' (2000a, p 9), the 'right to manage', using models from the business world, having become the replacement ideology. One aspect of the modernised social work environment has been the rise of agency social work, a system whereby private recruitment agencies supply contracted qualified social workers to what are predominantly statutory settings. Despite the significance of this phenomenon, it has been subjected to very little scrutiny. This chapter draws on literature from social work, health and business in order to illuminate the core issues surrounding the role(s) of agency social workers. The nature and value of the contribution made to social work by agency social workers is analysed within the context of the modernised service and the need for research into the costs and quality of agency social work is identified.

Background to agency work

The emergence of agency social work in the UK has been a phenomenon of the 1990s, its business counterparts having been in existence since the beginning of the 20th century (Black, 2006). The vast majority of available literature on agency work is concerned with business settings (for example, Booth et al, 2002; Blau, 2003; Engellandt and Riphahn, 2003; Forde and Slater, 2005). This literature has limited resonance with the complex political, ethical and statutory environment of agency social work. The business literature refers variously to 'agency workers' (Bronstein, 1991; Forde and Slater, 2005), 'temporary workers' (Druker and Stanworth, 1999) and 'contingency workers' (Bergstrom and Storrie, 2003; Daniel, 2006). Bronstein provides the following, generic definition: 'temporary agency working involves a triangular arrangement in which a temporary work agency hires a worker for the purpose of placing him or her at the disposal of a third party, the user enterprise, for a temporary assignment' (1991, p 292).

There has been a significant rise in the use of agency workers in Britain, with the number of such workers increasing from 50,000 in 1984 to 250,000 in 1999 (Forde, 2001, p 631). Across all industries in Britain, it has been estimated that 7% of the male workforce and 10% of the female workforce are in temporary forms of employment, with 2.8% of these workers (700,000) being employed on an agency basis (Booth et al, 2002). Employment agencies themselves currently account for 1.5% of small firms in the UK (Black, 2006). Such expansion can be located within the global economic changes brought about by neo–liberal reforms that seek a transient and flexible workforce that can respond quickly to changes in a faster-moving market place. Within the social work context, neo–liberal reforms have created a disparate, mixed economy of care in which state social work has become part of a quasi-market (Harris, 2003). This quasi-market has embraced agency social workers, whose characteristics and roles in the workplace are perhaps different from those of agency workers detailed in the business literature.

The literature from the business world identifies two types of agency worker, termed here the 'commodified' and the 'privileged' forms. Into the former category would fall low-paid, low-skilled workers, such as agricultural labourers whose working lives are contingent upon harvests/seasonal fluctuations, whereas the latter form of agency working encompasses the highly skilled specialists who can demand top prices for their labour, for example, consultant engineers. In the literature, these two forms of agency worker are seen as fitting the supply and demand needs of a range of industries. In addition, 'privileged' agency work is seen as offering personal fulfilment by way of highly paid and skilled 'portfolio career' paths (Handy, 1994; Fraser and Gold, 2001; Platman, 2004) in which a variety of different employment settings and projects are proactively sought by individuals rather than their seeking to build a career with a main employer. The attractiveness of 'portfolio' careers has been identified by Handy (1994) and Platman (2004) as a factor accounting for the rise in agency work.

A range of explanations has emanated from the commercial sector concerning the reasons why 'privileged' agency workers choose the comparative insecurity of agency positions over permanent positions, such as the higher pay for doing the same day-to-day job and the romanticism of being a 'free agent' who can pick and choose workplaces and working conditions (Handy, 1994; Engellandt and Riphahn, 2003; Platman, 2004). In contrast, the 'commodified' agency worker has been seen as "convenient, cheap labour" (Union of Shop, Distributive and Allied Workers, 2006, p 5), serving the supply-and-demand whims of businesses. Clearly, values, behaviours and issues regarding working conditions vary significantly between these two distinct forms of agency working found in the business world, with trade unions taking differing stances on the phenomenon of agency working but concerning themselves largely with the 'commodified' agency worker. Agency social work connects to some of the themes in this bifurcated perspective. For example, despite the argument that agency social work is located towards the 'privileged' end of the agency working spectrum, concern has been expressed about the lack of access of agency social workers to maternity pay, sickness pay and training opportunities (Carey, 2008a), issues usually raised in connection with 'commodified' forms of agency work:

> [Agency workers] are often employed, quite deliberately, on inferior terms and conditions. They rarely have access to sick pay and pensions. They receive little or no training. They're exposed to greater health and safety risks, and they have little protection or maternity rights ... Employers often use them to undermine established pay and conditions, and drive a cheap labour wedge through the existing workforce. (Union of Shop, Distributive and Allied Workers, 2006, p 1)

The discussion so far could be taken as implying that the rise of agency working has only benefits as far as employers are concerned, but this is not the case. Employers are concerned about the costs of using agency workers, none more so than their biggest employer, the National Health Service, which uses a wide range of agency workers. The issues involved in the use of temporary nursing staff within the NHS have largely been brought to national attention owing to issues of cost, although there are also significant questions surrounding patient care that merit further attention.

Development of nursing agencies

The use of agencies within nursing has been a feature of the NHS since its inception, through in-house bank and external agency working. (There are parallels here with the employment of agency social workers, given that nursing is also a highly ethical area of work in which many of the same considerations apply regarding the fit and the efficacy of employing 'privileged' agency nurses as temporary members of mainstream teams.) A 'bank' nurse is the term used for staff employed on NHS terms and conditions in times of sickness and absence. Often these staff already work as employees within the NHS, although arrangements between health authorities have not been uniform (Audit Commission, 2001; House of Commons Committee of Public Accounts, 2007). Agency nurses are supplied to health authorities by independent, profit-making agencies that operate in the commercial sector, negotiating rates of pay and commission levels. Agency and bank nurses are 'privileged' agency workers who receive higher hourly rates of pay than their counterparts on contracts of employment. The increasing use of agency staff within the NHS has, however, become a matter for public concern.

The Audit Commission (2001) calculated that 4% of the £18.9 billion pay bill for the NHS in 1999/2000 was spent on non-NHS staff and that over 50% of this spend was on nursing agency staff. Most of the concern voiced about the use of bank and agency nurses relates to the cost implications (Audit Commission 2001; House of Commons Committee of Public Accounts 2007), rather than to moral, ethical or motivational concerns. Martin Ward, Director of the Royal College of Nursing's mental health programme, has, however, stated that bank and agency workers present inherent risks to patient care, given the passing nature of their relationship with the care environment and the patients themselves (BBC News 1999). Concerns regarding the nature of communication, continuity of care and lack of familiarity with institutional policies and protocols have also been expressed by Manias et al (2003) in a small-scale case study involving agency nurse providers and hospital nursing managers. In an analysis of the use of agency nurses by a southern England health trust, Purcell et al comment that 'the use of temporary agency staff raised issues of quality control and continuity of patient care' (2004, p 718).

The House of Commons Health Committee addressed the issue of 'the over-use — indeed abuse — of agency and bank staff' (House of Commons Health Committee, 1999, sec 17) and the potential impact this may have both in terms of costs to the NHS and on the quality of patient care. The concept of a national 'in-house' bank of nurses – 'National Health Services Professionals' – was developed from the recommendations of the Health Committee, such an organisation being seen as a viable alternative to the use of a number of commercial agencies in terms of cost and quality and in responding to a workforce demanding flexibility in working patterns. Subsequently the Audit Commission (2001) undertook a review of the cost and the quality of patient care arising from the use of bank and agency staff, its findings being that there was little evidence of financial control or reliable data relating to this area of the NHS. A structural solution to the ongoing cost and quality issues in the use of bank and agency staff was suggested, in that the management of temporary staff was henceforth to be seen not as a temporary challenge but as an ongoing, permanent part of mainstream NHS business, with staff being managed and trained in the same way as permanent staff. However, the Healthcare Commission found that significant variations across the country, in terms of the use of bank and agency staff, had continued and stated that 'high usage of temporary staff is strongly linked to low levels of patient satisfaction' (Healthcare Commission, 2005, p 6).

Further parliamentary scrutiny (House of Commons Committee of Public Accounts, 2007) revealed a continuing lack of success in the management of agency and bank nursing staff, finding that the amount of money spent on temporary nursing staff had declined very little and very slowly, despite an increase in permanent staff. There was also still a lack of information on demand factors and actual usage of temporary nurses and the Committee noted that the use of temporary nursing staff might impact on the quality and safety of patient care if such staff were not subject to strict regulation regarding their mandatory training and total hours worked. This report went on to set a guideline of 6–7% of total salary spend as a reasonable level at which health trusts should hold their expenditure on bank and agency nursing staff, and again reiterated the need for the quality standards and reliable information that still appeared to be lacking across the NHS. However, success still seems to elude the NHS in the area of temporary workers and 'National Health Service Professionals' remains an unproven and costly managerial initiative (House of Commons Committee of Public Accounts, 2007).

In contrast to the situation with temporary nursing staff, the debate regarding the use of agency social workers within local authorities has not yet been presented as an issue of any national concern; hence, approaches have been at the level of individual local authorities. The particular issues surrounding agency social workers, the majority of whom work alongside mainstream, permanently employed staff within statutory settings, are now considered.

Development of social work agencies

Social work agencies such as Blake Beresford Thomas, Quality Locums and Reliance Care began to appear in Britain in the 1990s, at a time when recruitment difficulties began to be experienced by social services departments. They represent a significant but largely unexplored phenomenon of the past decade (for exceptions, see Kirkpatrick and Hoque, 2006; Carey, 2007). The 2000s have seen the consolidation under a New Labour government of fundamental structural and organisational changes to the way in which social work is delivered. The adoption of marketplace values, new managerialism, greater multi-agency working and consumerism (McDonald, A., 2006) has occurred during a period in social work history that has also witnessed increased formalisation and accountability in the social work profession (General Social Care Council, 2002). The past decade has also seen high levels of vacancy rates within local authorities for qualified social workers, as demand has outstripped supply (Parker, 2002; Coombs, 2005; Forde and Slater, 2005). This is the culture of change from which agency social work has emerged.

As we saw earlier, agency work in general may be seen as having several contradictory facets. It can be seen as falling within a romanticised view of self-employment, embodying flexibility and freedom, or it can be seen as a phenomenon that undermines hard-fought terms and conditions of employment and unionisation in deference to the supply and demands of certain capitalist systems (Burgess et al, 2003). As is the case with nursing agencies, the levels of payment received by agency social workers are at higher hourly rates than those of permanent workers, and hence are in agreement with this aspect of the 'privileged' form of agency working discussed above. Higher levels of earnings for agency workers are one factor held in common across the sectors, estimates of 20% higher wage rates for agency social workers than for permanently employed peers being claimed by Kirkpatrick and Hoque (2006) in their case study.

The existing literature pertaining specifically to agency social work is very limited and there is as yet no established body of knowledge about the contribution made by agency social work to its modernised environment, but there are suggestions of hostility towards it:

> If effective social work practice relies on teams working well together, agency social workers must wonder why those in permanent posts seem so eager to have an 'us and them' culture. The negativity endured by locums varies from perceptions that they are a waste of public funds to more personal accusations that they are out to make a quick buck – a brickbat that conveniently ignores the fact that they are plugging staff gaps. All this and a general feeling that, as temporary workers, they are second class citizens. (Sale, 2007, p 26)

Such views are perhaps too simple to characterise the complexity of agency social work, for example, as it emerges in the case study findings of Carey, including:

> the abundance of convoluted and ever-changing organisational and legal procedures; limited discretion and access to training; and brief, and superficial, relations with colleagues and clients. It is argued that agency social work provides more intense exposure to the uncertainty and change that epitomize care management. Such temporary employment may also help to further fragment state social work, and increase the superficial relations and hazards that encompass market-driven public sector employment. (Carey, 2008a, p 1)

Carey's construction of agency social work presents it as a complex phenomenon, full of contradictions and constantly negotiated relationships. The model of a 'triangular arrangement' postulated by Bronstein (1991) as characterising generic agency worker relationships (Figure 3.1) is clearly not sufficiently comprehensive to encapsulate the relationship patterns of the agency social worker's world, which might be seen as having a sextupular set of key work relationships. Agency social workers have allegiances to themselves, to their employment agency, to their host employer, to their service users, to the communities in which they work and to their colleagues (Figure 3.2). Managing the tensions and dilemmas produced by this range of allegiances is a particular challenge for agency social workers, all the more so when it is considered that the majority of agency placements are short-term in nature (Carey, 2008a).

The small-scale case study undertaken by Kirkpatrick and Hoque (2006) and that of Carey (2007; 2008a) represent the only specific academic enquiries into agency social work, their respective findings regarding the nature of the overall contribution that agency social workers make to contemporary social work being as yet inconclusive. For example, there are no known studies of agency social workers in terms of their effect on caseloads, case closures or interventions and there is no comprehensive research on the cost-benefits of employing agency social workers. The hourly rates of agency social workers are higher than those of their

Figure 3.1:The triangular world of an agency worker

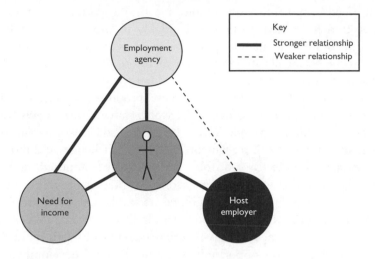

Source: Diagrammatic representation of Bronstein (1991)

Figure 3.2:The sextupular world of an agency social worker

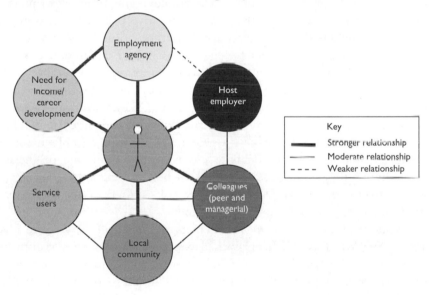

mainstream peers, although agency workers do not have associated employment benefits such as security of tenure and pension provision. Kirkpatrick and Hoque (2006) reported that some agency workers felt they were outsiders who were not valued as team members, whereas others had the opposite experience of finding their contributions and expertise welcomed by hard-pressed teams. Carey's (2008a) is the only study to date that has attempted to establish in depth the nature of the ways in which agency social workers practise and relate to others. His findings are that the particular pressures on agency social workers to conform and to deliver services at speed in unfamiliar surroundings lead to a working environment in which they find it essential to conform quickly to organisational and group norms and his pessimistic analysis is that relations with colleagues and service users seem to be essentially superficial and therefore present considerable risks to both themselves and service users.

These two case studies can be seen to have produced a range of differing perspectives on the nature of agency social work. Carey (2007) draws attention to the positive, 'upskilling' potential that the agency social work role offers, in that a range of different work placements, with new challenges and procedures, is readily available as a positive 'portfolio' career choice – although he balances this perspective with the views of agency social workers themselves, who often saw agency social work in a negative light. For example, agency social work was seen as deskilling in that tasks were often 'treadmill-like' – repetitive, involving less service user contact time than was experienced by mainstream social workers and characterised by fewer opportunities for professional development when compared with that of permanent peers. Kirkpatrick and Hoque (2006) present agency social work more positively, as a constructive choice that facilitates an escape from the oppressive nature of state employment. Other views put forward by Kirkpatrick and Hoque (2006) are less negative than those of Carey (2007; 2008a) and include the view that the decision to choose an agency social work post can be primarily expedient, fitting in with one's life circumstances at a certain point in time, rather than perhaps constituting a strategic career choice.

Apart from these two case studies we have only anecdotes regarding the day-to-day practice of agency social workers, such as: the mainstream social worker who was outraged when a new agency social worker had chocolates and flowers delivered to her at the area office as a 'golden hello' from the employment agency; the foster child who refuses to talk to a social worker if they are 'on the agency', as she knows they will not stick around for her; and the agency social workers who get on with a great deal of statutory, task-centred, performance-managed work in an efficient and industrious manner.

Despite the limited literature, there emerges a prevalent view of the advent of agency social work as a further privatised extension of new managerialism, with an allegiance to care management and competence-based, instrumental perspectives on social work (Hugman, 2001; Carey, 2003). The ability to 'hire-and-fire' agency social workers at short notice (Carey, 2008a) fits the ideology of new managerialism very well, even members of this 'privileged' workforce perhaps being viewed by management as 'commodified' and sharing this vulnerability with agency workers in general, whether or not they construct themselves as what might be termed 'portfolio-builders', 'escapees', 'treadmillers' or 'expedients'.

Background to the emergence of agency social work

Before attempting to account for the emergence of the specific phenomenon of agency social work, it is helpful to set a wider context by examining the changing nature of employment within the public sector, this being the sector in which the vast majority of social workers are employed and, indeed, where the vast majority of agency workers will also be working alongside them. The public sector has traditionally been associated with strong unionisation, security of employment, meritocratic career progression and final salary pension schemes (Andrew and McLean, 1995; Means et al, 2003). However, the impact of new managerialism (Harris, 1998b; 2003; Rickford, 2001), increasing workloads and stress on social workers (Means et al, 2003) and the falling value of pension schemes no longer makes local government the attractive employer of tradition. New managerialism, together with a negative media image, political interference, constant reorganisations and resource shortages (Carey, 2003), can all be seen as leading to the creation of a local authority workforce with low levels of morale (Jones, 2001; Caulkin, 2003; Revans, 2007).

In addition, the climate within which social work has existed since the permeation of New Right ideologies into local government has been one wherein the traditional autonomy of the professional social worker to exercise discretion over work priorities has been seriously challenged (Harris, 1998b; 2003; Evans and Harris, 2004). Key legislation such as the 1989 Children Act and the 1990 National Health Service and Community Care Act have further circumscribed areas of social work practice. Hugman (2001) sees the development of 'post-welfare social work', stemming from New Right ideologies, as having led to an emphasis on competence-based instrumental forms of work that Carey (2003) sees as essentially constituting a deskilling of social workers.

Overall, these developments suggest a climate that is not conducive to high staff satisfaction and retention (McDonald, A., 2006). Rickford (2001) describes the increasingly prescriptive and formal assessment processes that seemed to characterise social work and cites social workers who lament the lack of meaningful relationships with their service users. Carey, in an empirical study of statutory social work teams, notes that the emancipatory aspirations of many of those leaving qualifying social work courses soon disappear as 'mere fantasy in view of the daily grind in the office' (2003, p 126). Commentators such as Rickford (2001) and Carey (2003) reflect social workers' frustrations at being kept away from the 'social' or the 'community' by the increasing burden of paperwork that characterises contemporary care management. Given this rather negative picture of contemporary working life within local government, it would not be surprising if those social workers of a certain mindset (possibly one that is not risk averse, has an independence of spirit, places greater value on individualism and self-reliance than on teamwork and collegial support) opted for an alternative mode of employment once it became available. Indeed, it could be that the instrumental, task-centred nature that is the essence of agency work is well suited to a workplace increasingly dominated by a culture of performance management (Harris and Unwin, this volume, Chapter One). Alternatively, it could be argued that these 'privileged' agency social workers are in fact able to be the most creative and flexible, having the choice to move their labour elsewhere should they be prevented from working in a way that accords with their personal vision of social work. In theory, such independence might be used to envision agency social workers as street-level bureaucrats (Lipsky, 1980; Evans and Harris, 2004) par excellence, able to interpret rules without too much concern about the managerial and organisational consequences.

Commentators have variously asserted either that mainstream social workers' professional discretion has been seriously curtailed (Hadley and Clough, 1996; Lymbery, 2000) or, alternatively, that a measure of professional discretion continues to characterise contemporary social work (Baldwin, 2000; Evans and Harris, 2006). Despite the potential, however, for agency social workers to operate in ways that suggest discretion and autonomy, the case study evidence from Carey (2007; 2008a) indicates that the agency social workers in his study did not appear to be autonomous, discretionary, free agents respected for their skills and experience; rather, they largely complained of an inability to resist managers giving them a constant flow of routinised, high-risk cases which they were largely expected to respond to in a 'speedy' manner if their contracts were not to be terminated. Further, Carey goes on to state that, despite the many complaints of agency social workers about their working conditions, 'there was little evidence of tangible group resistance by employees to poor working conditions, strict eligibility criteria or the typically poor services provided to clients' (2007, p 110). Such a finding would not support the view that the scarcity value of agency social workers means that they can negotiate the best working conditions and move their labour elsewhere if conditions do not suit either their pocket or their ethics.

The picture that emerges of agency social work contrasts with a view of agency work in teaching, where a case study of supply teachers by Grimshaw et al (2003) postulated that agency positions may be sought as a form of 'individualised resistance' against the degradation of professional standards, brought about by an increasing predominance of managerial, rather than professional, standards within public service. Supply teachers can do the 'real' work (i.e. teach children), without the 'distractions' of inspections, performance management documentation and budgets. In contrast, the lack of resistance found in Carey's (2007) study could be interpreted as unsurprising, given that the very system of agency social work is itself a by-product of modernisation and agency social workers are hardly likely to 'bite the hand that feeds'. Alternatively, it may be that the complexities and contradictions in agency social work, such as those of uncertainty and unfamiliarity with locales, ever-changing operational systems and tensions with colleagues (Carey, 2008a), together with the short-term nature of most agency contracts, mean that the possibilities of 'cooperative resistance' between managers and agency social workers (Evans, this volume, Chapter Eight) are less likely to happen than with mainstream social workers. Agency social work may, therefore, be constructed as an essentially self-focused activity, with agency workers having a professional concentration on getting what they, as individuals, can out of the system, rather than having a professional orientation that concerns itself with helping to achieve social justice and service for individuals and communities (International Federation of Social Workers, 2001).

Ideologies of the self

Social workers as a profession are becoming increasingly aware of their potential to earn higher wages across different authorities and sectors, and while many commentators see such increased wage levels as just rewards, there are views that the professional and remunerative recognition increasingly being afforded to social workers may not be in the best interests of the individuals and communities with whom social work is carried out. Jordan (2004) is perhaps rather pessimistic in this regard and laments the tendency of state social workers to become self-serving in their concerns for professional and personal advancement, rather than being driven to improve the collective lot of the individuals and communities with whom they work. One might argue that the tendency of agency workers is even more likely to be to move between organisations, to those offering better terms and conditions in a work pattern that echoes that of agency workers in commercial and industrial settings. Such individualised behaviours are interpreted by Jordan as natural consequences flowing from mainstream social policies that encourage what he calls 'technologies of the self' (2004, p 9).

This underpinning culture of the self, which inherently discourages relationships with the role of the state and wider community, was given considerable legitimacy in the social work arena by the structural changes that were brought about by the Conservatives through the 1990 National Health Service and Community Care Act. This legislation created a 'mixed economy of care' wherein the state became a facilitator and enabler to a range of social care providers, rather than a core provider of social care itself (Giddens, 1998; Means et al, 2003). Principles of choice and individualism, paralleling the commercial consumer who 'shops around for the best deal', became the dominant ideology across social work, particularly in adult care services (Harris, this volume, Chapter Four). The structural changes brought about by the mixed economy of care were primarily designed, it was said, to give choice to the service user, but an additional consequence of the stimulation of the contract culture on both provider and purchaser services was to offer similar choice-making scenarios to social workers.

Jordan further argues that the underpinning ideology across the mainstream of a society that embraces 'projects of the self', rather than more collectivised ways of thinking, is likely to encourage individual social workers, especially those who are young or recently qualified, to look at their own worlds in this way (2004, p 9). Making a preferred choice to work for an independent social work agency rather than to be employed by a statutory agency may be a natural consequence of such an ideology, especially as private social work agencies have proliferated post-1990. Qualified social workers, for the first time in their history, have a range of employment settings competing for their skilled labour. Despite a claim that the public still largely views social workers and their organisations as unsound and untrustworthy (Jordan, 2004), the social work profession has recently become a more formalised profession via the establishment of the General Social Care Council in 2001 and the subsequent creation of a professional register for qualified social workers (General Social Care Council, 2002). This professional initiative has come about at the same time as social workers' terms and conditions of employment have become considerably enhanced, largely due to market forces rather than to any newly awakened appreciation by government or employers of social workers' intrinsic worth.

These improvements in social workers' positions of advantage and professional recognition might, however, be argued to further alienate them from sharing values and models of society with some of the disadvantaged individuals and communities with which they work. If agency social workers are to develop careers via the construction of very individualistic career paths, then it may be even harder for them to empathise with the values and perspectives of communities whose only hope of empowerment may lie in collective action rather than in individual advancement. Healy and Meagher contrast the British position with professional social worker minorities in North America and Australia who 'actively oppose attempts to improve the industrial and cultural recognition of social services work' (2004, p 249).

These 'abolitionists' see the pursuit of economic reward and professional recognition as elitist and anti-ethical, sidelining the genuine needs of service users and their communities. There has been no significant evidence of parallel movements within the British social work arena, apart from initiatives such as the Social Work Action Network (Ferguson, 2008, pp 5 and 129), suggesting that there is either widespread support for or at least acceptance of the individualistic progression path that has characterised the recent professional and material recognition of social work within Britain. In the following section the possible 'fit' of agency social workers within postmodernist perspectives on the nature of social work is considered.

Agency social work and models of social work

There are many different views about the role of social work in the modernisation agenda and whether established values, such as those of emancipation and empowerment, hold any sway in an increasingly circumscribed and prescriptive world of practice. Payne postulates that there are three main approaches to social work:

- *Reflexive-therapeutic* views see social work as promoting the well-being of individuals, their groups and communities via relationship-based 'therapeutic' interventions that are dynamic and reflexive. Increased awareness of the strengths within a person or a community leads to insight and helps to realise potential that brings about transformation in circumstances.

- *Socialist–collectivist* views see social work as essentially emancipatory, challenging social orders that are regarded as having caused the underlying disadvantage or oppression of individuals and their communities. Individuals and communities are encouraged to seek empowerment to change, rather than to fit in with, the prevailing social order.
- *Individualistic–reformist* views of social work seek to bring about individual/ group levels of change, rather than to challenge the wider social order. Social work is seen as supporting integration into wider society in ways that are mutually beneficial. (Payne, 2005a, ch 1)

Healy states that tasks within social work are extremely varied and lists a range of tasks, acknowledging that a primary task is often assigned by the institutional context:'risk management; implementation of statutory law; support and advocacy; therapeutic intervention; community education; community capacity building; research; policy development, implementation, and evaluation; social services administration' (Healy, 2005, p 3). Within these tasks can be seen the need for approaches that might embrace emancipatory models such as autonomy, choice and empowerment, while others might call for skills in rationing, risk assessment and enforcement.

Jordan (2004), looking back over a period of 25 years, believes that it is the latter type of tasks that have increasingly come to predominate within British social work. Dominelli (2004) also highlights an increasing tendency towards technicist ways of working at the expense of complex, relational ways of working within contemporary British social work. Payne's typology would similarly suggest that Healy's task list might demand a range of responses across the reflexive–therapeutic, social–collectivist and individualist–reformist spectrum. Contemporary practice theories, from critical–reflexive orientations to evidence-based practice approaches, assume that social workers have certain capacities, including those to reflect critically, to analyse, to use and build practice-relevant knowledge and to negotiate and use their context critically and creatively (Healy and Meagher 2004, p 243).

These perspectives present considerable challenges to social workers across all sectors, depending on the particular pressures within settings and the balance between resources, rationing and opportunities for creativity, innovation and discretion. Only the research of Carey (2008a) has begun to explore the nature of the fit between agency social work and ways of practising, his largely pessimistic analysis, as we have seen, being that much of the work carried out by the agency social workers in his case study was superficial and could be seen as contributing to further fragmentation of state social work. Carey (2008a) further emphasised that the short-term nature of most agency social work meant that agency social workers did not have the time to develop 'social capital' or collective ways of working, their time being even more pressured than that of mainstream colleagues in terms of being expected to rapidly 'process' their cases through to closure.

Conclusion

The introduction of agency social work, as a significant element of modernised social work, has raised a number of key questions in terms of the very nature of the modernisation agenda. To date, there has been no systematic evaluation of agency social work's contribution to issues of economy, efficiency and effectiveness (Audit Commission, 1989), nor, indeed, to ethics, on a national level. Supporters of agency social work will point to its flexibility, for both employer and 'privileged' employee, and its task-centred fit with the target-driven culture of performance management and will argue that the ability to work for a number of different employers adds a depth of experience and richness to a social work career, especially for those who are able to operate as street-level bureaucrats. Critics of the agency way of working will point to the divisive nature of differentiated terms and conditions, to the fleeting nature of agency social workers' contact with teams, service users and communities and to its contradiction with much contemporary social policy that is encouraging closer working relationships across local organisations and professionals (for example, Department of Health, 2003a).

Cynics may say that in a working environment where local team offices are being sacrificed for centralised call centres (Coleman, this volume, Chapter Two), where technology means that workers do not 'need' their own desk and where service users are worked with via computer screen more than they are face-to-face, then is it any longer necessary to have close working relationships with either service users or colleagues? The evidence presented in this chapter has been conflicting and, regardless of whether agency social workers perceive themselves as 'portfolio-builders', 'escapees', 'treadmillers' or 'expedients', are they not in fact all 'commodities' within a performance management culture that sees them as both instrumental and disposable? Agency social workers would appear to be dependent wholly on the approval of management and its 'right to manage' (Harris and Unwin, this volume, Chapter One). They are also denied a 'sense of belonging' (Carey, 2008a) with colleagues, service users and communities that, it could be argued, should still be at the core of modernised social work. Only when further research into this politically, commercially and ethically sensitive area of social work is carried out will we have better answers to the many questions that this chapter has raised.

Part Two
Modernisation and service users

FOUR

Customer-citizenship in modernised social work

John Harris

Introduction

The advance of consumer culture seemingly knows no bounds:'In contemporary society, almost no human need or activity avoids commodification, and consumer society ... is increasingly all encompassing' (Edwards, 2000, p 5). The hegemony of consumerism is evidenced by the growing influence consumerist ideas have exerted on the politics and practice of social policy (for discussions see, for example, Gilliatt et al, 2000; Baldock, 2003; Needham, 2006), including social work, with users of services being expected to take on greater involvement in arranging, and more recently managing, the services they receive:

> Despite different diagnoses and prescriptions, thinkers of the left, right and 'radical centre' share a normative commitment to liberate the user of public services from the role of passive recipient (or even victim) of producer-led services. The consumer-driven reorientation of public services has been a consistent thread of public service from the Conservative years through to the policies of New Labour. (Gilliatt et al, 2000, pp 333–4)

This chapter explores these developments. It begins by locating the origins of consumerism – in public services generally and social work specifically – in the Conservative governments' reforms of the public sector, before considering more recent trends in New Labour's modernisation agenda. It then turns to the issues, implications and limitations that recent developments raise, debating them in relation to a number of themes. The first is the way in which New Labour depicts the public sector as locked into its social democratic welfare state origins in terms of the rigidity and uniformity of its 'monolithic' service provision. In the modernisation agenda, the form and content of this portrayal of public sector provision is contrasted with the fluidity and flexibility of contemporary consumer culture. Second, businesses operating within that culture are seen by New Labour as having much to teach the public sector about how to transform its services. Third, at the centre of the transformation that New Labour requires, there emerges the figure of the customer-citizen with high expectation, forged in consumer culture, carried over into encounters with the public sector, and straining at the leash to make choices about the services s/he receives. Fourth, the emergent managerial role envisaged for customer-citizens is explored.

Charting the rise of the customer-citizen

The New Right ideas that were so influential on the Conservative governments from 1979 to 1997 placed a strong emphasis on citizens' rights to 'freedom' and 'choice'. The Thatcher governments saw these rights as having been suppressed by the bureau–professional regimes that characterised the post-war social democratic welfare state (Harris, 2003, ch 2; Coleman, this volume, Chapter Seven; Evans, this volume, Chapter Eight), which was alleged to have ridden roughshod over citizens' individual needs (Wilding, 1992). Social work was included in the New Right's stinging criticism of the public sector (Loney, 1986; Jones and Novak, 1993; Midgley and Jones, 1994) as the Conservatives overhauled the content and process of welfare services, with a declared commitment to the centrality of customer choice (Ranson and Stewart, 1994). This overhaul, it was promised, would lead to citizens being able to live their lives as they wished, with access to flexible responses to their customer preferences (Hoggett, 1991, p 247). Customer choice on the part of the citizenry was seen as preferable to the social democratic welfare state's reliance on professional judgement. A reduction in professionals' status was seen as going hand-in-hand with the enhancement of customers' status, greater responsiveness to their individual needs and making more choice in the services available to them (Exworthy and Halford, 1999, p 5).

After the fall of Thatcher, Major's contribution to this New Right discourse of the customer-citizen was the *Citizen's Charter* (Prime Minister, 1991), which symbolised the consolidation of consumerist discourse in the public sector. The Charter's impact on that discourse was profound; following its publication, a political consensus began to coalesce around the customer-citizen, in social work as elsewhere in the public sector. The strategic claim was that by transferring services and resources outside the public sector and putting in place quasi-market arrangements, the customer-citizen's experience of services would be transformed. The Labour Party also endorsed customer-citizenship, placing a new emphasis on the individual citizen and the desirability of empowering individuals as consumers against the dominance of the state in their lives (Pierson, 1998, pp 196–7). This represented a departure from the way in which the issue of professional power in the public sector had often been represented by the Labour Party, namely, that the way to limit professional power was to give citizens 'voice' and make professionals more democratically accountable (Plant, 1992, p 27). With its embrace of consumerism, the Labour Party produced its own *Citizen's Charter* (Labour Party, 1991) in which the citizen's status as a customer was emphasised. This ideological rapprochement through the two Charters marked the beginnings of a political consensus around the customer-citizen on a number of points: clear standards should be set out against which the performance of services should be judged; services should be flexible enough to meet individual needs; individuals should have a greater say in how their needs were met; dissatisfied service users should have access to complaints procedures (Prime Minister, 1991; Labour Party, 1991).

There has been critical commentary on these developments that suggests that the shift to consumerism in public services was a post-hoc rationalisation that flowed from changes in the role of government in relation to the public sector and, as such, was almost an accidental occurrence (Lewis and Glennerster, 1996; Baldock, 2003). Whatever its provenance, the early 1990s witnessed the establishment of an enduring consensus around the customer–citizen as a maker of choices from a mixed economy of social services. This consensus turned away from the public and collective nature of services, as espoused by the social democratic welfare state, in favour of the exercise of rational, self-interested, individual choice at the point of use of services. The consensus continued after New Labour came to power in 1997.

New Labour and the customer-citizen

The 'Third Way' thinking that was influential on what was now, under Blair, New Labour maintained the political consensus on the public sector in seeing the way forward for services as being inextricably intertwined with quasi-markets, provider diversity and customer choice (Giddens, 1998). Consistent with this thinking, when New Labour was elected it retained its support for customer-citizenship and the Conservatives' Citizen's Charter programme was replaced by 'Service First' (Cabinet Office, 1998), as an aspect of New Labour's declared aim to modernise the public sector (Cabinet Office, 1999). 'Service First' set out expectations about: standards of service; provision of information; consultation and involvement; access and choice; fair treatment; effective resource use; innovation and improvement; and collaboration with a range of service providers (Cabinet Office, 1998). Since then, a whole series of policy developments and organisational restructurings have taken place as part of the modernisation agenda, which have been meant to make services such as social work more business-like (Harris, 2003, ch 5) and the people who use them more like customers (Harris, 2003, ch 7). The latter are regarded as needing to be reconstructed from 'passive recipients' to 'active choice makers' (Clarke et al, 2000b, p 260; McDonald, C., 2006, ch 7; this volume, Chapters Five and Six) and services are seen as needing to accommodate higher expectations on the part of their customers, who are depicted as being increasingly knowledgeable about what they want from services and what they expect services to deliver (Clarke et al, 2007, p 67). 'If government is going to be effective at delivering services in the way people want them for today, it has to be modernised, it has to be updated' (Blair, quoted in Newman, 2000, p 46).

In using as its referent the active choice-making customer–citizen, New Labour talks 'both to and for the people directly, in order to reprimand an "unresponsive" public sector' (Scourfield, 2007, p 114) and empowers managers also to speak powerfully on behalf of customer-citizens. Given the historic allegation, beginning with the Conservative governments, that social workers are guilty of 'producer capture' (Giddens, 2003) – a form of professional self-interest that is inimical to customer-citizens' interests – managers can represent themselves as being on the side of customer-citizens against professionals (Barnes, 1997, p 32). 'Playing the user card' can be used by managers to support a particular policy, strategy or action based on what they purport to know about what users want or need (Gilliatt et al, 2000, p 335). This managerial alignment can be invoked to justify subjecting social workers to the disciplines of the quasi-market and managerial constraints within the organisations in which they work in the interest of services becoming 'customer-focused' and concerned with the empowerment of customer-citizens. Managers' concern with organisational efficiency is represented as their acting as agents for delivering the wishes or aspirations of customer-citizens (Newman, 2003, p 87):

> The consumer-citizen is constructed largely within his or her relationship with the state as opposed to a professional. The state 'manages' service delivery on behalf of the consumer-citizen, controlling the activities of professionals and circumscribing their professional autonomy. Professionals have a largely instrumental value to managers acting as key agents of the state. (McDonald, C., 2006, pp 120–1).

Although customer-citizenship is presented as extending service users' involvement, it is involvement premised on a universalised managerial set of expectations about what being treated well as a customer means (Clarke and Newman, 1997, pp 121–2). These managerial expectations formulate the customer-citizen's rights in a significantly different and narrower way, effectively leaving overall control with managers and sidestepping questions of justice, inequality and oppression (Ferguson, 2007). Thus, reliance on narrow definitions of customer satisfaction legitimates the power of management by giving a mandate for what is being done, without changing the underlying power relations, as this ministerial comment makes clear:

> the Government must now focus on customer satisfaction as a key driving force in public service improvement ... The Cabinet Office is exploring the possibility of developing a new standard measurement system that can identify and then track how satisfied customers are with the public services they get.... this will be a powerful force for change from the ground up – showing which areas of public services are leading the way in providing a good service to customers and which need to improve. (Hutton, 2005)

New Labour's general approach to public services, reviewed thus far, was reflected in its specific modernisation agenda for social work, *Modernising Social Services*, and its concern with developing customer–citizen choice (Department of Health, 1998). *Modernising Social Services* was followed by the *Quality Strategy for Social Care*, which proclaimed a 'new vision and culture' that would focus on 'extending choice, control and flexibility' and on ensuring that 'second best will never be good enough. We want everyone who uses ... social services to expect only the best' (Department of Health, 2000a, Foreword). 'The best' was defined as 'flexible, user-centred services tailored to individual needs' (Department of Health, 2000a, para 19). To achieve the best, the relationship between services and customer-citizens would have to be renegotiated: 'Staff will be working with people who are informed and know what they can expect. Users' expertise will be respected. Such empowerment can only lead to better outcomes' (Department of Health, 2000a, para 13). Since then, rhetorical references to consumerism have been made by the Audit Commission and the Commission for Social Care Inspection (Harris, and Unwin, this volume, Chapter One) and have occurred in statements about public services written and spoken by government ministers, in policy documents and in political speeches. In these pronouncements, services are presented as either abounding in choice for the customer-citizen or being required to move in that direction:

> In reality, I believe people do want choice, in public services as in other services. But anyway, choice isn't an end in itself. It is one important mechanism to ensure that citizens can indeed secure good schools and health services in their communities. Choice puts the levers in the hands of parents and patients so that they as citizens and consumers can be a driving force for improvement in their public services.
>
> We are proposing to put an entirely different dynamic in place to drive our public services; one where the service will be driven not by the government or by the manager but by the user – the patient, the parent, the pupil and the law-abiding citizen. (Blair, 2004, p 1)

Garrett has argued that such consumerist talk by New Labour, as part of a process of modernisation, is a smokescreen for the promotion of changes that mesh with neo-liberal political perspectives. Neo-liberalism

> holds that the social good will be maximised by maximising the reach and frequency of market transactions and it seeks to bring all human action into the domain of the market ... Human well-being can best be advanced by liberating individual entrepreneurial freedom ... the role of the state is to create and preserve an institutional framework appropriate to such practices. (Harvey, quoted in Garrett, 2008, p 278)

In this regard, referring to people using public services as consumers or customers references them to wider market/capitalist relations (McLaughlin, 2008, p 5).

Notwithstanding New Labour's concern to promote neo-liberal forms of engagement with public services, it is important to stress that this concern is not founded on antagonism to services being provided per se, as was the case with some variants of New Right thinking under Thatcherism. However, New Labour's commitment to the continuation of services is based on a distinctive public *service* ethos, not seen as being at odds with use of the private sector and the advocacy of competition (Carey, 2006), rather than on the public *sector* ethos of the social-democratic welfare state (Needham, 2006): 'Our third way for social care moves the focus away from who provides the care and places it firmly on the quality of services …' (Department of Health, 1998, para 1.7). As Needham shows, this public service ethos is seen as being underpinned by a customer orientation, which was endorsed in her research by politicians in central and local government, senior civil servants and senior local government managers. When Needham asked her research participants, "What do you think it means to treat local people as customers?", the most common response was that it meant personalising services around the needs of the individual user, rather than imposing assumptions about her/his needs (Needham, 2006, p 851). This response was consistent with a growing emphasis in New Labour's modernisation discourse, which has linked its long-standing preoccupation with choice with a more recently discovered desire for more personalised services.

There has been a goal for some years, across the political spectrum, of making social work services more attuned to the personal needs of their users. This goal dates from at least the Conservatives' community care reforms, with their emphasis on the social worker/care manager arranging services to meet the needs of a particular person, rather than requiring the person to fit whatever services were already available (Social Services Inspectorate, 1991a; 1991b). New Labour has presented 'personalisation' as the latest development in seeking to achieve this goal of individually attuned services in order to take consumerism to new levels of sensitivity and responsiveness. This is seen as necessary because of higher and still-rising consumer expectations of public services and, as part of that trend, the existence of a greater appetite for choice and personalisation (Needham, 2006, p 855), with New Labour portraying users of services as ever more refined and discriminating customer-citizens. The type of consumer 'who cannot possibly derive satisfaction from universally provided, collectively financed and state-allocated services' was identified as already emergent as a policy theme some years ago (Warde, 1994, p 223). This Conservative prototype has now become the fully fledged customer-citizen of contemporary political discourse. By now, the embedded nature of individualised consumerism sees customer-citizens as only having their individual interest in getting the best deal they can, rather than seeing services as being rooted in collective citizenship (Priestley, 1999; Pearson, 2000; Needham, 2006; Ferguson 2007; Scourfield, 2007; Tanner, this volume, Chapter Six). This view of customer-citizenship is located not just in consumerism, but in an implicit and particularly tantalising political vision of public services that would be experienced as akin to 'high-end' consumerism in the marketplace; the sort of consumerism that does not just provide choice but also personalises its products and services.

A milestone in the pronounced shift by New Labour towards personalisation was the Adult Social Care Green Paper, *Independence, Well-Being and Choice* (Department of Health, 2005) (see Ferguson, 2007, pp 77ff; 2008, pp 388ff; Tanner and Harris, 2008, chs 2 and 4), which saw increasing the use of direct payments and introducing individualised budgets as the principal routes to personalisation, with individuals able 'to make of their lives what they will' (Scourfield, 2007, p 109). The Green Paper's proposals were taken forward in the White Paper, *Our Health, Our Care, Our Say*, which indicated that proactive approaches were necessary in order to increase the take-up of direct payments: 'Direct payments should be discussed as *a first option with everyone*, at each assessment and each review' (Department of Health, 2006, para 4.25, my emphasis). The need to develop individual budgets was also emphasised in the White Paper; these are sums of money, allocated to individuals, that bring together the different sources of funding to which they are entitled, rather than an allocation that is just for eligible social care needs, as is the case with direct payments. The allocated sum for an individual budget can be taken as a cash payment for the purchase of services or used for service provision itself or a mixture of the two. This is seen as offering the advantages of direct payments but without the potential difficulties that some people would experience in becoming a budget manager and employer: 'Individual budgets offer a radical new approach, giving greater control to the individual, opening up the range and availability of services to match needs, and stimulating the market to respond to new demands from more powerful users of social care' (Department of Health, 2006, para 4.30). As Ferguson points out in his discussion of these developments, New Labour's advocacy of the reduction of the role of the state in the provision of services and the stress on individuals' taking on greater responsibility for their own lives is the 'central tenet of neo-liberal common sense' (Ferguson, 2007, p 394).

Politicians and civil servants have been at pains to point out that achieving such profound changes poses a challenging agenda. One example will suffice: David Behan, then Chief Inspector of the Commission for Social Care Inspection, began with the proposition that

> if we are to meet people's expectations and deliver the policy ambition of the White Paper, we need to develop a new way of commissioning. The challenge is to commission for personalised, bespoke care. The White Paper sets out a clear vision for the development of integrated services, which offer personalised care where people are able to exercise choice and control over their services. (Behan, 2006, p 1)

For those who see personalisation as being an agenda exclusively associated with services for adults, he emphasised that

> Every Child Matters (2003), the Children Act (2004), the National Service Framework for Children and the Education Bill currently before Parliament reflect themes of individualisation and personalisation of services. The creation of a mixed economy – a pluralism of provision – is seen as the key to delivery of greater choice for individuals and in driving up standards. (Behan, 2006, pp 1–2)

And he approached the personalisation agenda from a perspective rooted in customer-citizenship, which draws its knowledge of how things should be done from the private sector:

> Last week we held a seminar on commissioning. We received a presentation from someone from a commercial background. He had a clear message – putting the customer at the centre – the key to success is understanding what the customer wants and providing it. What he meant was that every single function in an organisation should be focused on the customer – even functions that don't see people who use services face-to-face. But in social care it hasn't always been clear who the customer is – too many intermediaries stand between the commissioner and the end-user. (Behan, 2006, p 3)

Customer-citizenship: issues, implications and limitations

We have seen that the customer-citizen has been the central figure in New Labour's drive to modernise social work services. In New Labour's modernising vision, the customer-citizen represents what it means to be 'modern' in relation to public services. The customer-citizen is seen as a quintessentially modern figure her/himself and public services are seen as needing to be modernised in order to be brought into alignment with her/him and what s/he represents. This analysis raises a range of issues, implications and limitations.

Inflexible services, stuck in the past

The New Labour analysis repeatedly refers to the 'one size fits all' model of public services, for example, 'Since every person has differing requirements, their rights will not be met simply by providing a "one size fits all" service. The public expects diversity of provision…' (Office of Public Services Reform, 2002, p 13). This alleged residual rigidity is seen as stemming from the origins of the social democratic welfare state, shaped by the experience of war-time and rationing:

Many of our public services were established in the years just after the Second World War ... centralised state direction ... developed a strong sense of the value of public services.... The structures created in the 1940s now require change ... The challenges and demands on today's public services are very different from those post-war years. The rationing culture which survived after the war, in treating everyone the same, often overlooked individuals' different needs and aspirations ... (Office of Public Services Reform, 2002, p 8)

The social democratic welfare state underpinnings of public services are attacked repeatedly as outdated in the modern world: 'we must respond to the individual's aspirations and needs, and we must reflect the desire of the individual to have more control over their lives. We must recognise that the one size fits all model that was relevant to an old industrial age will not satisfy individual needs' (Blair, 2003, p 17). Overall, the public sector has been portrayed as inherently inefficient, wasteful and unwilling to embrace change (Clarke et al, 2000a; Pollitt, 2003), with slow and cumbersome bureaucratic structures: 'like a dinosaur, too big, too slow-moving, too insensitive, insufficiently adaptable, and seriously underpowered as far as brains are concerned' (Pollitt, 2003, p 32). This critique of a rigid and antiquated public sector is the starting point for New Labour's analysis of customer-citizenship. It is seen as redundant in the modern world of consumer culture because today's society differs substantially from the austere society within which the post-war welfare state was constructed. In this analysis, 'one size fits all' services are in head-on collision with contemporary consumerism.

Consumer culture in the modern world

In New Labour's modernising discourse, Britain is depicted as a 'consumer society' or a 'consumer culture' in which a proliferation of goods and services enables a wide variety of wants and needs to be satisfied, as people express themselves through different and individual modes of consumption, a phenomenon made possible by 'post-scarcity values' (Featherstone, 1991): 'Rising living standards, a more diverse society and a steadily stronger consumer culture have ... brought expectations of greater choice, responsiveness, accessibility and flexibility' (Office of Public Services Reform, 2002, p 8). Bauman argues, but in more pessimistic vein, that people have become dependent on the market and that their identities are forged primarily by their roles as consumers:

Consumer conduct (consumer freedom geared to the consumer market) moves steadily into the position of, simultaneously, the cognitive and moral focus of life, the integrative bond of society and the focus of systematic management. In other words, it moves into the selfsame position which in the past – during the 'modern' phase of capitalist society – was occupied by work in the form of wage-labour.

> This means that in our time individuals are engaged (morally by society,
> functionally by the social system) first and foremost as consumers rather
> than as producers. (Bauman, 1992, p 49)

These changes in the wider economy, initiated by the private sector, are seen by
Williams as having produced a series of shifts that have been reproduced within
welfare provision: mass production to flexible production; mass consumption to
diverse patterns of consumption; production-led to consumer-led; from mass,
universal needs met by monolithic, bureaucratic/professional-led provision to the
diversity of individual needs met by welfare pluralism, quasi-markets, reorganised
welfare work and consumer sovereignty (Williams, 1994, p 49). New Labour
has reduced such shifts to a simple circular argument: consumerism = choice =
freedom = consumerism.

Learning from business

In advocating better and more desirable services that are more in tune with what
customer-citizens want, New Labour always presents the private business sector
in an ideal form, as the fount of wisdom and the provider of high standards of
service (in this regard, see the comments of Behan discussed above). The origin
of this veneration of business was the Conservative governments' concern with
turning public sector organisations into quasi-businesses (Harris, 2003, chs 2 and
3), underpinned by a belief that the private sector knows best, businesses do things
better and they should be beacons for the improvement of the public sector. This
Conservative belief in the efficacy of the private sector has been sustained by New
Labour discourse, which, as we have seen, makes frequent references to what is seen
as the nub of recent societal change, namely 'consumer culture', and to what are
presented as responsive knock-on effects in the ways in which goods and services
are provided by businesses. As we have seen, these business developments, allegedly
in response to consumerism, are contrasted favourably with portraits of rigid
models of service provision that are said to have characterised the public sector.
Like the Conservative administrations before them, the New Labour governments
have argued that, by learning lessons from the private sector, the public sector
will produce better and more desirable services, more in tune with what the users
of those services want (Farnsworth, 2006). Incorporating the discipline of the
market, managerialist beliefs and business practices from the private sector into
the public sector have been presented as the keys to success, particularly in local
government services (Cabinet Office, 1999). New Labour's drive to modernise
services so that they match the alleged expectations of customer-citizens is always
grounded in what are seen as the business requirements of the modern world
(Newman, 2000; Garrett, 2005, p 534).

Customer-citizens with high expectations

It has already become clear that the analysis underpinning New Labour's modernisation agenda sees the consumer culture of the modern world as being the seedbed within which customer-citizens' high expectations of public services have been sown and have flourished. Whereas users of the services provided by the post-war social democratic state are regarded as having been passive recipients, today's customer-citizens are depicted as active, knowledgeable consumers who construct their identities from the services and products they purchase in the market and are represented as bringing the same requirements to public services, with demands that those services should be responsive, flexible and diverse. In New Labour's discourse, public services are an aid to what we might call 'individual life projects': 'The good citizen is one who wholeheartedly engages in an ongoing project of the personality defined by continuous consumption ... "Freedom" is freedom to create personality and identity through the act of consumption' (McDonald, C., 2006, p 127). Whereas citizenship in the social democratic welfare state was a status, modern customer-citizenship is seen as a consumerist achievement embodying the 'notion of an active, reflexive and responsible citizen' (Moss and O'Loughlin, 2005, p 178):

> The reconstruction [from clients] ... to consumers or customers of market-produced services represented the invocation of a new identity.... The discourse of 'consumers' and 'customers' assumes that the ideal 'customer' or 'consumer' is one who is able to rationally access services through the market, 'buying' in services in an effective and efficient way to meet their own needs, irrespective of whether the provider is a state-provided or private service. (McLaughlin, 2008, p 5)

As part of this discourse, social work has been engaged in an extensive modernisation programme, with changes in policy, organisational design and systems of regulation, based on seeing users of its services as customers who require individualised and personalised services. These customer-citizens are depicted as the motor for the modernisation agenda because the 'active' consumer envisaged by New Labour 'requires modern public services to be adaptive, responsive, flexible and diverse'(Clarke et al, 2000b, p 261).

Does the customer-citizen reality match the New Labour rhetoric? That rhetoric is fed by a myth based on a comparison that celebrates the best experiences of 'high-end' consumerism in the market (though they are never identified as such), which the majority of us will rarely or never experience, and denigrates the very worst experiences in the public sector. In other words, the customer-citizenship rhetoric sounds suspiciously middle class (Pollitt, 1994, p 11) – or upper middle class. The exemplars of the demanding consumer cited by Behan, in the speech mentioned earlier, are telling:

> In the next few years people's 'voice' and their expectations will be a
> significant driver of the way services are commissioned and provided.
> The people who are now entering 'old age' will bring with them a
> range of expectations which will be more demanding than previous
> generations. Just note the recent writings of the baby boomers – Janet
> Street-Porter, Germaine Greer et al. – they have all laid out their
> expectations about their future care and how current models do not
> meet their ambitions. (Behan, 2006, p 2)

These celebrity exemplars of the demanding consumer will presumably not be
ringing their local authority contact centre in order to seek satisfaction of their
demanding expectations. When extolling such experiences and expectations of
the alleged benefits that the market provides, New Labour's portrayal ignores,
for example, everything-for-a-pound shops, dodgy back-street second-hand car
dealers and fast-food restaurants. Many of the users of social work know this 'lower
end' of the market all too well. In the daily struggle to get by, they may have
difficulty in aspiring to participate even in this end of the market experience, let
alone permit themselves to dream of immersion in New Labour's depiction of
public sector consumerist utopia. This is the customer status and experience that
many people carry into New Labour's customer-citizenship and their interaction
with social work. Many do not have high expectations of what being a customer
involves and extolling the desirability of consumerism in public services does not
necessarily have the effect of heightening their expectations. In any case, users of
social work have been shown to have difficulty in making demands as customers
because they have little conception of what type of help to expect from both
statutory and independent sector services (Ellis, 1993; Davis et al, 1997; Clark et
al, 1998; Richards, 2000).

In essence, New Labour's modernisation agenda celebrates choice but ignores
the act of consumption itself. Consumption is a skilled accomplishment. We learn
to behave as consumers and our learning is located within a class position that
intersects with a range of other social divisions in our biographies. Consumerism
is not a ready-made experience that all possess, simply waiting to be unleashed
by the statements in policy documents that henceforth it will be the basis for
engagement with public services. Whether or not, or the extent to which,
customer-citizenship is accomplished varies according to the roles of others,
authority relations and users' experiences of managing earlier situations, as well
as the amendment and application of any skills acquired to a particular service
context (for example, the accomplished customer-citizen has to consume the
fire service, the library and social work in different ways [Gilliatt et al, 2000,
pp 337–8]). Furthermore, the repertoire of skills available will be shaped by the
users' location within the intersections of the social divisions of age, class, disability,
gender, 'race' and sexuality. The impact of all of these variables on the extent to
which customer-citizenship is accomplished will shape the range and content of
the services that are secured.

The limitations on the possibilities of customer-citizenship that arise from the ways in which these variables play out in people's lives and in the specific circumstances in which they seek assistance are ignored by New Labour. In its modernisation discourse, the user is a discerning agent who exercises choice in the marketplace of public services (Newman, 2005, p 49). For New Labour, 'the "freely choosing" consumer – with expectations of choice formed in the market place – is the central rhetorical figure' (Clarke, 2004, p 130).

The customer citizen as choice-maker

As we saw earlier, New Labour argues that customer-citizens with high expectations derived from consumer culture will not be satisfied with only *public sector* services; they will aspire to have access to a *market of public services*, with a diversity of providers. Thus, New Labour has characterised users of public services as customers who not only have expectations about choice but who also will increasingly see those expectations fulfilled because consumerist choice is seen as central to delivering the changes that will modernise public services, as this ministerial comment indicates: 'We are also determined that citizens should be empowered and have a voice and a choice in the services they receive. This is the new context in which local government and local partners must deliver improvement' (Woolas, 2006). In any market, active choice from options is the key to the authority of the customer (Keat et al, 1994), but there are a number of implications and limitations in the highlighting of the issue of choice in the New Labour discourse – implications and limitations on which the spotlight seems rarely to fall.

First, the reality, rather than the political rhetoric, of choice is that people in receipt of public services often have no choice of provider or no provider at all; in the case of social work, customer-citizens may well be told that they will not receive a service until they get worse (Needham, 2006, p 856) and 'most users of social services are not in a position where they can shop around and take their "custom" elsewhere' (Butcher, 1995, p 161). In the absence of adequate resources, it is difficult to see how the New Labour vision of the customer-citizen as choice-maker is supposed to function; choice can only operate in the context of surplus capacity, and for that to be achieved, services would have to be expanded (Needham, 2006, p 852).

Second, the New Labour discourse sees user demand as an alternative to professional assessment, steadily assuming a more prominent role as a distributional principle. It is unclear how the much longer established distributional principle of 'need' is to be squared with user demand. 'Need' disturbs the privileged place occupied by 'choice', fuelled by user demand, in the New Labour modernisation agenda, since need can never be simply 'what people want'. 'Need' implies the existence of an objective condition, or at least something that has to be uncovered and articulated, and to date such conditions have been determined through processes of 'needs assessment' (Barnes, 1998). It is difficult to see how individual customer choices can replace professional judgement. Individual customer choices cannot determine the overall pattern of services, which have to respond to the overall level of needs (of existing and potential users) or, at least, to those needs that have been deemed to be capable of being met by public services. Thus, the concept of 'need' leads into the question of what should be provided for whom. That question is inherently political, and the political response to it hitherto has been located within a framework of professional discretion (Evans and Harris, 2004). The question is merely obscured – it does not disappear – by shifting to an emphasis on customer–citizen choice.

Third, relying heavily on customer–citizen choice in public services, in the manner portrayed by New Labour (as a bundle of preferences waiting to be satisfied), would lead to an ever-increasing demand for public services (Needham, 2006, p 856). This is clearly not New Labour's intention, as there is a parallel concern to keep a firm grip on public expenditure. Here, New Labour's invocation of consumer culture as a model for public services, as in the following rendition, breaks down: 'One approach to understanding what customers want is "social marketing" – finding out across the whole community who the "customer" is and what they want, so that councils can market existing services more effectively and develop better ones' (Behan, 2006, p 3). In the private sector marketplace, this is indeed the case, as the intention is to encourage as much consumption (and profit generation) as possible. In public services, however, the relationship between demand and resources is usually fraught, and subject to active management; only people whose needs are defined as satisfying certain policy criteria receive a service (Flynn, 2007, p 145). In this context, the state is concerned predominantly with *restricting* demand, through mechanisms such as eligibility criteria, assessments of need, charging policies and prioritising service allocation through resource panels and so on. Far from being involved in encouraging choice, social workers are usually preoccupied with managing scarce resources, the excessive demand for those resources and what it is 'reasonable' for someone to expect by way of a response to their needs, in the light of what is available. While the consumerist rhetoric has been turned up in volume, services have been increasingly targeted, means-tested and risk-assessed, with attention focused more sharply on the most disadvantaged (Kirkpatrick, 2007). As one social worker, reflecting on 25 years of experience, put it: "Although there was always an element of rationing resources, today, under the guise of managerialism, with its focus on routines and procedures, one is largely engaged in explaining why needs cannot be met" (quoted in Rogowski, 2001, p 15). This reflection captures the social worker's position as the node at which New Labour's modern customer–citizen-oriented approach meets the long-standing issue of rationing and the ranking of competing risks and needs. Unlike a private business in the marketplace, the social worker cannot abdicate in favour of customer choice and cannot avoid the questions of who should (and should not) get a service and what are the appropriate levels of service (quantity and quality) for those who are to be served.

Fourth, New Labour's emphasis on customer-citizens having a primary interest in picking and choosing between services to further their 'life projects' has a number of limitations. It hides the reality of how many people come into contact with social work. Most of them do not choose to use social work in the first place. Often they approach services in stressful conditions (Barnes and Prior, 1995). Contact with social work may be misunderstood and/or unwelcome. It may well have been initiated by someone else on her or his behalf. Some people involved with social work are more or less captive as a result of their life experiences, or through aspects of their social context that have a coercive element (Forbes and Sashidharan, 1997; Clarke et al, 2007, p 95; Flynn, 2007, p 162; Bain, this volume, Chapter Five). Those who are making contact with social work in their own right, 'rather than trying to access a particular commodity ... are looking for their circumstances or conditions to be improved or remedied' (Clarke et al, 2007, p 112). Once in contact with social work, the lives of many are subjected to surveillance, regulation and formalisation. New Labour's presentation of service users as enterprising, active, choice-making customer-citizens isolates its idealised depiction of their experiences from such material and emotional circumstances and is at odds with those circumstances in its reference to customer-citizens being in control of their own lives through a series of rational impersonal transactions. While this may be consistent with reinforcing the neo-liberal message that citizens should avoid dependence on the state and take on more individual responsibility when they engage with public services, it is out of kilter with the often complex interpersonal relationships that exist between service user and social worker (Hadley and Clough, 1996, p 196; Hoggett, 2000, p 147), within which 'choices' are made:

> There is a fundamental conflict between the impersonal and formal relations of contract which prevail in the market and the relationships which prevail in social services and which place a high premium on personal and informal contacts. Factors which play a very limited role in commerce – the helping and caring roles of individuals, family members and local networks – are the essence of the work of social services. The statutory responsibilities of official agencies are also a crucial part of the social services framework in a way they are not for a normal commercial enterprise. Another key distinction arises from the fact that SSDs provide public rather than consumer goods. Whereas the ordinary entrepreneur needs to satisfy only the customer, workers in social services have a 'multi-dimensional agenda': they have to satisfy service users (who may have carers or families with conflicting interests and needs), but also have important responsibilities to the common, public, interest. (Langan, 2000, pp 163–4)

As Langan makes clear, consumerism sees people as independent individuals, whereas social workers are involved in negotiating complex issues of independence, dependence and interdependence:

> Are the social services offered to a particular person just for him or her, or even for that individual at all? Is it not the case that others always benefit directly or indirectly from the intervention, not just the identified service user?... The provision, or withholding, of a service may satisfy one or more of the possible customers, but only directly or indirectly at the expense of others whose needs or interests may be in conflict with those of the 'satisfied customer'. There are always multiple customers or service users and often conflicts of interests and perception between these different people. Workers inevitably have to mediate between different and sometimes conflicting interests and norms within any social situation. (Smale et al, 2000, pp 91–2)

This everyday complexity of social work is sidelined by the notion of rational, self-interested customer–citizens making choices. It is as though being a competent, choice-making customer–citizen will happen because New Labour's rhetoric decrees it. In reality, people who have been disadvantaged may need massive amounts of support in order to acquire the assertiveness that making choices as a customer–citizen implies, as the experience of self-advocacy demonstrates (McNally, 2000). Furthermore, in some circumstances being in need and functioning as a customer–citizen may be a contradiction (Biggs, 2000), let alone the preoccupation that some people may have, not with choice, but with finding *any* service (Barnes, 1997, p 34):

> The notion of users of social care services exercising rational choice in a way which is consistent with the notion of economic agents maximising personal benefits ignores the reality of the way in which people come to be in the position of 'needing' such services and the way in which such services are used ... Entry to the social care system is often an indication of lack of choice rather than the positive exercise of choice ... [or it] has the characteristics of the 'least worst' option rather than a positive choice. (Barnes and Prior, 2000, p 85)

The emergent managerial role for customer-citizens

Social work has been subjected to a range of changes that mimic the rationale and operation of private businesses (Harris, 2003). As a consequence, it has increasingly had a narrow dual focus on individual service users and on the internal demands of the organisations in which social workers are employed, rather than outwards, towards the communities in which social work, and the individuals with whom it works, are located. In the process a sense of place is lost (Coleman and Harris,

2008, pp 590–1), reinforced by a key aspect of this individualistic, inward-facing orientation – the primacy of information technology and the sense of social work's primary task being to feed the organisation's demand for information on individual customer-citizens (Harris and Unwin, this volume, Chapter One). Modernised social work is seen as a collection of processes that have to be performed, shaped by the demands of information technology systems (Parton, 2008), rather than what a classic social work text described as 'reflective consideration of the person-situation configuration' (Hollis, 1972). The next stage in these trends appears to be detaching, or semi-detaching, social workers from customer-citizens. The rationale of personalisation (discussed earlier) is that individualised customer-citizens who are disenchanted with collective provision and able to make choices can be self-reliant, self-managing, self-maintaining and committed to the arrangement of their own personalised packages of services; access to services can, as it were, be Ikeaised,[1] a process by which more responsibilities and risks can be shifted on to customer-citizens to assemble services and support themselves:

> This involves 'offering' individuals ... active involvement in action to resolve the kind of issues hitherto held to be the responsibility of authorized governmental agencies. However, the price of this involvement is that they must assume active responsibility for these activities, both for carrying them out and, of course, for their outcomes, and in so doing they are required to conduct themselves in accordance with the appropriate (or approved) model of action. This might be described as a new form of 'responsibilization' corresponding to the new forms in which the governed are encouraged, freely and rationally, to conduct themselves. (Burchell, quoted in Scourfield, 2007, p 115)

As Burchell makes clear, customer-citizens can seek more flexible services, but in order to do so they must become more flexible themselves: more autonomous, managerial and entrepreneurial. This contrasts with the New Right's take on consumerism, which continued to position the service user as a recipient of services, but as a more knowledgeable and discerning recipient, with the social worker being inculcated into a calculative rationality and budget consciousness (Harris, 2003, ch 3). Social workers having been enjoined to become rational calculative practitioners, it is now the turn of customer-citizens to develop these attributes: 'New Labour's perspective on citizenship appears to focus less on what the citizen can expect from the state in terms of social rights, and more on how the citizen *should be* – in this case, active, responsible and enterprising' (Scourfield, 2007, p 112, original emphasis). In addition, the customer-citizen must take on functions, and their associated risks, that would previously have been undertaken by social work, such as managing public money, record keeping and achieving outcomes (Scourfield, 2007, p 116). Whereas the New Right-inspired Conservative governments were concerned to make social work organisations more managerial and to get service users to think of themselves more as consumers accompanied by social workers as their 'user-champions' in the marketplace (Drakeford, 2000, p 109), in New Labour's modernisation discourse the personalised customer-citizen is seen as assuming a new and extended set of responsibilities in which consumerism and managerialism come together in her/his person. The accomplished customer-citizen's relationship to services is based on being consumer-savvy and managerially competent; 'self-manager' might be a more appropriate term for the personalised customer-citizen than 'service user'.

This progression towards a managerial role for customer-citizens is, perhaps, the most significant development in New Labour's consumerist aspirations to date. It is part of a wider trend in which managerialism – originally developed to run organisations – has become ever more pervasive, its instrumental rationality becoming more extensive (Hancock and Tyler, 2008). It is now reaching into the sense-making of service users, shaping their discursive and material resources. In Habermasian terms the 'system rationality', located in the state and the economy and associated with the maintenance of capitalist exchange relations, is impacting on the 'lifeworld' through 'steering media':

> Media such as money and power ... encode a purposive rational attitude towards calculable amounts of value and make it possible to exert a generalized, strategic influence on the decisions of other participants which *bypass* processes of consensus orientated communication. Inasmuch as they do not merely simplify linguistic communication, but *replace* it ... the lifeworld contexts in which processes of understanding are always embedded are devalued in favour of media-steered interactions: the lifeworld is no longer needed for the coordination of action. (Habermas, quoted in Hancock and Tyler, 2008, p 36, original emphasis)

The intrusion of system rationality into the customer-citizen's lifeworld is seen by Habermas as a process of 'colonisation' in which the structures of thought, language and action are regulated by instrumentality and utility, and the communicative possibilities are curtailed, with managerialism reconfiguring the most intimate communicative everyday activities. (For example, other people are 'resources' or 'providers' rather than sources of meaning or interdependence.) In this sense, the self-managerial role envisaged for the personalised customer-citizen by New Labour is consistent with and legitimates the tenets of neo-liberalism referred to earlier. Personalisation is not just a political idea; it is a (micro-)political force that is anti-personal in not being as interested in how people understand their lives as it is in representing how the world is and how people are meant to be and behave within it. These micro-politics of everyday life are the sites on which experiences and understandings mediate and are mediated by the relations and processes of commodity culture (Lefebvre, 2000). In this context, New Labour's modernisation agenda subjects customer-citizens' subjective experiences to managerialism in defining (implicitly) what it means to be a 'good' service user, in assertions about what people (should) want, and how they (should) want to live their lives. In addition, the promised 'empowerment' attached to self-management (the work involved is mentioned very rarely) may be intertwined with the co-option of the self-managing customer–citizen into the management of scarce resources through rationing (see the discussion of choice-making in the previous section). Furthermore, as the balance shifts increasingly towards what consumers can do for themselves, central government is empowered, owing to the more narrowly defined kinds of services that customer–citizens can demand (Heffernan, 2006, p 142), and the organisation is empowered by the achievement of a greater degree of flexibility (Gilliatt et al, 2000, p 347).

Conclusion

As we have seen, the way in which the users of social work are portrayed in the modernisation agenda and are meant to conceive of themselves, as customer–citizens, has important implications for them and for social work. New Labour has little concern with whether service users see or want to see themselves as customer–citizens, but great concern that this is what should be achieved; a customer focus that embodies a view of people as competent economic and social actors, capable of pursuing their own best interests (Drakeford, 2000, p 24). As was suggested earlier, the origin of this perspective is neo-liberalism

> that both describes and prescribes society as made up of atomised individuals with their own distinct interests, capacities and resources. It involves a rejection of any social theory that acknowledges that people are more than atomised individuals, that they have shared identities through which they and their interests are formed, and that society is constituted by bonds of mutuality that go well beyond the instrumental transactions between atomised individuals. (Muetzelfeldt, 1994, pp 139–40)

This neo-liberal discourse has promulgated entrepreneurial customer–citizen selves: individualistic, autonomous, competitive, self-interested, rational and informed (Froggett, 2000, p 7); selves who use 'choice to maximise their individual utility based on their self-interest' (Muetzelfeldt, 1994, p 148). We have seen the dominant place that this conception of the self as customer–citizen has occupied in New Labour's modernisation agenda, encapsulating the breadth and depth of changes occurring in 'consumer society'. People are now considered to perceive and position themselves primarily as consumers, constructing their identities though the choices they make as customers and expecting public services to offer that identity to them in ways that reflect their experiences in the market. New Labour represents these expectations as sweeping into public services and highlights the alleged antagonism between customer–citizens' interests and those of service providers, occasioned by its drive to individualise services and open them up to choice. Thus, the rhetorical figure of the customer-citizen has been the lynchpin of New Labour's modernisation discourse.

The drift of this chapter has been that a more realistic appraisal of the implementation of the modernisation agenda sees it as seeking to *construct and install customer-citizenship as a mode of engagement with services* that is in tune with the tenets of neo–liberalism, dominant in the wider society. Of course, social workers rarely experience New Labour discourse in this fashion. The political and policy appeal to them is expressed in terms of the desirability of the drive for personalisation, discussed earlier. (After all, they work in what used to be referred to as the *personal* social services.) Social work values and motivations predispose them to be receptive to messages that are wrapped in the language of individualisation and personalisation, messages that may mask the impact of managerialism on service users' lives and may lead to social workers not engaging critically with, or challenging, its instrumental nature (White, this volume, Chapter Seven; Evans, this volume, Chapter Eight). In addition, the danger of making independence and choice the central organising principles of policy and practice

> is to forget how and why the public sector emerged in the first place – to ensure that those who are necessarily dependent are treated with respect and dignity, to ensure a collectivised approach to risk and to ensure that secure and reliable forms of support outside of the market or the family are available. (Scourfield, 2007, p 108)

Furthermore, we have noted that public services are not a locus that makes for straightforward shifts to consumerist ideas and practices, given their limited resources. We need to be wary of mistaking the customer-citizen rhetoric for the reality of resource constraint and rationing, depicted bleakly, as:

> A pressurised public authority com[ing] to rely on pre-selected 'packages of care', which are not really tailored to individual needs, so the experience becomes more like that of a 'consumer' under a communist regime – queuing up for commodities which are strictly rationed by the authorities according to their own criteria of risk and need, and then being given something which does not fit or suit and certainly is not chosen. (Jordan and Jordan, 2000 p 23)

This bleak picture is located within three sets of processes that can be identified as being intertwined in pursuit of New Labour's customer-citizenship: McDonaldisation – the principles of efficiency, predictability, calculability and control now permeate social work organisations (Ritzer, 2000; Dustin, 2007; Harris and Unwin, this volume, Chapter One; Coleman, this volume, Chapter Two); Disneyisation – customer-citizenship is an example of theming that rarely connects with the 'real world' (Bryman, 2004); and Ikeaisation – self-assembly and self-management are now seen as desirable on the part of customer-citizens. These three sets of processes indicate some of the power and sophistication inherent in New Labour's discourse around the figure of the customer-citizen. However, we should be careful of assuming that the existence of a discourse is the same as the success of a discourse; being made *subject to* a discourse is not the same as being *subjected by* a discourse:

> One of the central arguments of Foucault was that large-scale public systems ... rely for their smooth operation on widespread internalisation of the norms according to which they actually operate ... Welfare users are neither lawyers nor bureaucrats, they must understand almost instinctively what they can ask for and how they will get it. The internalization of these norms is a long cultural process. The public cannot quickly be made to learn new rules for the consumption of welfare and it appears that if those rules cannot be fitted to the daily order of their lives, they will never learn them at all. (Baldock, 2003, pp 67–8)

Baldock's argument appears to be borne out by empirical research. On the basis of a project looking into the meanings and experiences of consumerism for providers and users in the police, the health service and social care for adults, Clarke et al conclude that:

> the terms in use to describe the relationships people have to public services are in flux. Their fluidity and contested character reflect the turbulent combination of changing publics and changing public services. It is clear that both providers and users of services are engaged in 'making up meanings' to express their experiences and expectations, and their ambitions and anxieties. It is also clear that the 'consumer' has failed to capture popular and organisational imaginations. It commands little enthusiasm and, indeed, appeared largely as a figure *against* which people constructed their desired relationships. (Clarke et al, 2007, p 138, original emphasis)

If the resistance to New Labour's image of the customer-citizen and the attempts made to renegotiate the new 'rules' of engagement with services found by Clarke et al are typical, it may turn out that we are witnessing New Labour achieving some success in changing terminology but facing continuing struggles about and against changes in substance.

Note

[1] I am grateful for discussions with Lydia Harris-White and for her contributing the concept of Ikeaisation.

FIVE

Modernising children's services: partnership and participation in policy and practice

Katrin Bain

Introduction

After its landslide victory in the 1997 general election, the New Labour government published a series of White Papers, Green Papers and reports setting out its agenda to modernise government and public services. The agenda was rooted in the redefinition of the relationship between the state and citizens: 'At the heart of the modern welfare state will be a new contract between the citizen and the government, based on responsibilities and rights' (Department of Social Security, 1998, p 80). The literature exploring this new contract has so far focused on health, education and adult social services (see, for example, Dwyer, 2000; Harris, 2003; Clarke et al, 2007). In all of these areas, policy is very much phrased in the terminology of consumerism (Harris, this volume, Chapter Four). Consumer-oriented services that meet the needs of citizens are described as offering good quality, value-for-money, individualised services or care packages, a choice of services and services that are easily accessible. In the areas of health, education and social services for adults, an attempt has been made to offer choice to service users, for example in choosing a hospital, a school, or buying care packages through direct payments. Choice is one important element in the modernising agenda that is seen as contributing to more personalised public services that empower the individual (Department of Health, 1998). The reformed public services are urged to acknowledge service users as individuals and to actively involve them in service planning and delivery. This emphasis on service user involvement, expressed in terms of partnership and participation, is the focus of this chapter.

The chapter explores the content and implementation of the modernisation agenda's new contract between citizens – in this case parents – and the state in children and families social services. It draws on an analysis of national policy documents and qualitative interviews with four managers and 11 front-line children and family social workers in one English local authority. The data are part of an empirical study, conducted in 2005, on the representations of citizenship in policy and social work practice. The chapter begins by offering an overview of children's services, including recent policy developments. It then moves on to look at three approaches to parental involvement: 'working in partnership with parents', 'parental participation' and 'consumerist citizen involvement'. Each of these approaches is considered in relation to policy and how policy is implemented in social work practice and stock is taken of the potential each offers to parents to play an active part in the social work process. The chapter concludes by reflecting on the possibilities and limitations of each approach, especially in the light of the restructuring of children's services following the 2004 Children Act.

Children and families social services: key themes and working principles

Following the 1989 Children Act and the 1990 National Health Service and Community Care Act, social services departments established specialist teams for the provision of services to children and adults, a tendency that was consolidated and strengthened by the 2004 Children Act, after which separate departments were introduced. Nevertheless, the key legislation for children's services is still the 1989 Children Act, which is based on the premise that children should be brought up by their families whenever possible, while at the same time making provision for state intervention to protect children where necessary (Hill, 2000, p 161). With regard to child protection, the 1989 Children Act introduced the concept of significant harm as the threshold for compulsory intervention in family life by social workers, on behalf of the state, in the best interests of the child (Department of Health, 2003b, p 3). Within the Act, harm is defined as ill-treatment or the impairment of health and development (section 31(9)). In order to establish whether a child is experiencing significant harm 'his health or development shall be compared with that which could reasonably be expected of a similar child' (section 31(10)). Concerns about significant harm trigger a social work response:

> Where a local authority has reasonable cause to suspect that a child is suffering, or is likely to suffer, significant harm, the authority shall make, or cause to be made, such enquiries as they consider necessary to enable them to decide whether they should take any action to safeguard or promote the child's welfare. (1989 Children Act, section 47)

This aspect of children's services' responsibilities is referred to as child protection and often forms the main focus of social work (Commission for Social Care Inspection, 2005a, p 16). In practice, this often means protecting children from their parents, or at least one of their parents, and can lead to involuntary use of services (Commission for Social Care Inspection, 2005b, p 32).

In pursuit of social work's child protection responsibilities, the government has set out clear timelines for all stages of the process, within which social workers are expected to work, and local authorities are audited regularly with regard to their achievement of targets set by central government (Commission for Social Care Inspection and National Statistics Office, 2005). Some professionals are critical of this approach:

> "I think it is one of social services' biggest faults that the government lays down what it is going to give you a tick and a star for.... That is the agenda to such a great extent that they forget about the other things that are much more preventive." (Sarah, fieldwork manager)

The provision of preventive services and support to families outside the child protection process have remained in the background, even though there are provisions for them in the law (Commission for Social Care Inspection, 2005a). Indeed, the law states a clear commitment to children being brought up, whenever possible, within their families and this is expected to be facilitated by local authorities' duty to provide preventive services (1989 Children Act, section 17) in order to support parents and stabilise family situations. However, because the general duty to provide these preventive services is not attached to individual rights to receive such services, local authorities may fulfil their legal duty by offering family support only to parts of the community. The Commission for Social Care Inspection has raised concerns about the high threshold for receiving family support services and acknowledges that resources are allocated to child protection work rather than to family support (Commission for Social Care Inspection, 2005a, p 16). The *Children Act Report 2000* confirms that help for families whose children are not at risk of maltreatment is not always available (Department of Health, 2001b, p 36).

High-profile inquiries into the deaths of children (Reder et al, 1993; Department for Education and Skills et al, 2003) may help in explaining why prevention and support outside the child protection process are underused. The inquiry report into the death of Victoria Climbié – the most recent high-profile inquiry at the time of writing questions this bifurcation into preventive and protective responses: 'It is not possible to separate the protection of children from wider support to families. Indeed, often the best protection for a child is achieved by the timely intervention of family support services.... The needs of the child and his or her family are often inseparable' (Laming, 2003, p 7).

In response to the Victoria Climbié inquiry report, the government initiative *Every Child Matters* (Department for Education and Skills, 2003) introduced a model of a pyramid of services (Figure 5.1) that together formed the integrated children's services, which are set out in the 2004 Children Act. These services range from universal services such as health and education, through targeted services such as therapy, family support and children's centres to specialist services, including child protection. *Every Child Matters* was concerned in part with seeking to strengthen targeted services and thereby offering families wider access to support services.

Figure 5.1: Integrated children's services

Specialist

**Services for
children
at high risk**
For example:
Child protection
Adoption and fostering

**Services for families with
complex problems**
For example:
Children and families social services
Targeted parenting support

Targeted

**Services for children and families
with identified needs**
For example:
SEN and disability
Speech and language therapy

**Services for all children in targeted
areas**
For example:
Sure Start
Children's centres

Universal

Services for all children and families
For example:
Health – GPs, midwives, health visitors
Education – early years and schools
Connexions – 13–19

Source: DfES (2003, p 21)

The concern to strengthen support services in *Every Child Matters* is consistent with section 1(1) of the 1989 Children Act, which insists that the welfare of the child should be paramount. The welfare principle is reflected in the emphasis on the need for social work to be 'child-centred'. This results in social workers practising first and foremost in the interests of the child and seeing the child's interests as potentially competing with those of the parents:

"And one of the professional values [is] that I am very child focused, so as much I will work in partnership with parents and I view that as very, very important. At the end of the day I would definitely say that I was a person that worked in the best interests of the child ... I would say that I work in the best interests of the child while trying to work in partnership with parents." (Anne, social worker)

This emphasis results in the child generally being considered to be 'the client' in children and families social services. In an ethnographic study conducted during 1997 in a local authority children and families team, Scourfield (2003) found that when asked the question "Who is the client?", social workers clearly stated that it was the child. His study also found that child protection workers did not perceive work with women and men, for its own sake, as part of their task. This approach to practice is consistent with that advocated in government guidance for the assessment of children in need and their families: 'Working with families is not an end in itself; the objective must always be to safeguard and promote the welfare of the child' (Department of Health, 2000c, p 13). Nevertheless, parents have an important part to play in the child protection process as a dimension of the child–centred approach, as most children will continue to live with their parents. Social work intervention is, therefore, often targeted towards parents, and social workers have regular contact with them. This relationship is often referred to as 'working in partnership with parents'. The following section looks at how 'partnership working' is understood in policy and social work practice and at the opportunities that the concept offers for participation on the part of parents.

Partnership with parents

The term 'working in partnership with parents' was first introduced in the guidance concerning the implementation of the 1989 Children Act as the central principle for family support services; the same terminology then also became used in relation to child protection. Even though the term itself is not used in the 1989 Children Act, the principles underpinning the Act are seen as embodying partnership-based practice (Department of Health, 1991, p 2; 2000c, p 5).

Earlier research into working in partnership with parents assumed an understanding of partnership as active parental participation and appraised practice against this understanding (Corby et al, 1996; Sinclair and Grimshaw, 1997; Aldgate and Statham, 2001; Hall and Slembrouck, 2001). These studies found that parents generally valued the opportunity to attend meetings but found it difficult to participate and to challenge social workers' decisions, as they wanted to be seen as cooperating with social services. All of the studies concluded that the parents involved had not been given sufficient opportunities to participate and offered recommendations for overcoming these limitations. Following the concerns expressed in these early studies of the implementation of the 1989 Children Act, government policies and guidance have continued to promote partnership with parents. The discussion that follows traces the understanding of partnership in these documents. Within them, parents are not understood as active participants and it is, therefore, not surprising that official promotion of a policy of partnership with parents does not automatically lead to enhanced parental participation.

The government guidance *Working Together to Safeguard Children* sets out 15 principles for working in partnership with families:

1. Treat all family members as you would wish to be treated, with dignity and respect.

2. Ensure that family members know that the child's safety and welfare must be given first priority, but that each of them has a right to a courteous, caring and professionally competent service.

3. Take care not to infringe privacy any more than is necessary to safeguard the welfare of the child.

4. Be clear with yourself and with family members about your power to intervene, and the purpose of your professional involvement at each stage.

5. Be aware of the effects on family members of the power you have as a professional, and the impact and implications of what you say and do.

6. Respect the confidentiality of family members and your observations about them, unless they give permission for information to be passed to others or it is essential to do so to protect the child.

7. Listen to the concerns of children and their families, and take care to learn about their understanding, fears and wishes before arriving at your own explanations and plans.

8. Learn about and consider children within their family relationships and communities, including their cultural and religious contexts, and their place within their own families.

9. Consider the strengths and potential of family members, as well as their weaknesses, problems and limitations.

10. Ensure children, families and other carers know their responsibilities and rights, including any right to services, and their right to refuse services, and any consequences of doing so.

11. Use plain, jargon-free language appropriate to the age and culture of each person. Explain unavoidable technical and professional terms.

12. Be open and honest about your concerns and responsibilities, plans and limitations, without being defensive.

13. Allow children and families time to take in and understand concerns and processes. A balance needs to be found between appropriate speed and the needs of people who may need extra time in which to communicate.

14. Take care to distinguish between personal feelings, values, prejudices and beliefs, and professional roles and responsibilities, and ensure that you have good supervision to check that you are doing so.

15. If a mistake or misinterpretation has been made, or you are unable to keep to an agreement, provide an explanation. Always acknowledge any distress experienced by adults and children and do all you can to keep it to a minimum.

(Department of Health, 1999, p 76)

These 15 principles describe the professional position social workers should adopt when working with families. On the face of it this position is based on respect, clarity and consideration for the family's position when using services. On closer inspection the principles can be divided into two categories. The principles in the first category (1, 3, 6, 8, 10, 11, 14 and 15) safeguard social workers against accusations of professional misconduct and minimise complaints. The principles in the second category (2, 4, 5, 9, 12, 13) emphasise the need for the careful exercise of statutory powers in the context of child protection. Principle 7 is the nearest to partnership as manifested in practice. It acknowledges the family's position but leaves the power to define the problem and what intervention is necessary with the social worker. These 15 principles demonstrate that the understanding of partnership in this policy area differs from the common understanding of partnership as 'a contractual agreement among equals' (Smith, 2005, p 81). In fact, the concept of partnership adopted in these policy documents tends to confirm and reinforce the existing power relationship between social workers and parents; the 15 principles could almost be read as advice offered to social workers on how to minimise resistance from parents. This limited understanding of partnership is often seen as being consistent with the statutory role that children's services have:

> **Interviewer:** *"You said, 'Working in partnership with parents'. Could you explain what that means?"*
>
> "Um ... I suppose I mean, essentially it is about cooperation, um ... but ... really we do have, we mostly work with children that are on the Child Protection Register, so sometimes it doesn't feel, although we say the words like cooperation or working in partnership then we have got as a local authority a very specific brief, and a format that we have to follow, and sometimes it doesn't fit that comfortably ... So that's the hurdle we have to get over, and I think it is about the skill of the individual workers in trying to work with parents, and saying 'Look I know that you don't want social services involved in your life, but that there is a plan, we feel that your child is being harmed and is at risk, and there is a plan that we need to work together with you, and the quicker that plan gets progressed then the quicker the child

gets off the register.' I think it is being open and honest with parents as well." (Helen, team manager)

Indeed, the power relationship between social workers and parents prevents the possibility of a partnership based on an agreement among equals. Not only do social workers have an advantage with regard to knowledge, including legal knowledge, but also the potential to remove a child represents the ultimate power of children and families social services. Lapierre's study (2008) of women who have experienced domestic violence found that this power makes it hard, if not impossible, for parents to make alternative suggestions or to disagree with social workers' suggestions: "So in a way they were saying to me 'do as you're told or we'll take your kids away'" (Angela, woman/mother); "… but I couldn't answer her back because she had my kids basically, she had control over my children" (Sharon, woman/mother) (quoted in Lapierre and Bain, 2008).

Even though it is widely used, the terminology of 'working in partnership' has limited value in characterising the citizen–state relationship between social workers and parents in child protection practice, for at least three reasons. First, it can give parents a false sense of being equal partners, as the common-sense understanding of partnership would suggest. As shown above, this is not the understanding of partnership in policy or in practice. Extending the existing approach to encompass the potential for an equal partnership is impossible because in the area of child protection the safety and well-being of the child (rightly) overrides the parents' interests, when necessary.

Second, the same partnership terminology is used for inter-agency working. Both working together with parents and inter-agency working are covered in the same guidance (Department of Health, 1999). The *Collins Dictionary of Social Work* uses the latter as the definition of partnership (Pierson and Thomas, 2002, pp 336–7). This terminology fails to differentiate between the two kinds of partnership working and this conflation is also a feature of practice, as can be seen in the following quotation: "an initial assessment, which would mean going out and seeing the family in their own home environment obtaining their permission to work together so that we can actually get a bigger picture about what is going on and speak to the variety of agencies that are involved" (Tara, social worker).

Third, in current practice little distinction is made between the family support that parents use voluntarily and child protection, where compulsory state intervention in family life is possible. The practitioners interviewed see their work as a continuum, with family support as a possible precursor to child protection:

"Yeah, if they were seen as 'children in need' we would make a plan and that would involve the parents and the key professionals like the health visitor and the school, objectives and what we can do and what they need to do, targets really … If with all that support put in place looking at all the practicalities really but working with them and then we would agree this plan and then we take it from there but if the parents fail to [do] this and this and there are no improvements then we would look at taking it to case conference and maybe registering the children and then again it would go through the process of having this support but having core groups and making it quite clear that if the objectives aren't met when we review the case it could mean looking at legal action." (Amandeep, social worker)

This stance is reflected in the restructuring that followed the 2004 Children Act, which emphasises integration of services and information sharing between agencies, and understands services as lying on a continuum (Department for Education and Skills, 2003, p 1). While this provides the possibility of widening access to preventive services, it also entails the risk of escalating to intervention in order to safeguard children and shifting the focus towards child protection in services such as children's centres, which currently offer general information and support to families (Smith, 2005, p 191). As an alternative to a continuum model of services, having a clear boundary between services to support families and interventions to protect children would give parents and social workers a clearer idea about the possibilities and limitations of parental participation. It would also open up new possibilities for strengthening the idea of 'working in partnership' and shaping it towards citizen participation.

Following this consideration of the limitations of the concept of 'working in partnership with parents', the next section explores the potential for parental participation in the existing configuration of policy, provision and practice.

Parental participation

Participation as an objective for children's (and adult) social services was introduced in the White Paper *Modernising Social Services* (Department of Health, 1998). The aim is 'to actively involve users and carers in planning services and in tailoring individual packages of care; and to ensure effective mechanisms are in place to handle complaints' (Department of Health, 2003c, p 50). Participation, therefore, goes beyond 'partnership' and aspires to offer service users a key role in shaping the services they use. Further, it is understood as an important tool for involving those users who use services involuntarily, as is often the case in child protection (Department of Health, 2001b, p 81). With so much pinned on what participation can achieve, its meaning needs to be clarified.

Arnstein (1969) has identified eight levels of citizen participation, ranging from 'non-participation' via several 'degrees of tokenism' to 'citizen power' (Figure 5.2). Arnstein's typology is relevant for children and families social work, as it specifically takes into account the power relationship between different actors, such as the one described above between parents and social workers. As will be shown below, Arnstein considers most areas of participation suggested in children's services policy as 'tokenism'. Access to information is the lowest 'token' offered, but she acknowledges that it can be used to promote participation: 'Informing

Figure 5.2: Arnstein's ladder of citizen participation

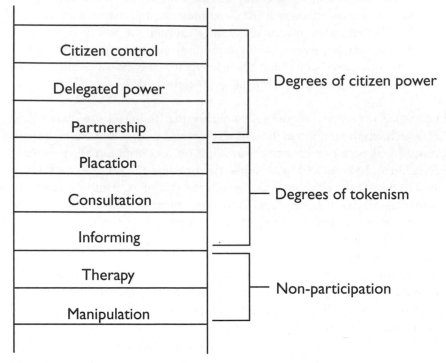

Source: Arnstein (1969, p 217)

citizens of their rights, responsibilities and options can be the most important first step toward legitimate citizen participation. However, too frequently the emphasis is placed on a one-way flow of information – from officials to citizens – with no channel provided for feedback and no power for negotiation' (Arnstein, 1969, p 219).

In the six principles of working in partnership that address information flow (identified above), the direction of the flow is from the worker to the parent. The same is true of the majority of documents the family receives. Local authorities provide leaflets for parents with general information about services offered. In the interviews conducted, social workers said that these leaflets are given to parents during the first visit as well as being available at their offices. In addition, during social workers' involvement, parents should be informed about decisions and receive copies of assessments, plans and reports. These should be explained to parents in order to ensure that their content is fully understood (Department of Health, 2000c, p 42). Such information sharing may be limited in cases where the child may be at risk: 'If you have concerns about a parent's ability to protect their child, consider carefully what the parents should be told, when and by whom, taking account of the child's welfare' (Department of Health, 2003c, p 16). In the case of a child protection conference, the social worker's report is shared with the parents before the conference, whereas all other professionals bring their reports to the conference (Department of Health, 1999, p 54). This limits the opportunity for parents to prepare their responses, although social workers are enjoined to ensure that they take parents' and children's wishes into account and offer them opportunities to record their views (Department of Health, 1999, pp 58–9): 'At the conclusion of either an initial or core assessment, the parent(s) and child, if appropriate, should be informed in writing, and/or in another more appropriate medium, of the decisions made and be offered the opportunity to record their views, disagreements and to ask for corrections to recorded information' (Department of Health, 2000c, p 32). This offers parents a channel for feedback and negotiation. Given the uneven distribution of power (mentioned above), it is questionable how far parents would feel that they could use this channel and, in any case, it is unclear to what extent it is offered to them by social workers. Inspections conducted by the Commission for Social Care Inspection found that parents were not sufficiently involved in the referral process, to the point where they were not even informed about a referral or that information had been requested from other agencies (Commission for Social Care Inspection, 2005a, p 35).

Moving up Arnstein's ladder of citizen participation, the next level is consultation, which is promoted in government initiatives such as the Quality Protects programme. The government acknowledges that consultation is currently underdeveloped and should be extended (Department of Health and Social Services Inspectorate, 2003, p 26). In order for consultation to be meaningful it has to be combined with other elements of participation. Otherwise

> people are primarily perceived as statistical abstractions, and participation is measured by how many come to meetings, take brochures home, or answer a questionnaire. What citizens achieve in all this activity is that they have 'participated in participation.' And what power holders achieve is the evidence that they have gone through the required motions of involving 'those people.' (Arnstein, 1969, p 219; see also, Croft and Beresford, 2002)

This position is shared by the Commission for Social Care Inspection, which considers consultation only to be meaningful if people's opinions and feedback influence policy. Consultation has increased, but so far there is little evidence that this has resulted in changes to service delivery (Commission for Social Care Inspection, 2005b, p 28). Therefore, the Commission for Social Care Inspection advocates meaningful consultation with and participation by service users in all stages of service delivery and evaluation, yet, in the interviews conducted, only one of the social workers said that service user feedback is an important influence on her day-to-day work. Information and consultation as potential forms of proactive citizen involvement are supplemented by provisions for reactive citizen involvement (Beresford and Croft, 1993, p 12). Reactive citizen involvement refers to the involvement of citizens after things have gone wrong. The 1989

Children Act makes provision for complaints in section 26, as amended in the 2006 Representations Procedure (England) Regulations. It sets out the formal complaints procedure that service users can follow if they are not satisfied with the services received.

As has been established thus far, the opportunities for parents to have their say and influence practice are limited. While existing policies offer a good starting point, they are currently stuck at the 'tokenism' stage and need to be developed further in order to offer more potential for parental participation that does justice to the government's pledge to make families equal stakeholders in the process of planning and delivering services. This would take participation towards the higher levels of Arnstein's ladder of citizen participation, where service users have 'enough power to make the target institutions responsive to their views, aspirations, and needs' (Arnstein, 1969, p 217). One of the five key commitments of New Labour's modernisation agenda, reviewed at the outset of this chapter, is to make services responsive to users' needs, offering personalised choices instead of 'one size fits all' services (Harris, this volume, Chapter Four). The next section considers parental participation in the wider context of the modernisation agenda.

The wider context of modernisation

The modernisation agenda has been influenced by private sector principles. It is assumed that people's experience of the private sector is positive and they are expecting a similar experience from public services (Harris, this volume, Chapter Four): 'People are exercising choice and demanding higher quality. In the private sector, service standards and service delivery have improved as a result. People are now rightly demanding a better service not just from the private sector, but from the public sector too' (Cabinet Office, 1999, p 10).

In order to fulfil these alleged demands from 'people', one key commitment of the modernisation agenda is to transform services 'to meet the needs of citizens not the convenience of service providers' (Commission for Social Care Inspection, 2005b; Department of Health, 1998; see also Department of Social Security, 1998; Cabinet Office 1999, p 13). Choice is considered a key element in achieving this. The government has introduced the element of choice in a variety of services, such as choice-based lettings, direct payments in social care and choice of hospitals and schools. Choice is understood as the opportunity for citizens 'to select outcomes which are particularly appropriate to them' (Office of Public Services Reform, 2005, p 3). Choice can be divided into economic choice, where money follows the service user's choice, as in the case of direct payments, and non-economic choice, where choice is not followed by financial payments but still involves selection between alternatives, for example, options such as appointment times or choices about treatment (Policy Commission on Public Services, 2004, p 26). With the exception of children with disabilities, there is no provision in children's services for direct payments. In addition, as we have already seen, the availability of family support services is very limited and parents are seldom in a position to choose a service provider. The limitation of choice in a consumerist sense is most apparent in child protection. Most parents do not choose to become involved with social workers over child protection issues, as the majority of referrals received by children's services come from other agencies, such as nurseries and schools. Once a case becomes known to social workers, non-compliance with the services offered may be interpreted as neglecting the children or putting them at risk, which then allows for compulsory intervention in family life: "They don't have choice, they can't tell us to go away and they can't go, or generally can't go, somewhere else" (George, social worker).

Nevertheless, the Commission for Social Care Inspection considers that choice is a valid concept for child protection and widens the consumerist take on choice towards empowerment:

> A note of caution is needed in the ongoing debate about 'choice'. In social care when we talk about choice, let's be clear that we are talking about more than acting as a consumer; we are talking about real choices, which affect how people are able to live their lives. But many people who use social care services are not in a position to make choices – indeed, it may not even be their choice to receive social care. There are many reasons why choice may hold not much meaning for people who rely most on care services, but their needs and wishes should still count. (Commission for Social Care Inspection, 2005b, p v)

The social work participants in the research were less positive about consumerism and choice. So far as the social workers were concerned, being a 'consumer' is linked to retailing and the exchange of products for money. The term also does not do justice to the social workers' understanding of their role as professionals:

> "We are not in the marketplace, we intend to genuinely help people with difficulties, and we are not doing it for economic gain or financial gain, so in my opinion using customer [or] consumer suggests that you are in the marketplace, and you are trying to market your product, trying to make a gain, which is not the case in this situation." (Daniel, social worker)

Indeed, the rhetoric of choice is so at odds with the reality of child protection that it can mean little more than making sure that the parents understand the consequences if they decide not to comply with the intervention:

> "They have choices as to whether they are going to undertake some of these things, that will bring about change, or they are going to carry on the same, and hope that it will all go away, that's what I meant, people have choices, in whether they're prepared to do their side of the bargain ... you have got to choose whether you are prepared to

do those things, but clearly if none of it gets done, and your child isn't able to develop properly, this is a choice that we look at permanency somewhere else, so when you say choice I think you have to be clear to people what their choices are, which is to get stuck in and get it sorted out for their child, not for us, not to keep social services happy, but because they want the best, you know they want things to change for their child." (Sarah, manager)

Consistent with this viewpoint, the Public Administration Select Committee recommended that the government should acknowledge the limitations on choice (Office of Public Services Reform, 2005, p 4). In its response, the government did not accept the recommendation; it saw choice as an opportunity for service user involvement and wanted to focus on the advantages rather than the limitations (Office of Public Services Reform, 2005). Although there may have been some advantages in the government's modernisation agenda in terms of increased choice for adult service users (Tanner, this volume, Chapter Six), NHS patients and parents with regard to the education of their children, in children's services the concept of choice has so far offered parents little potential for involvement.

Modernising children's services – where do we go from here?

This chapter has drawn on policy documents and data gathered in interviews with managers and social workers in order to illustrate how the citizen–state relationship is constructed in parent–social worker interactions in children's services. More specifically, it has considered the possibilities for parental partnership and participation and for tensions between the common-sense understanding of the terminology used and the intended meanings in policy and practice.

As we have seen, the widely espoused idea of 'working in partnership with parents' is primarily used in a rhetorical and misleading way. The existing power relationship between social workers and parents, as well as the context in which social workers have to carry out their work, prevents the development of partnership in the sense of 'a contractual agreement among equals' (Smith, 2005, p 81). At best, partnership is used in practice to describe a genuine interest in the views of parents and taking these views into account in the decision-making process. Yet the vision set out by the government for public services includes the aim of empowering people, which goes further than the current understanding of partnership: 'The government has a clear and non-negotiable vision of revitalised and improved public services, designed around the needs of individuals, rooted in the values of community, empowering people and offering choice' (Platt, 2005). Thus, recent iterations of the modernisation agenda focus on individual choice, support for independent living and giving people a greater say in how the services they receive are delivered. Children's services are implicitly included in this agenda, even though the examples used in policy documents are limited to voluntary use of services (see, for example Department of Health, 1998). The high level of involuntary use of children's services, and the statutory powers attached to it, make it a special and testing case for the implementation of the modernisation agenda, as we have seen.

Children's services are governed by the 1989 Children Act, which attempts to reconcile the need for child protection with minimal and supportive intervention in family life. However, government guidance and performance targets have shifted the focus to child protection, which has resulted in family support taking a back seat. The 2004 Children Act sets out the timeline for establishing integrated children's services incorporating health, education, family support and child protection. This restructuring dangles the prospect of being able to refocus social work towards supportive, preventive services that parents use voluntarily. However, in the current climate, with high-profile inquiries into child deaths, it runs the risk of extending the emphasis on child protection to other services and discouraging parents from using these services for fear of becoming known to children's services.

The statutory power and responsibility to protect children from harm has led to a child-centred practice where the focus is on children and parents are viewed solely in relation to their capacity to offer a safe environment for them. As most children continue to live with their families, it would be beneficial to refocus the social worker's perspective towards the family as a whole and acknowledge that parents have needs of their own. This would enable the provision of holistic support to strengthen the family. The Commission for Social Care Inspection acknowledges that:

> Many children will be known to the new integrated children's services because of the social care needs of their parents or guardians. By failing to address the adults' needs, such as mental ill health and substance misuse, the solution to support children will only be partial. Collaboration is needed to ensure that both the child's and adults' needs are met. (Commission for Social Care Inspection, 2005b, p 168)

If this aspiration is to be realised in practice, resources need to be (re-)allocated accordingly. The government and audit processes could support such a shift by strengthening the role of family support in performance targets and inspection reports. In the absence of this macro-shift, it will be left to front-line social workers and their managers to build on the opportunities provided by following legislation and official guidance in order to give parents (and children) a voice and create opportunities for participation.

Conclusion

Being a social worker in children's services is not an easy task. It has been well documented that such social workers are overloaded and that there is little stability in teams. In addition to the organisational challenges of high workload and staff turnover, the decisions about services are difficult ones: 'Support is complex to assess, to get right and to deliver, especially for parenting, because of the balance between the neglect of family problems and intrusion into family life, not to mention ideas of what satisfactory parenting is, how and when this needs support and who should decide that' (Quinton, 2004, p 79). In contrast, service users have clear expectations of social workers and how they want their relationship to be. Service users want to be:

- respected;
- listened to;
- provided with accessible information;
- in control of their lives and able to solve problems independently, if possible;
- experts about their own families' needs;
- part of the team around the child.

(Croft and Beresford, 2002, p 390; Policy Commission on Public Services, 2004, p 58; Quinton, 2004, p 191)

The expectations of service users show that they value the interpersonal skills of social workers. It has been argued that, with the introduction of the modernisation agenda and the shift towards a consumerist perspective, these skills, which were traditionally associated with social work, have been seen as less relevant (Harris, 1999, p 104). However, these skills have been endorsed in some quarters as having continuing resonance for consumerist public services:

> Professionals must be technically competent, but this by itself is no longer enough. We need professionals who are responsive to the needs of consumers as individuals and who develop relationships built on respect for opening up choices. This requires professionals to develop 'soft' skills such as listening and empathy together with the attitudinal attributes that allow them to co-manage care with their clients. (Policy Commission on Public Services, 2004, p 58)

Thus, what is valued in social work, the statements in policy documents and the expectations expressed in service users' views are not that far apart, but it is up to social workers to give the rhetoric of partnership, participation and choice meaningful content on a case-by-case basis. A first step would be to acknowledge the statutory powers within children's services and the limitations for parental participation that these entail. It is important to communicate this clearly to the parents rather than to pretend that they are equal partners, as the rhetoric of partnership suggests. The same is true for other limitations, such as resources. It is pointless to talk about choice if there is only one provider operating in the area and the intervention is compulsory. At the same time, parental involvement can be widened within the existing restrictions as the following examples show:

- ensuring parents have copies of reports prior to meetings taking place so that they can consider the content and prepare a response;
- offering advocates to support parents in putting their views forward;
- setting up family group conferences so that families can find solutions for themselves.

For all three of the above, provisions exist in legislation and guidance and it is up to social workers and managers to make use of them.

Parental participation in children's services is a challenging task, owing to the limitations described in this chapter. It requires skills and initiative from social workers in seeking to develop it on a daily basis; when successful it can help to overcome resistance and empower service users.

SIX

Modernisation and the delivery of user-centred services

Denise Tanner

Introduction

There is a growing affinity, at least on the surface, between research evidence about what service users say they want from health and social care services and messages conveyed in social policy. A key theme from research findings and literature generated from the experiences of adult service users is the central importance of the services and support that enable them to improve the quality of their lives, as distinct from improving the quality of services as an end in itself (see, for example, Beresford and Branfield, 2006). An intrinsic requirement, from their perspectives, is that services and interventions should enhance the degree of choice and control that they exercise over their lives. These broad concepts are common across adult service user groups, even though there may be varying nuances of meaning and emphasis within this, reflecting a diversity of situations, backgrounds, impairments, personalities and so on (see, for example, Campbell and Oliver, 1996; Faulkner, 1997; Joseph Rowntree Foundation Task Group, 2004; Taylor et al, 2007). The vision for 'modernising' adult social care outlined in the Green Paper, *Independence, Well-being and Choice* (Department of Health, 2005), appears sympathetic to such service user aims and concerns at this fundamental level. It acknowledges that everyone has the right to control her or his own life (para 1.1) and that, in support of this value, 'Services should be person-centred, seamless and proactive. They should support independence, not dependence and allow everyone to enjoy a good quality of life, including the ability to contribute fully to our communities' (para 1.3). This vision is reinforced in the White Paper *Our Health, Our Care, Our Say* (Department of Health, 2006), with its 'three simple themes, which came from people themselves', namely, 'putting people more in control of their own health and care'; 'enabling and supporting health, independence and well-being'; and 'rapid and convenient access to high quality cost-effective services' (para 1.5).

This chapter examines specific areas of conflict and constraint in achieving this 'modernising' vision of services that promote independence, well-being and choice, focusing mainly on older people's experiences of social care services. It begins by summarising what quality of life means from older people's perspectives, incorporating consideration of both research evidence and theories of successful ageing. It then discusses four areas of practice in which various facets of the modernisation agenda's managerialism appear to be obstructing the delivery of user-centred services. First, the tension between the need for timely intervention that supports older people's coping strategies and the managerial policies and practices that seek to ration, restrict and delay service provision is discussed. Second, the significance of disjunctions between policy discourses, managerial concerns and service user understandings and prioritisations of need is explored. Third, the service user requirements for a 'whole person' focus in assessment and service provision are compared with policies and practices associated with restricted and fragmented professional roles and responsibilities. Fourth, the extent to which the operation of the 'care market' militates against the exercise of choice and control by service users is discussed. The chapter proceeds to consider the potential of current policy directions, in particular the extension of direct payments and the introduction of individual budgets, to deliver support that is more closely attuned to the needs and preferences of service users.

Quality of life and 'keeping going' from the perspective of older people

Research based on older people's views and experiences identifies the following themes as key to a good quality of life: social relationships; social roles and activities; health; a positive psychological outlook; home and neighbourhood; financial circumstances; and independence. It also highlights that the reasons why these factors are important to older people's quality of life are that they are related to the enjoyment of freedom to do as they want, pleasure and satisfaction, enjoyment of social attachments and feelings of security (see, for example, Bowling and Gabriel, 2007). Other research centred on older people's experiences and perceptions indicates that a key concern for them is 'keeping going' against the odds and maintaining their perception of independence (Tanner, 2001a; 2001b; Townsend et al, 2006). 'Keeping going' entails maintaining those aspects that give their life quality. When this becomes difficult, help is valued that supports them in maintaining functioning or standards in relation to the dimensions of their lives that are most important to them. Thus, for example, older people value low-level support that helps them to maintain standards within the home (Clark et al, 1998); they value community environments and facilities that help them to retain the ability to get out and about and to feel safe in their communities (Holland et al, 2005); and they welcome opportunities and support to maintain friendships and fulfil valued family roles (Godfrey et al, 2004; Nazroo et al, 2004). Another common theme in research, including cross-cultural research, on older people's perspectives is their resourcefulness and resilience (for example, Johnson and Barer, 1997; Aronson, 2002; Cliggett, 2005). In order to 'keep going' as long as possible, older people want access to forms of help that support their own preferred strategies and that are available at the time when they experience a threat to their sense of being able to cope (Tanner, 2007).

The development and evaluation of policy and practice is aided by reference to theoretical models of successful ageing, as well as by evidence from older people themselves. Successful ageing is seen as the effective management of the shifting balance of gains and losses encountered in later life; older people are able to maintain well-being by optimising strengths and resources and by deploying strategies to negotiate losses and difficulties (Baltes and Carstensen, 1996). Strategies include substituting alternative goals for those that are no longer attainable and drawing on other resources to compensate for losses and impairments (Steverink et al, 1998; Godfrey, 2001). A significant implication of this understanding of how the ageing process can be successfully negotiated concerns the capacity of services to respond to older people when they reach a critical phase; this occurs when there are few remaining opportunities for the substitution of goals and resources. How older people manage these processes has to be understood in the context of their whole life course and in relation to their subjective as well as objective experience. This indicates the need for complex and sensitive assessments of 'risk', as well as for timely intervention from the older person's perspective. It also highlights the different levels at which intervention needs to operate: building the reserves that people bring to the stage of later life; seeking to mitigate the challenges they encounter during the ageing process; and providing access to compensatory support to help them deal with difficulties and losses (Grundy, 2006).

Timely intervention that supports older people's coping strategies

In what ways, then, do social care services promote older people's quality of life, providing adequate and appropriate support at the time they feel they need it? Looking first at the role of assessment, the 1990 NHS and Community Care Act, implemented in 1993, gave local authorities a duty to assess need for community care services. According to the assessment guidance, assessment was to be seen as a service in its own right, enabling individuals to understand their situations better and identifying available options to help them manage their lives (Department of Health, 2003d). However, although the 'gateway' to assessment is wide in terms of the statutory responsibility to carry out assessment of anyone who appears to be in need of services, it seems that access to assessment is itself limited by practitioners', service users' and carers' awareness of the service restrictions that operate in practice. Although, in legal terms, eligibility criteria apply to access to services and not access to assessment, in practice individuals are screened out from receiving assessment if exploratory questions by the person receiving the initial contact or referral suggest that they are unlikely to be eligible for services (Ellis et al, 1999; Gott et al, 2007). This in effect denies them the potential benefit of assessment as a route to identifying wider support options. If an assessment is carried out, it seems that its process and outcomes, perhaps inevitably, are influenced by practitioner awareness of service availability, or lack of it. One study based on interviews with 28 practitioners carrying out assessments referred to 'the inextricable link between process and context. More specifically, it was evident from the analysis that practitioners' awareness of the constraints and limitations of the resource context influenced the assessment process and their decision-making' (Foster et al, 2006, p 131).

Moving from assessment to access to support services, while there is a clear-cut duty to assess need, the legal obligation to provide services is more restricted. In direct contrast both to research evidence about the nature of support that older people value and theoretical models of successful ageing, statutory social care practice remains heavily dominated by the operation of eligibility criteria that restrict access to social care services to those with prescribed high-level needs. Thus, eligibility criteria are a tool to ration services according to the level of available resources (Clements, 2004). The framework for eligibility for social care services is provided in *Fair Access to Care Services* (FACS) guidance (Department of Health, 2003d). This sets out four bands of eligibility, according to whether the risks to independence are 'low', 'moderate', 'substantial' or 'critical'. Local authorities are able to decide at which band of risk they will target their services according to availability of resources. In response to resource shortfalls, an increasing number of councils are setting their eligibility threshold for access to services at a higher level. For example, 73% of councils were expecting to restrict their provision only to those with critical or substantial levels of need in 2007–08 (Commission for Social Care Inspection, 2008b). A similar pattern has been noted in Sweden, where a decline in the proportion of older people receiving home care services has been shown to be attributable not to the improved functioning and abilities of older people, but to a recasting of the threshold of 'need' (Larsson, 2006). There is evidence of a growing divide between people who are eligible for services and those who are not, the latter becoming 'lost to the system' and experiencing a poor quality of life (Commission for Social Care Inspection, 2008b).

The need for social care services to move away from a predominant focus on risk, narrowly defined, and towards much wider intervention to promote the quality of later life is now well recognised (Department of Health, 2002b; Wistow et al, 2003; Department for Work and Pensions, 2005; Department of Health, 2006; Office of the Deputy Prime Minister, 2006). There are efforts to 'invert the triangle of care' so that there is more emphasis on proactive intervention to promote the well-being of the whole community, rather than reactive, high-intensity services to meet the needs of a few (Association of Directors of Social Services, 2003). Government funding (£60 million over two years) has been granted to 29 sites to establish and run pilot projects to explore how different partnership arrangements between councils with social services responsibilities, older people, Primary Care Trusts and the voluntary, community and independent sectors can 'provide truly integrated preventative approaches for local older people across the whole system' (Department of Health, 2006, para 2.1). The language of 'prevention' in this and other policy documents has increasingly been replaced by concepts of 'promoting independence' or 'enablement': 'By "promoting independence", we mean an approach that is focused on ensuring that everything possible is done to ensure that people are able to remain living in their own homes, with choice and control over how they live their lives' (Care Services Improvement Partnership, 2007a).

As well as providing a more positive and inclusive perspective than the concept of prevention, this approach is also more compatible with a focus on measuring outcomes. The pilot projects focus on three key areas: providing low-level support to improve health, well-being and independence; reducing acute admissions or occupancy of beds; and supporting older people to live at home or in supported housing, as opposed to in institutional care. The areas of activity of the different projects include community development, access to information, health promotion, low-level support, case finding, telecare and post-hospital discharge support.

A national evaluation of the pilot projects is under way and interim findings suggest that, in comparison with non-pilot sites, the projects are effective in reducing the days of emergency hospital bed occupancy, improving access to services for excluded groups and improving partnership working between the statutory, community and voluntary sectors. The projects are also reported as assisting the focus on promoting older people's health and well-being to become more integral to the wider strategic agenda (Care Services Improvement Partnership, 2007b). However, the projects only have two-year funding and, although funding included a requirement that effective projects must be sustainable in the longer term, it is not clear how this will be achieved or, more significantly, how positive models or lessons can be adopted in other areas without the additional funding and other incentives that attach to pilot projects.

Using acute hospital bed occupancy days as a key indicator of effectiveness could disadvantage projects that are concerned with broader quality of life outcomes. Research has identified that the outcomes valued by older people fall within three categories: achieving change in physical, social or psychological functioning; maintaining health and well-being or preventing deterioration; and service processes, that is, the way that services are accessed and delivered (Glendinning et al, 2006). This research suggests that services are more focused on *change* and *process* outcomes than on those concerned with *maintenance* and *prevention*. It is important that evaluation of pilot projects incorporates measures of maintenance and prevention outcomes, as well as change outcomes. However, this poses methodological challenges, not least because these outcomes are more likely to be delivered in the longer term than in the timescale of two-year projects. It is also the case that many preventive initiatives that have developed have been provided in the voluntary sector. Small, localised services may not be well coordinated with wider provision, thus limiting access, or they may serve only a restricted geographical area (Thompson and Postle, 2007). Funding provided through the statutory sector is often short-term and therefore a relatively easy target when budgets have to be cut. Services concerned with maintenance outcomes are likely to be particularly vulnerable in this regard (Glendinning et al, 2006).

Basing practice on service user understandings

As already demonstrated, the 'needs' for which older people want support relate to the dimensions that are perceived as significant to their quality of life. Although there are common themes, as identified by Bowling and Gabriel (2007), what is experienced as a 'need' is individually defined; meaningful assessment has to engage with the older person's understandings, taking account of their past, present and anticipated future lives (Clarke and Warren, 2007). This indicates the need for a high level of interpersonal skills and sensitivity on the part of the assessor (Powell et al, 2007). Guidance for the Single Assessment Process, the framework for a single coordinated assessment for older people, states:

> Older people are the most important participants in the single assessment process. There are two reasons for this. First, the assessment is about and for them. Second, of all the experts in the care of older people, the greatest experts are older people themselves. They will know when they are having difficulties, the nature of those difficulties, and what might be done to resolve them. (Department of Health, 2002c, p 1)

Despite this policy recognition of the centrality of older people to the assessment process, there is evidence that the focus of assessment and decisions about whether, when and what services are accessed remains largely in the hands of practitioners and managers. The findings of Foster et al's (2006) research on assessment practice suggest that the topics that provide the focus for assessment are significantly shaped by practitioners' assumptions and perceptions, influenced in turn by organisational priorities and the broader service environment. In their study, this led to certain areas being excluded from discussion, militating against person–centred assessment. These findings echo those of Richards (2000), who observed that assessments were mainly led by agency agendas and that older people's thoughts and feelings were sidelined in this process: 'If user–centred and agency–centred objectives were not clearly distinguished and the assessor tried to understand the elderly person primarily though gathering standard information required by the agency, attention was distracted from the elderly person's narrative and the insights it provided' (Richards, 2000, p 46). Practitioner concerns with completing organisational requirements and adhering to policies and criteria obstruct the ability to 'tune in' to the older person. Baldock and Hadlow's (2002) study of assessment of older people who were 'housebound' found that the underpinning constructs and language used by practitioners were fundamentally different from those used by older people. Whereas practitioners engaged in 'needs-talk', characterised by a focus on resources, abilities and disabilities, older people used 'self-talk', concerned with themselves, their feelings and relationships.

Wider political and social discourses that have flourished under the managerialism that characterises the modernisation agenda also obstruct service user-centred assessment when they construct older people in ways that run counter to the understandings and perceptions of older people themselves. There is evidence, for example, that the concepts of 'independence' and 'frailty' are construed differently by policy makers, managers and practitioners, on the one hand, and older service users, on the other. These different understandings have consequences for the process and outcomes of assessment and for older people's identities. In social care practice, the concept of 'promoting independence' is often interpreted to mean minimising the amount of service use by the individual concerned. This relates to issues of rationing, targeting and eligibility criteria, discussed previously. Secker et al (2003) highlight differences in policy constructions of 'independence' and what this means to older people. Whereas, in policy terms, independence refers to an objective state where the older person is not reliant on others (or, more usually, not reliant on using services), independence in older people's terms is about subjective feelings of being in charge of their lives. Secker plots the objective and subjective dimensions of independence on two intersecting axes. This shows that it is possible to have a high state of objective reliance on services and at the same time to experience feelings of independence. A relevant example is an older person who achieves feelings of independence by using services that enable her not to be a 'burden' on her family (Godfrey et al, 2004). Conversely, it is possible to have a low level of reliance on others but to experience feelings of dependence if there is no sense of having choice, being in control of how one's life is lived or of having a valued identity. However, promoting independence in practice often seems to be pursuing an objective of ensuring someone does not use services long-term, rather than attending to subjective dimensions of well-being.

As well as the objective of minimising service use, the concept of independence is closely affiliated in policy and practice with notions of self-responsibility and individualisation (Ferguson, 2007). This is another area where central policy concepts are interpreted in ways that are antithetical to the meanings and preferences of older people. There is much research evidence that older people value interdependence and reciprocity in their personal, social and community relationships (Phillips et al, 2000; Barlow and Hainsworth, 2001; Godfrey et al, 2004; Powell et al, 2007; Tanner, 2007). This holds true for different ethnic groups (Grewal et al, 2004). However, in social care practice, individuals are to a significant extent divorced from their social relationships: 'need' is seen primarily as a product of individual, rather than social, circumstances (Barnes, 1997); services are delivered in individual care 'packages', to the exclusion of group or community interventions; and older people are viewed, in one-dimensional terms, as recipients of services but rarely as potential 'givers' or resources (Barnes and Shaw, 2000).

Another key concept in policy and practice that has different meanings for older people is that of frailty: 'The way in which frailty among older people is conceptualised and interpreted has profound implications for policies, organisational practices and personal experiences of care across the life course' (Grenier, 2007, p 426). Grenier highlights the significance of the concept of frailty in determining eligibility for services. She compares discourses about frailty in care practice and academic writing with the understandings of older women. She notes that, in practice and much academic writing, frailty is related to physical deficits and risk, but as far as the older women in her study were concerned, frailty was related to a feeling of loss of control over their circumstances:

> While judgements primarily about the bodies of older women take precedence in professional care practice, older women's lived experiences point to the personal interpretations of physical changes. Such tensions challenge whether frailty is located in the body or in personal and emotional experiences ... While such socially and emotionally-defined experiences are subjugated in the dominant discourse, they are the primary themes in older women's accounts. Nonetheless, it is the dominant conceptualisations that shape the context of care, organisational practices, social representations and the lived experiences of older people. (Grenier, 2007, p 437)

Grenier points out a number of ways in which the dominant construction of frailty is problematic. It gives priority to physical functioning; in so doing, it condones simplistic forms of assessment that bypass social and emotional dimensions of experience. Service rationing is done on the basis of the narrow physical construction of frailty; it ignores the way in which frailty in later life is structured by social and economic disadvantage across the life course. It discounts individual and cultural differences in the meaning and significance of physical frailty. Also, it implies negative attitudes and responses, through its entanglement with notions of pity, blame or burden (Grenier, 2007, p 438). She argues that attention needs to be given to preventing frailty and to addressing the subjective experiences of frailty, rather than to restricted concerns with responding to physical frailty.

While the first section of this chapter considered the impact of overt processes that prevent practice from responding to the needs of older people, namely targeting and rationing of services, this section has identified more covert processes that obstruct user-centred practice. It has been argued that although policy and practice guidance recognise that service users should be placed at the centre of assessment, practice is permeated by organisational, managerial and wider social discourses that are at odds with the understandings of older people. Since older people's discourses are often hidden or marginalised, the aim of user-centred practice is not realised.

Adopting a whole person focus

Service users (not just older people) want social care services to treat them as 'whole people', and to experience services as joined up and coordinated (Hudson et al, 2005). This section considers three obstacles to this being delivered in practice: partial and restricted assessments; fragmentation and restricted roles within social work and social care service delivery; and lack of coordination and integration of the wider service network.

FACS guidance on assessment (Department of Health, 2003d), mentioned earlier in the chapter, makes clear that decisions about eligibility for services should be based on risks to independence if care is not provided. It states that the assessment of risk should be wide-ranging, covering freedom to make choices and involvement in family and wider community life, as well as health and safety and the ability to manage daily routines. However, as indicated in the previous section, in practice eligibility decisions tend to be based on the assessment of physical functioning and self-care, neglecting consideration of life history and social and emotional needs (Stanley, 1999). Foster et al (2006) showed that assessment was often partial, excluding areas that practitioners decided were of less relevance, such as mental health, personality, preferences and social and recreational activities, regardless of whether or not this accorded with the older person's view. This restricted view is directly counter to what service users want from social workers: 'They see a distinct value and contribution in social work practice which addresses both their personal, psychological needs and the broader issues and problems that face them. They see these two aspects of their lives as closely bound and inseparable' (Beresford, 2007, p 50).

Evidence from older people demonstrates the value they place on this broader and integrated approach to their lives, even though this is insufficiently acknowledged in policy and practice. A study that looked at the experiences of patients (who were mainly older people) with case management by community matrons found that the psychosocial support provided by community matrons was a 'crucially important component' of the role, even though this aspect was not recognised at all within Department of Health guidance (Sargent et al, 2007, p 517). These points relate back to the discussion in the previous section about the disjunction between service users' understandings and perspectives and those of practitioners. Managerial requirements surrounding assessment, arising from the need to control resources, are the lens through which older people's needs are viewed, and this blocks and distorts the ability to engage with older people's needs (Chevannes, 2002). The more that assessment is restricted to prescribed areas, removing it from a 'whole person' focus, the greater the likely discrepancy between what practitioners 'know' on the basis of their assessment and the needs, views and experiences of service users (Beresford, 2003). Yet it is this professional knowledge, filtered through managerialist requirements, that determines access to social care services.

A related obstacle to a whole person focus is the fragmentation of roles that has developed within care management, and indeed within the modernisation agenda more broadly. Social work is conceived as 'a series of separate tasks for skilled practitioners, and discrete experiences for service users' (Jordan, 2007, p 17). Increasingly the responsibilities for assessment, coordination of care and review are separated out and allocated to different personnel and/or teams. Consequently, service users do not experience the care management process as integrated, continuous and coordinated but feel 'passed on' from one worker to another (Ware et al, 2003). One of the consequences of this fragmentation is that the relationship-based components of the social work role are undermined (Postle, 2001, 2002; Ware et al, 2003; Lymbery et al, 2007). Yet engaging with issues such as an older person's life history, mental well-being and social and emotional needs is likely to depend on the formation of a relationship conducive to exploration of these often sensitive and complex areas. The lack of time and opportunity to form these relationships, along with the perceived lack of relevance of relationships to the care management 'task', are major barriers to 'whole person' assessment. In terms of intervention, the emphasis is on the role of the practitioner as a 'manager' of 'care services', not on the social worker's deployment of professional skills in working with people. These two approaches to the professional role are described as, on the one hand, the 'technical rational', where the role is a mechanistic one of acting as an agent for the delivery of a commodity from one body to another, and on the other hand, the 'professional artistry' view, where the role involves judgement, moral dimensions and intuition (Fish and Coles, 2000). Relationships are central to the factors that give quality to older people's lives, as reviewed earlier in the chapter. This applies to service relationships as well as to personal and social relationships, with relationships with practitioners and care providers a central component in defining a quality service from the perspective of service users (Harding and Beresford, 1996; Qureshi and Henwood, 2000; Beresford, 2007). Social workers cannot act to promote well-being without being 'professional artists' and involving themselves in relationships.

A third obstacle to the achievement of a 'whole person' focus relates to the poor coordination of services that form part of the network of provision needed to deliver the well-being agenda. People do not compartmentalise their lives into different types of problems – health, housing and so on; these aspects all interrelate to comprise their whole experience (Oldman, 2002). The need for comprehensive and integrated provision between not just statutory sector agencies, but also the voluntary and private sectors, has been increasingly recognised in policy. Thus, the Social Exclusion Unit's *Sure Start to Later Life* report identifies a range of services as being relevant to preventing decline and promoting well-being for older people. As well as health, housing and social care, these include: information; advocacy; social activities; lifelong learning; volunteering; finance and benefits; safety and environment; and transport (Office of the Deputy Prime Minister, 2006). Similarly, Standard 8 of the National Service Framework for Older People (Department of Health, 2001a) is concerned with promoting the health and well-being of older people through a coordinated programme. However, a review of progress on achievement of the framework standards noted the lack of a coordinated approach to well-being and highlighted the need for partner organisations to work together towards this goal (Healthcare Commission et al, 2006). One of the barriers to delivering outcomes-focused services identified by Glendinning et al's (2006) review was divisions between health and social care services that obstructed a holistic response to the older person's needs. The research included study of practice examples that were seen to be delivering user-focused outcomes. However, the researchers note the lack of continuity between the focus of these particular projects or services and other, more mainstream services that the older person was receiving:

> there appeared to be significant disjunctions between these examples of good practice and service users' wider lives. For example, day centres could provide excellent quality services, with a high emphasis on process outcomes, for those who attended. However, support for users to maintain their own social networks outside the day centre was non-existent. The most striking disjunction, acknowledged by many managers and practitioners, was between short-term reablement services and longer-term home care services. Here resource constraints and poor relationships with independent providers meant that home care services were often inflexible, of poor quality and insufficiently responsive to the outcomes desired by older users. (Glendinning et al, 2006, p 63)

Thus, while reablement services were closely oriented to delivering change outcomes based on goals identified by older people, and to improving morale and confidence, not just physical functioning, this approach was not carried through in the more mainstream services. Services such as those that come under the umbrella of 'reablement' or intermediate care tend to be time limited. Although they may be based on principles that accord with older people's needs and preferences, there is a need for these principles to be incorporated within mainstream provision (Young and Stevenson, 2006).

The care market: delivering quality services from older people's perspectives

As highlighted earlier in the chapter, the exercise of choice and control over their lives and, as a means to that end, choice and control over services, is central to service users' requirements of social care services. This applies to older people, as to other service user groups (Qureshi and Henwood, 2000). Arguments about the problems inherent in applying the concept of the active and informed 'consumer' to those who become eligible for social care services are now well rehearsed (Caldock, 1994; Barnes, 1997; Higgs, 1997; Biggs, 2000; Harris 2003; this volume, Chapter Four). There is such diversity within the social category of 'older people' that, while some may be able to exercise their consumer power and purchase services within the private sector, those who are less physically, socially and economically advantaged are likely to be denied these opportunities. It is, of course, the latter section of the older population who are most likely to be the users of social care services, particularly as eligibility criteria for services tighten. When Hardy et al (1999) interviewed a sample of older people, their carers and care managers, they found that older people exercised little choice at any of the key stages of the care management process: defining their own needs, making decisions about services or reviewing the intervention. Similarly, Hey (1999) interviewed older people identified as 'frail', key members of their care network and social workers and found that few older people adopted the role of 'consumers' in relation to care services. Most had low expectations of care services and tended to place trust in their own 'coping' ability; any choice exercised was likely to be in the form of refusing services or deferring decisions. In discussion of choice, it is important to remember also the barriers to choice experienced by carers. It has been argued that their choice is constrained by the expectations inherent in their relationship with the person they are caring for and by organisational factors that restrict information and resources. Choice is likely to be particularly problematic if it involves the carer wanting to reduce or relinquish caring responsibilities (Arksey and Glendinning, 2007).

In relation to different services within the care 'market', there is fairly clear evidence about what older people want from home care services. The following factors were identified by older people as important in a quality home care service: reliability and continuity of staff; kindness, understanding and cheerfulness of staff; competence of staff to undertake the required tasks; willingness to be flexible; and understanding of the needs and preferences of the service user (Qureshi and Henwood, 2000). However, a review of home care services for older people noted a number of concerns, including issues concerning the recruitment and retention of home carers and, from older people's experiences, issues related to the quality of the service received, such as timing and length of visits and reliability of staff. The report concluded that home care services in many areas were overstretched. It highlighted the need for changes in the way home care services are commissioned and delivered, in particular, to reach a wider population of older people and address preventive objectives:

> A definition of 'home care' that limits state-funded support to a prescribed list of tasks, delivered by a certain type of agency, does not make practical sense to older people and their families. A more flexible and holistic response is needed, that is more closely attuned to what people actually want and need. (Commission for Social Care Inspection, 2006, p 7)

A study exploring the perspectives of home care workers in Northern Ireland confirmed that concerns about the stress and demands of the job and irregular and unsociable hours were relevant factors in poor staff retention (Fleming and Taylor, 2007). As the Commission for Social Care Inspection report found, these factors that pertain to the care market have a direct impact on the quality of the service experienced by older people. Lack of staff, poor recruitment practices, limited time allocated for tasks and tightly prescribed care plans all militate against achievement of the quality standards important to older people. Home care workers have themselves noted the need for more time to be spent with service users and the stress that they feel when they are unable to deliver this. As one home care worker is reported as saying, "One of my clients said to me one day when I was rushing to get to the next call, 'how can you be caring when you are always rushing me? That's not very caring'. I realised she was right. There are times you barely have time to be pleasant" (Fleming and Taylor, 2007, p 72).

The importance that older people attach to their relationships with care providers was mentioned earlier in the chapter, but this is one area where choice is virtually absent. Resource rationing and prioritisation indicate that care workers are oriented to 'tasks', rather than to the emotional and social needs that are bound up in relationships. As one Australian study concludes, the right to choice

> does not extend to the right to choose a worker whom one knows and likes, or to spend non-instrumentally oriented time with her or him. The policy in this context precludes the notion that older people have the right to participate in the design and execution of services that suit them. (Russell and Schofield, 1999, p 88)

Some of the deficiencies in current home care provision have been related directly to the marketisation and privatisation of home care, which originated with the Conservative reforms of community care and have been retained as key dimensions of New Labour's modernisation agenda for social care. Arguments that an expansion by the statutory sector of in-house provision would better meet older people's needs are effectively silenced by the discourse of modernisation, which promulgates 'a seemingly incontrovertible narrative' about the merits of marketisation and privatisation (Scourfield, 2006, p 24).

With regard to institutional care, research with 'frail' older people in care homes has highlighted four interrelated dimensions that are important for quality of life, from their perspectives: being able to express their identity and maintain a sense of self; a care environment in which they can exercise control, choices or rights; the ability to form and maintain personal relationships; and being able to engage in meaningful activities (Tester et al, 2004). Tester et al noted that, although good practice principles have been incorporated in care home standards, there is still evidence that care staff do not have time to get to know and understand older people as individuals. There are arguments that the marketisation of care prioritises interests that contradict those of older people:

> Far from providing a plethora of small-scale, responsive, customer-focused services which the privatizers and marketers promised ... the residential care market has displayed far more traditional tendencies to monopoly and standardization. The future of private provision is set to be one of large-scale warehousing, physically located on far fewer premises and offering little by way of choice. In the process, large not to say grotesque, profits will have been made by a handful

> of individuals, on the basis that yet further profits are to be extracted from the sector. The world of equity specialists, venture capitalists and buy-out deals may seem remote from the day-to-day operation of social welfare and of social policy analysts. Yet the line that links the person in the dayroom and the person in the boardroom is a direct one and the language that it speaks is that of cash flows, more than care, and of the quantity of earnings, much more than the quality of service. (Drakeford, 2006, p 936)

Failure to adequately manage the care home market can lead to home closures, with adverse consequences for the individual older people displaced, as well as for choice and diversity within the residential care sector more generally (Glasby and Henwood, 2007). It also seems that national and local policies in respect of care homes and, in particular, the working relationships developed between local authority commissioners and care providers may influence the motivations and professionalism of care home managers (Matosevic et al, 2007). This in turn is likely to affect the quality of care experienced by older people. Issues of quality in care homes are particularly salient when account is taken of the social marginalisation and barriers to the exercise of citizenship faced by older people who become care home 'residents' (Scourfield, 2007).

In discussing the quality of services from service users' perspectives, it is important to note that, although broad themes are discernible, there are considerable differences in terms of what is important to individuals (Beaumont and Kenealy, 2004). For example, it has been shown that, in relation to home care services, individuals have different standards of quality, influenced by a number of factors; it is therefore proposed that quality standards should be negotiated by care providers with each individual (Patmore, 2001). This raises significant concerns about traditional approaches to evaluating quality on the basis of applying a uniform set of standards. Not only do these tend to ignore individual differences, they also often bypass or underplay the views and experiences of people who use services regarding the criteria that are important to them. Further, traditional approaches to quality assurance tend to rely on overly bureaucratic systems for defining and measuring quality; these then undermine the flexibility of services and their responsiveness to service users' needs (Beresford and Branfield, 2006). The challenge is to develop ways of defining and evaluating quality that are centred on the perspectives of service users, that allow for negotiation of differences at the level of service provision to individuals and that are straightforward to implement and use in practice.

Current directions

This section considers the potential of directions set out in the current modernisation policy agenda to deliver outcomes that meet the needs and preferences of older people. As outlined at the beginning of the chapter, one of the main thrusts of recent policy statements is supporting independence and 'putting people more in control of their own health and care' (Department of Health, 2006; 2007b). Key strategies in achieving this vision are the expansion of direct payments and the introduction of individualised budgets.

Direct payments allow individuals to receive a cash payment so that they can purchase for themselves services that will meet needs assessed as eligible. Individual budgets bring together different funding streams and give individuals control over how this budget for different components of their care is spent. This agenda and its underpinning values are set out in a document on adult social care, *Putting People First*, which is a collaboration between central and local government, professional and regulatory bodies. This states:

> The time has now come to build on best practice and replace paternalistic, reactive care of variable quality with a mainstream system focused on prevention, early intervention, enablement, and high quality personally tailored services. In the future, we want people to have maximum choice, control and power over the support services they receive.
>
> We will always fulfil our responsibility to provide care and protection for those who through their illness or disability are genuinely unable to express needs and wants or exercise control. However, the right to self-determination will be at the heart of a reformed system only constrained by the realities of finite resources and levels of protection, which should be responsible but not risk averse.
>
> Over time, people who use social care services and their families will increasingly shape and commission their own services. Personal Budgets will ensure people receiving public funding use available resources to choose their own support services – a right previously available only to self-funders. The state and statutory agencies will have a different not lesser role – more active and enabling, less controlling.
>
> (Department of Health, 2007b, p 2)

To what extent will this further 'modernisation' and 'transformation' of adult social care, as it is heralded, address the problematic issues that have been raised in this chapter?

Although there has so far been limited take-up of direct payments by older people (Commission for Social Care Inspection, 2004b), research does suggest that direct payments have the potential to increase their feelings of choice and control over their support arrangements and to improve their social, emotional and physical health (Clark et al, 2004). However, Clark et al's research also highlights that access to adequate support to manage the financial and administrative demands of direct payments was crucial to making the scheme work, from older people's perspectives. The same issue about the crucial role of support is identified in the preliminary findings of the evaluation of individual budgets (IB) pilots:

> A strong theme to emerge was the importance of support outside of the users' own caring networks. Access to free brokerage, professional advocates and/or mentoring by someone who has been through the process were seen as crucial to getting the most out of IBs. Without this support interviewees thought it would be difficult for IBs to work for people with complex support needs, who have little family support, or who do not want to rely on their families for help with managing their IB. (Individual Budgets Evaluation Network, 2007, p 4)

In addition to the need for support, there are a number of reasons why direct payments may not deliver the outcomes required by older people. Direct payments do not bypass assessment and are only received when needs have been assessed as being eligible according to the criteria. They do not, therefore, overcome the partial and restricted assessments identified as problematic earlier in the chapter. In terms of the flexibility to support older people's own strategies for 'keeping going', although a direct payment may provide greater flexibility, it is unlikely to increase the resources available to promote well-being without increased funding and a widening of eligibility criteria. Thus, Clark et al (2004) found that, while direct payments enabled older people to make choices, such as using a personal assistant to help access social activities, this meant 'juggling' the allocated care hours and/or paying additional costs themselves. For both direct payments and individual budgets, it is not clear how assessment based on service user-defined outcomes will combine with managerial decisions about eligibility and cost ceilings on payments. It is also questionable just how much flexibility will be permissible, given that the recent history of social care has been that of a 'regulatory and centralizing state' (Scourfield, 2007, p 111; Harris and Unwin, this volume, Chapter One), with tightly prescribed criteria and procedures. Restrictive criteria and cumbersome monitoring systems, spawned by concerns about cost efficiency, limit the flexibility to deliver service user-centred outcomes, but also constrain the ability of practitioners to engage fully with service users' perspectives (Ellis, 2007). This fundamental tension was highlighted in an annual Commission for Social Care Inspection report:

> There is a tension between councils having to focus on narrowly defined adult social care (out of necessity to manage budgets) and meeting broader objectives to improve health and well-being and ensuring personalised care. The standardisation and explicit decision making that goes with targeting services sit uneasily in practice alongside the personalisation agenda that is about self-assessment,

individual direction and arm's length accountability for expenditure decisions. (Commission for Social Care Inspection, 2008b, p xiii)

In other words, many of the same problems arise with direct payments and individual budgets as with traditional care management.

It is suggested that 'cash for care' policies are motivated by concerns to contain costs and that the funding made available through direct payments does not reflect the real costs of the care required (Timonen et al, 2006). The low rates of pay made available through the limited funding allocated to direct payments may make it difficult to recruit suitable staff (Leece, 2007). If caring becomes more individualised, a possible contraction of the care market could place informal carers in the position of feeling obliged to step in and assume the role of personal assistant, even when neither they nor the older person concerned see this as an avenue for promoting their independence. Although there is the potential for informal carers (who are not co-resident) to be paid by an older person through a direct payment, thus potentially promoting feelings of independence, the financial remuneration works out even lower if the carer is also taking on the task of managing the direct payment or individual budget (Ellis, 2007). Consideration also has to be given to the impact that rendering informal care relationships as commodities to be purchased in the care 'market' has on the interpersonal dynamics of caring relationships and on how individuals construct their own identities vis-à-vis significant others (Henderson and Forbat, 2002; Ellis, 2007).

There are inherent inequalities in relation to who is most likely to benefit from such schemes. For example, people from minority ethnic groups appear to be under-represented among users of direct payments (Butt et al, 2000). There is also evidence that direct payments tend to be restricted to those who are perceived by assessors as having higher levels of ability (Timonen et al, 2006), with relatively low rates of take-up by people with mental health problems, people with learning disabilities and older people (Commission for Social Care Inspection, 2004b). A key factor seems to be the attitudes of professionals who gate-keep access to direct payments. Ellis's (2007) observations of practitioners undertaking assessments showed that older people were often discounted as appropriate candidates to receive a direct payment, based on ageist judgements about their dependence. This demonstrates that direct payments will not in themselves prompt assessment practice that is attuned to individual service users' understandings. Although self-assessment is promoted as the way forward for service users to have greater control (Department of Health, 2007b), early indications from the pilot experience of individual budgets are that, while some people found self-assessment empowering, others found the process confusing and were unclear about how an individual budget could be used (Individual Budgets Evaluation Network, 2007). Again, this suggests that 'cash for care' schemes give rise to additional requirements for information, support and advocacy that will have to be addressed if such initiatives are really going to deliver increased experiences of control for service users.

More fundamentally, critics argue that, although direct payments and individual budgets appear on the face of it to meet service users' requirements for increased choice and control, these initiatives are primarily about promoting the role of the private sector, rather than increasing the provider role of the public sector. It is argued that the model that underpins cash-for-care initiatives is one of individualised consumerism rather than of collective citizenship (Priestley, 1999; Pearson, 2000; Scourfield, 2007). Ferguson (2007) sees direct payments as exemplifying the personalisation now dominating adult social care. He argues that this will not address wider issues of inequality and powerlessness. Scourfield points out that

> A danger of using independence and choice as central organising principles is to forget how and why the public sector emerged in the first place – to ensure that those who are necessarily dependent are treated with respect and dignity, to ensure a collectivised approach to risk and to ensure that secure and reliable forms of support outside of the market or the family are available. (Scourfield, 2007, p 108)

He argues that policies such as direct payments construct service users as 'autonomous, managerial and enterprising individuals' (p 108) who are responsible not only for themselves but also for managing public funds and for managing the risks that arise from this. He sees this as problematic in two ways. First, not all individuals are able to undertake and discharge these responsibilities. For example, research has noted that sometimes older people are overwhelmed by their difficulties and unable to take an active role in relation to their assessments and care plans (Richards, 2000). A similar point is made about the promotion of self-care and independence in health policy; people with 'intensive clinical needs' may be too ill or frail to achieve these aims (Sargent et al, 2007). There may be other social factors, for example related to social class, gender, ethnicity and 'culture', that make some individuals less able to adopt a consumer–citizen role (Baldock and Ungerson, 1994). Scourfield (2007) argues that there is a danger that those who cannot fulfil the status of 'autonomous, managerial and enterprising individuals become 'subordinated citizens'. Second, reiterating Ferguson's (2007) point, relying on predominantly privatised solutions to socially constructed problems (such as 'old age') will not address social and economic inequalities; at best, such solutions will respond to some of their consequences. To ensure adequate social care that is responsive to social inequalities and diversity, there are arguments for the expansion of state provision (Scourfield, 2006) and for clear public responsibility for managing the care market, so that the rights and interests of the most vulnerable sectors of society are protected (Beresford, 2005; Drakeford, 2006).

Conclusion

This chapter has argued that, in order to meet the requirements of older people and promote their well-being, policy and practice need to support older people's strategies for 'keeping going'. At a community level, this means acting to boost the resources and diminish the threats faced in relation to areas known to be important to quality of life, namely, social relationships, roles and activities, physical and mental well-being, home and neighbourhood environments, financial circumstances, and independence. At an individual level, it means engaging with each older person's perspective about the factors that contribute to their sense of well-being and offering appropriate support at the critical juncture when usual coping strategies are not sufficient to deal with new or ongoing challenges and losses. It also means paying careful attention to the processes by which help is provided, so that each older person's senses of self and self-worth are maintained.

A key theme of the chapter has been the centrality of relationships to older people's well-being. One aspect of this is the nature of older people's relationship with their families, friends and communities. They want to maintain or develop relationships that provide a sense of belonging and value and this means relationships in which they are givers as well as receivers. Older people who are not able to engage in the more commonly promoted forms of citizenship, such as employment, volunteering and community involvement, can nevertheless contribute through their relationship with others (Jordan, 2007). This is borne out by research with older people, which demonstrates the value that they place on interdependence and the reciprocal nature of their relationships (Godfrey et al, 2004; Tanner, 2007). Research has shown that even older people in objectively adverse circumstances can obtain a sense of self-worth through supporting others (Tanner, 2007). In this regard, a relevant question is posed by Jordan:

> Why then does the government emphasise independence and choice as central to the well-being of these [service user] groups, when it is obvious that *inter*dependence is the reality for them, even more than for the rest of us? One part of this seems to be that, in a highly individualistic culture of self-responsibility and self-development, it is only someone who can be represented as exercising choice who can be accorded respect and value. (Jordan, 2007, pp 67–8)

This is a key area where policy discourses are discordant with the meanings and perspectives of older people.

A second aspect of the central importance of relationships relates to the nature of support services. Older people value their relationship with social care assessors and service providers who take the time to engage with their perspectives and intervene in ways that support their preferred ways of coping and help them to maintain a sense of self. Social work would seem to have a central role to play, since 'it deals in relationships, which are the main components of well-being and of its destruction' (Jordan, 2007, p 128). Service users do not want social workers who are simply navigators and organisers, but social workers who form supportive relationships and get directly involved, or are 'hands on' in their approach (Beresford, 2007). To the extent that current policy initiatives suggest much narrower conceptions of the social work role, this is not hopeful for delivering the relationship-based interventions valued by older people.

In these two respects – the nature of relationships with families and communities and the nature of relationships with service providers – the modernisation policy discourse of 'independence, choice and control' fails to engage adequately with what research tells us about maintaining and promoting older people's well-being. At a fundamental level, this stands to create a barrier at the outset between practitioner understandings on which intervention is based and those of older people. It seems that policy is making selective use of service user evidence and only taking on board those elements that appear to be compatible with existing agendas. The result is likely to be a distorted reflection that bears only a partial resemblance to what older people want from support services. While the resources to intervene for the promotion of well-being, broadly defined, are important, so too are the underpinning values – respecting diversity in relation to what gives life quality, responding to individuals' preferred coping strategies, valuing relationships and promoting reciprocity and interdependence.

Part Three
Modernisation and professional practice

SEVEN

Quiet challenges? Professional practice in modernised social work

Vicky White

Introduction

A growing number of writers have presented social workers as having been turned into unreflective people-processors by waves of managerialism over the last 30 years and, more recently, by the intertwining of managerialism with New Labour's modernisation agenda. The chapter begins by outlining this position before questioning it and moving on to consider the 'discretionary space' within which social workers operate. This space is seen as being constructed by social work's location as a state-mediated profession and the duties social workers perform on behalf of the state, within that location. Next, the concept of resistance is explored, followed by consideration of what constitutes resistance in the current context of modernisation. The chapter concludes that, while evidence of a continuing commitment to externally based radicalism is important for social work, so are the opportunities for 'quiet challenges' by social workers as they go about their day-to-day work in the discretionary spaces social work provides.

Unreflective people-processing?

A number of commentators have claimed that we have witnessed the demise of the 'autonomous reflective practitioner' (see, for example, Dominelli and Hoogvelt, 1996) and have regarded social work as having been robbed of its 'radicalism and transformatory potential' (Butler and Drakeford, 2002, p 7; see also, Jones, 2001; 2005; Powell, 2001; Ferguson, 2008). In this vein, Postle has suggested that one of the strategies practitioners have employed to cope with the changing nature of their work has been no longer to challenge or question 'inherent dissonances'. Drawing on the work of Lipsky (1980), Postle maintains that this approach involves practitioners adopting a 'client–processing mentality' through which they 'psychologically adapt themselves to their jobs in order to cope with dissonances ... this approach lends itself to an apparent willingness to follow procedural models of working' (Postle, 2001, p 20).

The alleged rise of the unreflective, people-processing practitioner seems to render increasingly redundant proposals for alternative 'radical' approaches to practice. In the face of these pessimistic claims, this chapter considers what capacity exists within modernised social work for 'radical' approaches to the interests of service users and social workers. Contrary to the arguments of much of the existing literature, the continuing existence of professional discretion is identified as offering 'spaces' for resistance, indicating that while the influence of managerialism is central to the modernisation agenda, it is possible to interrupt and disturb it at some points. Identifying the possibilities for resistance to the dominant modernising discourse of managerialism is consistent with the core place that has been accorded to such resistance in documenting, theorising and researching workplace cultures and behaviour more generally, as we shall see later. Within that literature, the possibilities for resistance are seen predominantly as lying within the existing frameworks of power rather than being concerned with wholesale transformation of those frameworks. Such an approach to power relations may be viewed by some as offering a weak form of resistance. However, this focus opens up the use of the discretionary space within practice in forms of resistance that do not have to be synonymous with large-scale transformative radicalism. It can encompass a range of 'quiet challenges' by social workers, working in and against managerialism for more critical forms of practice that seek to engage with furthering service users' interests. In seeking to develop this argument, the initial considerations are: where does the discretionary space within social work originate? What kind of profession is social work?

Social work as a state-mediated profession

Much has been written about how the state shapes the agenda of social work practice (see, for example, Howe, 1986; Aldridge, 1996; Harris, 2003; White, 2006), and this writing emphasises that 'the critical characteristics of social work practice ... do not derive from the prescriptions of professional social workers' (Howe, 1986, p 2). In this sense 'state social work' depicts more accurately the field of social work usually referred to as the 'statutory sector'. Given that the statutory duties of social work are undertaken on behalf of the state, it is the state context that draws the parameters of the spaces within which the problems and possibilities of social work practice are located.

Johnson's analysis of professional work (Johnson, 1972) can be used to illuminate social workers' experiences of state social work and the discretionary spaces it provides. He viewed professions as occupational power structures which could be classified into three categories: collegiate, patronage and mediated. In the case of mediated professions, an agency, usually a state organisation, acts as mediator between the profession and its clientele in deciding with whom the profession will work and what should be provided for those people with whom the profession engages, within the parameters of legal frameworks and resource allocation (Johnson, 1972, p 77). Through this process, power is delegated to the professionals concerned and their status is legitimated by the functions they perform on behalf of the state (Hill, 1997, p 209). State-mediated professions:

do not resist the extension of state power for they have no choice but to be public employees. On the contrary they generally welcome the extension of state power, for it is the only source of such power as they themselves possess; indeed, these occupational groups owe their very existence to the power of the state. (Cousins, 1987, p 97)

Social work can be considered as being located within just such a state-mediated professional organisational structure, as the basis within and through which social workers operate (Hugman, 1991, p 201). Thus Johnson's concept of the state-mediated profession makes sense of the overall features of social work's position and functioning, but the analysis remains at that general level. It does not move on to consider how state mediation shapes the nature of professionals' work and the discretionary space it affords. Derber's work (1982; 1983) can be used to move into these areas of consideration.

Derber's historical approach to professional work highlighted the extent to which professionals have become engaged in salaried rather than independent employment. He was concerned with what distinguished professional work from other types of work; just what was it that made professional work distinctive? The particular aspect of its distinctiveness that he pursued was the extent to which professionals control their work in situations of 'dependent employment', for example state employment (Derber, 1983, p 309). In order to explore this aspect, Derber examined the way in which professional work is controlled. He argued that in any sort of work, professional or otherwise, there are two potential components of control: control over the *means* of work (technical subordination), that is over the execution of work, and control over the *ends* of work (ideological subordination), that is over the goals or purposes of work. He maintained that, although professionals lack control over the *ends* to which their work is put, they nevertheless retain considerable discretion over the *means* of undertaking their work, unlike many other workers. The exercise of discretion in the *means* of undertaking professional work provides a 'domain of freedom and creativity' (Derber, 1983, p 316) or, we might say more modestly, discretionary space, within which professional work is carried out.

In the case of social work, its *ends* are established by the state. It is, in Derber's terms, 'ideologically subordinated' but, he argued, the *means* by which the state's ends are achieved rely on the discretion of social workers (and see Hugman, 1991, p 202):

> Keeping social workers' focus on individual pathology and away from social oppression was of major importance to state agencies ... and formed the basis for a highly sophisticated ideological co-option, where social workers' moral concerns for the well-being of their clients could be accommodated in a form of practice which served institutional ends. (Derber, 1983, p 333)

Derber's distinction between the *ends* and *means* of professional work suggests that social workers, as state-mediated professionals, may retain considerable degrees of what he termed 'technical autonomy', that is, control over *how* they do their work (Derber, 1983, p 335). Mashaw made a similar distinction for some areas of state employment (such as social work), identifying specialist skills and intuitive judgements that are used in the 'professional treatment model', with professionals accorded discretion about how tasks are performed within general frameworks (Mashaw, 1983, ch 2), a position supported by Hill: 'The organisational or planning activities at the top of hierarchies set contexts for, but do not necessarily predetermine decision-making at field levels, where very different tasks are performed and very different problems have to be solved' (Hill, 1997, pp 187–8).

The classic study that illustrated the discretion within these organisational spaces, which state-mediated professionals have in deciding how to undertake their work and how to go about solving problems that may differ from those at the top of hierarchies was Lipsky's *Street-level Bureaucracy* (1980). He placed a particular emphasis on street-level bureaucrats' face-to-face contact with people using their services:

> On the one hand, service is delivered by people to people, invoking a model of human interaction, caring and responsibility. On the other hand, service is delivered through a bureaucracy, invoking a model of detachment and equal treatment under conditions of resource limitations and constraints, making care and responsibility conditional. (Lipsky, 1980, p 71)

Lipsky suggested that, in these circumstances, street-level bureaucrats like social workers have discretion because the nature of the services they provide requires human judgement that cannot be programmed and for which machines cannot substitute (Lipsky, 1980, p 161; of course, this position is now less tenable – see Coleman, this volume, Chapter Two). In similar vein, Challis argued that social services departments' implementation of central government legislation required social workers to have a degree of discretion if they were to deal with the idiosyncrasies of people's lives (Challis, 1990, p 6). Further, Hudson suggested that it is in the interests of such agencies not to fetter the discretion of street-level bureaucrats, because they are engaged in carrying out much of the difficult rationing of services in situations where demand exceeds supply. It is the exercise of the discretion they possess in carrying out this function that is the source of their power over service users (Hudson, 1989). These three factors – the difficulty of programming human judgement, the consequent need for the exercise of discretion and the power inherent in its exercise – shape the space within which social work operates. The detailed construction of the space depends on three further factors:

- *expertise* – a body of knowledge that can be learned and transmitted;
- *indeterminacy* – work within areas of uncertainty which are portrayed as only susceptible to specialist, esoteric and non-transferable professional skills;
- *invisibility* – working situations in which detailed surveillance of work is difficult (Hill, 1997, pp 209–10).

While social workers' claims to the exercise of discretion on the grounds of expertise may be contentious and contested, indeterminacy has been a significant dimension in social work's general claim for a significant degree of discretion in its operation: 'Professional insulation from external controls is likely to be greatest where the outcomes of professional activities are relatively vague and intangible ... This may be a factor in professional attachment to casework' (Sibeon, 1991, p 27). Within their casework, social workers have been found to exploit indeterminacy in using their own preferred methods of work (Pithouse, 1987, p 49) and it is the autonomy to do so which, traditionally, has been the basis on which the job has been routinely undertaken (Pithouse, 1991, pp 45–6), as an 'invisible trade' (Pithouse, 1987). Social workers have, then, been regarded as state-mediated professionals who have a degree of 'technical autonomy' (discretion) over the *means* by which they carry out the *ends* of the state, within a professional treatment model.

Social work's subordination to statutory duties

The legal underpinning of social work, through its mandate of statutory duties, is the tangible manifestation of the state's *ends* (or goals) in social work; statutory duties define the responsibilities to be exercised by social workers on behalf of the state. Anleu argued that this legal underpinning affects the environment in which social work is practised (Anleu, 1992, p 41). Howe went beyond seeing the statutory mandate as a contextual consideration that affects social work and, instead, regarded it as determining the nature of social work much more directly (Howe, 1986, p 160). Aldridge presented the state as unequivocally shaping social work and setting its agenda in tasks that are determined by the government of the day (Aldridge, 1996, pp 182–3). Social work is, therefore, in a subordinate position in terms of both how it is defined and how it is organised:

> Social work is 'overdetermined' by the economic and social formation so that its status is best seen as relatively subordinate rather than as relatively autonomous. Put at its most uncompromisingly straightforward, state welfare is an element within the state apparatus, and as such will be to some extent articulated with it at both ideological and material levels ... What passes for social work is the product of the varying capacity of certain institutions and agencies to give it particular definition, to shape what it is that constitutes legitimate professional knowledge and the manner in which the delivery of services should be

> organised. In both respects, this means that the nature of social work
> is an accomplishment, a construction ... (Webb, 1996, p 173)

If the nature of social work is a construction, what we have witnessed over the past two decades is a political and policy reconstruction project as social work has undergone major structural and ideological changes, beginning with the Conservatives' reforms of community care/adults' services and children's services and culminating in New Labour's modernisation agenda. These changes appear to have left many social workers feeling disillusioned, disgruntled and under siege (White and Harris, 2001; 2004). For example, when Gupta and Blewett interviewed social workers they found that administration and performance targets dominated the work of social workers:

> What is measured is paper output not work with children. All managers care about is getting the assessment finished on time ... We are scrambling around to find more children to be adopted or else we lose our three star status and hundreds of pounds, yet adoption may not be right for these children. (Gupta and Blewett, 2007, p 177)

Similar concerns arose in reflections from social work practitioners participating in discussions on the impact that the organisational context has on their work, as part of a post-qualifying social work programme, across 2007–08. These social workers felt that their performances were being scrutinised inside their organisations, in terms of their potential contribution to moving their employing local authorities up league tables and improving on their star ratings (also see Foster and Wilding, 2000), as well as by the external audits on which these rankings are based; the emphasis was on targets, standards and outcomes – on quantitative rather than qualitative measures of their practice (Harris and Unwin, this volume, Chapter One). They felt that a persistent theme of management was that social workers' loyalty was owed to maximising their contributions to the mission statements and corporate goals of their employing organisations 'rather than to the code of ethics of their professional body' (Foster and Wilding, 2000, p 154). They were often set unrealistic timescales for assessments in children's services and faced restrictive use of *Fair Access to Care Services* (Department of Health, 2003d) criteria in adult services, as well as pressure from national standards frameworks and performance indicators, on a daily basis. They experienced management oversight and supervision as having become more intense as a result of a desire to control and direct front-line practitioners, in ways that corresponded with Hughes' evocative reference to the 'glass cage of total exposure' (2005, p 615). A key dimension of this exposure is computer-based performance monitoring, a commonplace practice that allows managers to collect data and analyse a wide range of staff activities. Ball and Wilson liken this to Foucault's image of the panopticon, where observers can observe unseen (Ball and Wilson, 2000, p 539). Information technology, quality systems and performance reviews were seen by the social workers as forms of increased scrutiny and inspection of their day-to-day work, ensuring that only 'core business' is undertaken.

Westhues et al (2001, p 42) see the origins of these changes in the application of business principles to the development and delivery of human services, replacing social work managers with 'business'-oriented managers, who are more comfortable with a marketplace emphasis (Westhues et al, 2001, p 42; see also Harris, 2003). Consistent with this insertion of a more business-like approach into social work, the social workers identified an increasing emphasis in their practice on cost-consciousness, cost control and achieving 'Best Value'. Social workers spoke of having to seek authorisation from managers to spend even a pound; this resulted in their 'dressing up' assessments, through embellishment and exaggeration, in order to acquire more resources for service users and carers. The views of these social workers are characteristic of a widespread disquiet that social work has moved from being a bureau-professional service to a service that is increasingly subject to external regulation and output controls (Harris and Unwin, this volume, Chapter One). It is claimed that the changes involve reorienting the identities of social workers so that they adopt managerial values and align themselves with managerial concerns (Halford and Leonard, 1999, cited in Davies and Thomas, 2002, p 462). The increasing commodification and marketisation of social work is seen as having resulted in the "end of expertise" and declining professional autonomy (Dustin, 2007, p xi) and has been accompanied by increasingly voluminous and prescriptive requirements (see, for example, Garrett, 2003; Tanner and Harris, 2008, ch 2) concerning *what* social workers must do and *how* they must achieve New Labour's goals. In Derber's terms, this amounts to the extension of the subordination of social workers from their ideological subordination to the state's *ends* and into the state's technical subordination of the *means* by which they undertake their work. At the same time, this state intervention into the *means* of undertaking social work seems to have undermined the basis for social workers' ideological co-option, leading to widespread dissatisfaction with the *ends* the state is seeking to pursue through social work (Harris, this volume, Chapter Four; Evans, this volume, Chapter Eight).

The extent to which 'technical subordination' has occurred is much debated in terms of whether discretion continues to be exercised in social workers' everyday decision making (Baldwin, 1998, 2000, 2004; Ellis et al, 1999; Bradley and Manthorpe, 2000; Evans and Harris, 2004; 2006; Evans, 2006; Hughes and Wearing, 2007, p 88). Drawing on Kirkpatrick et al (2005), Lawler argues that the increase in performance management and greater proceduralisation has reduced the autonomy of front-line staff and constrained and regulated their decision-making (Lawler, 2007, p 128). The loss of discretion reported by a wide variety of state social workers is consistent with the introduction of proceduralised, managerialised approaches to practice (Dustin, 2007, p 26). A front-line manager in children's services offers the following comments on professional autonomy and discretion: "I think we have a lot less professional autonomy because of all the compliance tasks that must be done … I've got three pages of compliances and I think that generally it's the professional autonomy that has been removed on a lot of levels" (Thomas and Davis, 2005, p 723). Similar comments are offered by child care social workers:"Our professional judgements are constantly undermined if it doesn't suit the performance targets".'Decisions are often made on the least expensive option not necessarily the one based on the social worker's recommendation' (Gupta and Blewett, 2007, p 175).

How are we to explain the disjunction between the kinds of analyses constructed by Johnson and Derber, which see state professionals such as social workers enjoying discretion in their work, and recent more pessimistic accounts of the disappearance of such discretion as social workers allegedly become unreflective people-processors? In retrospect, Johnson's and Derber's analyses can be seen as being contingent upon a particular historical moment, that of the post-war social democratic state. In that welfare regime, social rights were accorded to service users as 'client-citizens' (Roche, 1987, p 369), with state power as the 'caretaker' of their social existence, intervening in their lives 'to encourage the passive consumption of state provision' (Keane, 1988, p 4).This was a 'clientelist relationship between the citizen and the state' (Powell, 1997, p 209). For Marshall, social rights were 'not designed for the exercise of power at all ... they concern individuals as consumers, not as actors' (Marshall, 1981, p 141). If citizens were expected to consume social work in this way, there had to be state provision that embodied expertise and professionalism in the delivery of social services (Marshall, 1975, pp 205–6). Faith in disinterested professionalism, as the exercise of public service, enjoyed cross-party political support and became a cornerstone of the post-war social democratic consensus on welfare (Marquand, 1988) and this was the institutional basis for the exercise of discretion in social work. Indeed, such was the privileged position occupied by social work at this historical moment that it was able to have aspirations not only to exercising technical autonomy but also to using that autonomy to challenge its ideological subordination to the state-defined ends of social work, by counterposing a range of alternative paradigms (radical social work, feminist social work, anti-racist social work and so on) against the state's formulations.

In contrast, in the widespread pessimistic analyses of current developments, the incursion of managerialism into social work practice has reversed the process and has moved from a sole concern with the *ends* of the state, which characterised social work in the social democratic welfare state, to an accompanying focus on the *means* by which those *ends* will be realised, through detailed prescription of the nature of social work practice and monitoring of the outcomes (Harris and Unwin, this volume, Chapter One).While this general trend is undeniable, and aspects of it are explored in other chapters, is it still possible, contrary to the arguments reviewed thus far, for social workers to resist the counterproductive and damaging effects of the dominant discourse of managerialism? Where there is ambivalence and uncertainty, is there the possibility of resistance (Harris, 2003, p 184)? It may be that social workers, at least for some of the time, are able to hold on to social work values and defend their professional practice, rather than being totally dominated by managerialising and modernising discourses. In any case, those discourses experience difficulty in extinguishing professional discretion, for reasons identified by Lipsky (1980). As mentioned earlier, Lipsky saw the work of street-level bureaucrats as happening in services in which discretion is necessary in order to meet a variety of human needs; discretion is necessary simply to do the job. However, the vague, ambitious and often contradictory goals of street-level bureaucracies create another area of discretion: the space in which to translate nebulous policy into practice. Finally, Lipsky recognised the discretion that street-level bureaucrats themselves have to create space in order to advance their own values, interests and needs (see Evans and Harris, 2004, pp 883–90).

There is evidence that, instead of being subordinated and stifled by managerial control, some social workers have used these kinds of spaces and that practice has continued to develop (White and Harris, 2001; 2004). This suggests that, while social workers may be *subject to* managerialism, they are not necessarily and inevitably always *subjected by* it. Resistance may have flickered under the gale of modernisation that has hit social work, but perhaps it has not been snuffed out.

Resistance – the challenge to managerialism?

Braverman's work on labour processes was enormously influential in understanding changes in the workplace and how they affected people's working lives (Braverman, 1974). He was criticised for neglecting workplace resistance but Jermier et al (1994, p 4) have argued that this was not the case. The following quotation from Braverman indicates why workplace resistance emerges:

> But, beneath this apparent habituation, the hostility of workers to the degenerated forms of work which are forced upon them continues as a subterranean stream that makes its way to the surface when employment conditions permit, or when the capitalist drive for a greater intensity of labor oversteps the bounds of physical and mental capacity ... it renews itself in new generations, expresses itself in the unbounded cynicism and revulsion which large numbers of workers feel about their work, and comes to the fore as a social issue demanding solution. (Braverman, 1974, p 151, quoted in Jermier et al, 1994, p 5)

From this beginning in the work of Braverman himself, the labour process studies that built on his work had a great interest and attention in documenting and theorising workplace resistance (Jermier et al, 1994; Harris, 1998a; Thomas and Davies, 2005). This was originally conceptualised within a Marxist frame of reference, with a central place accorded to class struggle:

> 'Real' resistance in and around capitalist work organizations could take many forms, but would derive from only one source: revolutionary class-

consciousness. Thus, the meaning of resistance was straightforward and was to be interpreted as struggle against the fundamental defining feature of the capitalist mode of production: exploitation of labour through the generation and extraction of surplus value. (Jermier et al, 1994, p 2)

Thomas and Davies concur that 'the antecedents of workplace resistance were derived from essentialist expressions of class-consciousness and were the outcome of a capitalist mode of production' (2005, pp 711–12). Studies in the main focused on the 'prototype male blue-collar worker' and became 'the blue-print for understanding all forms of resistance, carried out by all categories and types of worker engaged in workplace opposition' (Thomas and Davies, 2005, p 712; Jermier et al, 1994, p 9). In early studies, given that the antecedents of resistance were located in class struggle, other social divisions – such as gender, 'race', sexuality, disability, age and ethnicity – were rendered invisible. This 'all or nothing view of resistance', driven purely by class conflict, was found to be increasingly inadequate in relation to understanding resistance (Thomas and Davies, 2005, p 712).

In response, more recently the concept of resistance has been widened to include new categories of workers that were previously overlooked, in order to understand its complexities (Thomas and Davies, 2005, pp 712–13) and with increasing recognition that 'the nature of resistance will vary across space and time' (Jermier et al, 1994, p 9). One aspect of embracing this variation is the move away from 'grand narratives' about resistance, and greater attentiveness to the meanings that workers themselves attach to their forms of resistance in the workplace. A more 'bottom-up' approach (Collinson, 1994, p 26) allows capturing of the responses of social workers to the practices of managerial control. The dissatisfaction in which resistance is rooted has been seen as going 'well beyond the ranks of a small numbers of politically committed individuals.... [it] embraces very large numbers of workers who might not think of themselves as "political"' (Ferguson, 2008, p 4). This cautions against seeing managerialism as having 'a cohesive and fixed meaning' and, instead, points to ways in which it might be 'negotiated, contested and resisted' (Davies and Thomas, 2000, p 552); individuals respond to managerial and modernising discourses in many and complex ways.

What constitutes resistance?

Drawing on research in the late 1990s and the 2000s, Thomas and Davies (2005) suggest that there has been greater questioning of what 'counts' and what does not 'count' as workplace resistance. They undertook research focused on the effects of 'New Public Management' on social workers and managers from two contrasting local authorities. The interviews explored issues of 'change, professional performance expectations, and feelings of "comfort" and "fit" with new managerial subjectivities promoted within the New Public Management discourse' (Thomas and Davies, 2005, p 722). From this study, the authors identified a variety of forms of workplace resistance. These ranged from 'subtle acts and behaviours', for example, ignoring requests for information and writing letters of complaint, through to distancing the self from managerial discourses by challenging and reinterpreting standards and procedures, the latter characterising the actions of front-line managers cited in other studies:

> "There are so many rules and procedures and everything else that ... you know, no-one's got the memory of an elephant, so everybody's got a whole load that they can't remember. So there's a sort of ignoring of certain things ... and in a sense I think that's quite tolerated." (Evans, 2006, pp 158–9)

> "I still really live by the tenet that rules are there to be broken and so I see procedures and guidelines as a way of enabling us to work but not necessarily as being the way we should always work and so I see them as being something that is, if you like, it's a framework, but that does not stop you putting different material on the inside. It doesn't stop you putting different pictures in. It doesn't stop you challenging." (White, 2006, p 126)

Social workers also may engage in a variety of forms of resistance. First, workers often mystify or conceal their knowledge of service users in order to acquire resources ('dressing up assessments', referred to earlier). Collinson (1994, p 25) refers to this as strategic manipulation of knowledge and information. Second, another resistance strategy is to deliberately delay paperwork or assessment plans so that managers are manipulated into taking a particular course of action. For example, one of the post-qualifying social workers mentioned earlier often left decisions about cases until last thing on a Friday afternoon, especially if accommodation for children was needed, in order to bypass some of the decision-making procedures. Third, apparent cooperation with a social work task may often conceal resistance. Such forms of resistance centre on 'destabilizing truth and challenging subjectivities and normalising discourses' (Thomas and Davies, 2005, p 727). These forms of resistance to managerialist discourse and practices are often subtle and small scale, and such local, individual struggles are rarely part of a wider campaign; they do not 'result in radical rupture or apocalyptic change' (Thomas and Davies, 2005, p 720). Rather, resistance operates in complex ways, rather than being a simple bifurcation of all or nothing, so that resistance by one person might be viewed as compliance or indifference by another (Jermier et al, 1994, p 2): 'Resistance and consent are rarely polarized extremes on a continuum of possible worker discursive practices. Resistance frequently contains elements of consent and consent often incorporates aspects of resistance' (Collinson, 1994, p 29).

A less active form of resistance than those considered so far is what Collinson (1994) calls 'resistance through distance'. This describes the way in which workers try to escape or avoid the demands of managerial authority and to distance themselves, either physically, mentally and/or symbolically, from the organisation and its prevailing power structure. Workers avoid being associated or allied with managers and adopt an 'us and them' attitude. On the basis of a series of interviews, Jones (2001) maintains that 'the depth of the divisions between the front-line practitioners and their managers' was a surprise to him. He goes on to say that 'if a 'them and us' culture is a measure of proletarianization then I have no hesitation in describing state social workers as being thoroughly proletarianized. I heard no positive word about managers' (2001, p 559). Moving into management is often dismissed by social workers for this very reason. It is seen as requiring compromise and conformity in order to move from being one of 'us' to one of 'them'. A practitioner experienced acting as a manager in a community adults team in this vein, as follows: "We're split on two floors. The manager never came to see upstairs people and I often said to him, 'you ought to come upstairs for a cup of coffee with us, we want to see you', but he never did" (White, 2006, p 136).

This practitioner went on to explain that, when she became acting manager, she had to make a conscious effort to speak to social workers. This experience as acting manager made her think about the personal compromises she would have to make in order to accommodate to the management culture:

> "You could be behind that door and nobody would ever know that you are there. I hated that. It's just something about the role that cuts you off. And so I'm glad really that I didn't take that on permanently. It still wouldn't interest me. You know, I'd be stuck behind that thing all day [points to computer] and in meetings. But, the meetings, again, are so far from the reality of everyday work." (White, 2006, p 136)

Similarly, in an earlier study, a social worker in children's services stated:

> "I wouldn't want to be a manager. I have found my little niche. I do what I can. I don't feel I can compromise myself, to the extent that I would have to, to go up the career ladder. In some ways you can feel a rebel, self-righteous that you haven't." (White, 1991, p 61)

Distancing through 'us and them' formulations can lead to another form of resistance through distancing, cynicism. Cynicism can be the last resort for resistance: a way of escaping the encroaching logic of managerialism that provides an inner space for workers when other avenues for opposition have dried up (Fleming and Spicer, 2003, p 160). For such workers, compliance with organisational goals does not mean that they have internalised the values of the managerialised organisation. Finally, resistance through distance can also involve withdrawal from active participation in the workplace. Often, dissatisfaction and unhappiness in social work is expressed in individualised ways – absenteeism through sickness and stress, moving job or leaving the profession (Collins, 2007).

In stark contrast to resistance through distancing strategies, Collinson suggests there is also 'resistance through persistence', when workers (drawing on organisational knowledge and professional skills) demand greater involvement in the organisation, by monitoring practices, challenging decision-making processes and generally making management more accountable (Collinson, 1994, p 25). For example, in one study women social workers exercised influence by responding to departmental consultation documents on specific areas of practice, either through their teams or on an individual basis (White, 1991). Social workers using such strategies draw on a wide variety of knowledge (for example: technical, organisational, procedural, local, regional, cultural, historical, legal, economic, strategic/political and self), which those in more senior positions may not share and which can be used as an important 'weapon of resistance' to challenge and disrupt the power of managerialising and modernising discourses. Social workers can control the flow of information upwards, play on the essentially private nature of their work and exploit management's reliance on their goodwill, on which service provision depends.

Thus far, implicitly and at one point explicitly (see Jones, 2001), boundaries have seemed to exist between social work practitioners and managers. However a recent survey 'found that 89 per cent of senior managers had been involved in social services work' (Ackroyd et al, 2007, p 15) and this would seem to keep alive the possibility that some of them, at least, might seek ways of preserving rather than constraining practitioner discretion. Ackroyd et al maintain that, in social work services, professional values have remained 'surprisingly robust' and management practice has been shaped or partially captured by professional ways of thinking (Ackroyd et al, 2007, p 20). Such differentiations within management suggest that organisations are not fully integrated and consensual wholes, even across different levels of management, as envisaged by mission statements or organisational visions. They are stratified on a number of different levels and, as a consequence, the goals of senior managers and front-line workers may be different, with the possibility of overlapping interests and alliances between local managers and social workers (Harris, 1998b; Causer and Exworthy, 1999, pp 84–5; Evans, this volume, Chapter Eight). A recent study discovered that procedures offer scope for interpretation and that social workers were able to exercise substantial discretion, with the support of front-line managers (Evans, 2006, p 277; this volume, Chapter Eight).

Very few writers have examined the idea that managers themselves may resist the imposition of managerialism. However, LaNuez and Jermier suggest that managers may engage in organisational sabotage. They define sabotage as a 'deliberate action or inaction that is intended to damage, destroy or disrupt some aspect of the workplace environment' (1994, p 221). Managers' resistance by sabotage is similar to that of workers. Managers may deliberately work without enthusiasm, take time off, engage in deliberate inaction by withholding relevant information, and fail to adhere to established policies, procedures and rules, or intentionally denigrate the organisation and its products or services (1994, p 242). Salaman (1979) notes that, despite the efforts of higher managers to 'design and install "foolproof" and reliable systems of surveillance and direction', there will always be 'some dissension, some dissatisfaction, some effort to achieve a degree of freedom from hierarchical control – some resistance to the organization's domination and direction' by other managers (Salaman, 1979, p 145, cited by Gottfried, 1994, p 105) and this resistance is found at many different levels in the organisation.

Conclusion: transformative radicalism *and* quiet challenges?

There have been calls to find 'more effective ways of resisting the dominant trends within social work and map ways forward for a new engaged practice' (Jones et al, 2004). Some writers argue that the way forward is to work outside the state context, towards global resistance: 'radical resistance involves tapping into a long tradition of radical social work and applying it in a global context' (Powell, 2001, p 165). Ferguson and Lavalette (2005) have linked such a strategy to what they argue is the most significant social movement of our time, namely, 'the anti-capitalist movement' or 'global justice movement', which they think will 'play a significant role in the discovery of a new, engaged social work practice' (2005, p 208). This movement was first encountered in a demonstration in Seattle in 1999, when 80,000 people brought the proceedings of the World Trade Organisation to a halt, and was followed by other demonstrations elsewhere in succeeding years. Ferguson and Lavalette stress the importance of these movements and ask whether 'individual social workers, as well as national and international organisations, are prepared to engage with these movements, and on what basis' (2005, p 220). They contend that there are two points of convergence between contemporary social work and the new movements: the rejection of and resistance to marketisation and managerialism and the 'overlap between the values of social work and the values of anti-capitalism … the promotion of social change; the commitment to social justice; and emphasis on human rights, empowerment and liberation' (2005, p 221; see also, Lyons et al, 2006; Lyons, 2007). However, they argue that values alone are not enough for a renewal of engaged social work practice, there is the 'question of organisation'.

Ferguson and Lavalette maintain that, after Seattle and the anti-war movement, there has been a 'rediscovery of the effectiveness of collective action and organisation' (2005, p 222). These movements have provided an opportunity 'to create new, much stronger, and much more radical, networks of social workers and service users, both nationally and internationally … the pessimism and despair that has surrounded social work practice for so long can be replaced by the hope that … another social work is indeed possible' (2005, p 223). Nationally, a number of events have taken place which demonstrate that social workers are interested in collective resistance: for example, a conference in Nottingham (2006), 'Affirming Our Value Base', which drew over 1,500 participants; one in Liverpool (2006), 'Social Work in the 21st Century'; and in Glasgow (2007), 'Social Work a Profession Worth Fighting For' reasserted social work's social justice agenda, launched *Social Work and Social Justice: A Manifesto for a New Engaged Practice* and initiated

Community Care's campaign 'Stand up for Social Work'. Lymbery argues that collective resistance can also occur by 'reconfiguring professional associations so that they are more politically engaged' (Lymbery, 2001, in Hughes and Wearing, 2007, p 11) and Meagher and Healy call for coalitions of professional associations (Meagher and Healy, 2003, in Hughes and Wearing, 2007, p 11). Consistent with this emphasis on externally based resistance, Powell finds it difficult to visualise how social work can carry on radical resistance within a state that is 'privatising social services or operating quasi-markets. It seems axiomatic that radical resistance has to be carried on outside the state in civil society' (2001, p 159).

Despite the undoubted significance of the forms of external resistance identified, there is also a need for practitioners to engage in resistance in the workplace; they can be 'in and against' current forms of social work.[1] This involves recognising and engaging with management and professional agendas in organisations in order to provoke change from within. One social worker commented that she thought social work had been, to date, a "quiet profession" and she reflected a view expressed by many other social workers interviewed in the same study, that social work needs to stand up and be counted" (Cree and Davis, 2007, p 159). Regardless of the extent to which social workers move towards standing up to be counted, this chapter has suggested that opportunities for resistance can be found in the nooks and crannies within existing organisational frameworks. Some commentators may view this as offering a weak form of resistance, as compared to the vision of transformative radicalism offered by the proponents of anti-capitalist/ global movements. However, as Thomas and Davies remind us 'the effectiveness of small-scale localized struggles in effecting larger scale change should not be underestimated ... the global is a construction of aggregated local events and discourses, not something that stands entirely outside of them' (2005, p 733). This focus on 'quiet challenges' opens up a view of discretion and resistance that does not have to wait for the fruits of large-scale transformative radicalism to ripen. It encompasses a range of more subtle challenges through which resistance will continue because, amoeba-like, it will adapt and mutate (Powell, 2001, p 87).

While there is no doubt that social work inhabits a 'frosty climate' and is 'haunted by uncertainty' (Bauman, cited in Powell, 2001, p 23), Bauman's uncertainty can be reclaimed 'as fertile ground for the development of ideas and suggestions of ways forward for those with the courage to engage' (McDonald, C., 2006, p 19). This courage to engage and to make a difference continues to be the major reason why people come into social work. The challenge in seeking to make a difference involves negotiating 'the slippage between the potential and ideals of social work as a professional activity and the reality of social work as organisational work' (Lymbery and Butler, 2004, p 10). As Lymbery points out, 'a restored belief in the role of social work at the level of practice can then provide the basis for a renewal of confidence in social work's ability to impact on other levels – a classic example of a "bottom-up" approach to change' (Lymbery, 2001, p 381). Such an approach is likely to involve resistance to managerialising and modernising discourses; on a day-to-day level, subtle acts and quiet challenges can contribute to that resistance.

Note

[1] The phrase 'in and against' was coined by the London Edinburgh Weekend Return Group (1979), which argued that in struggles against the state, state workers held a contradictory position, working in and against the state.

EIGHT

Managing to be professional? Team managers and practitioners in modernised social work

Tony Evans

Introduction

A key concern in many accounts of modernised social services is the fractured nature of the relationship between social workers and their managers. Managers, it is argued, have changed. While they used to share the professional concerns and commitments of the practitioners they managed, this is no longer the case. Managers' concerns are now largely organisational; their focus is the implementation of policy and their commitments are economy, efficiency and effectiveness. The relationship between managers and practitioners is now fundamentally antagonistic, characterised by the conflict of different worldviews Jones, for instance, argues that the traditional role of the social worker, focusing on the needs of service users, has been distorted by managers, who have sought to control practice and have transformed social work, imposing 'hard-nosed commercial logic' (2001, p 560).

This picture of 'the management' and the relationships of managers and practitioners in contemporary social services has come to be largely taken for granted. It is the default position when practitioners talk about their managers, but often in order to contrast their own positive experience with what management generally is considered to be like: 'They're all glorified accountants, not interested in practice; but my manager is not like that, my manager is different.' Interestingly, practitioners seem to want their managers to have some of the managerialist attributes of which they are critical in general terms; they complain, for example, when individual managers are not sufficiently efficient and effective. Managers are as often praised by practitioners for fighting for resources as they are criticised for imposing cuts; they often work with practitioners to mitigate the impact of the latest IT 'solution'; and they share practitioners' concerns that the latest organisational change is just shifting the deckchairs on the *Titanic*. This impression is anecdotal; it cannot, on its own, be used to dismiss the idea of the prevalence of hard-nosed management identified by Jones. However, it does suggest that we should be careful not to take this view for granted, but to examine it against the evidence and consider its implications for professional practice.

This chapter considers the origins of the characterisation of managers as creatures of managerialism. Within the critical literature on managerialism it is possible to identify two different strands of analysis, presenting different pictures of the relationship between managerialism and management and between managers and practitioners. One strand focuses on managerialism as the dominance of managers; the other emphasises managerialism as a set of ideas, practices and skills which engage managers to varying degrees. The equation of managers with managerialism, suggested by the first strand, is called into question by research evidence and, further, the second perspective suggests the need to decouple the connection made between managers and managerialism. In the light of these arguments, findings are presented from a case study of a social work team to illustrate, develop and explore these observations.

The advance of managerialism

Over the last two decades, managerialism – the idea that managers should be in control of public organisations and that they should run these organisations in line with business principles and concerns – has been increasingly prevalent within public sector services (Pollitt, 1993; Harris, 2003). The advance of managerialism has been closely associated with the influence of neo-liberalism on government policy since the 1980s. Neo-liberalism is critical of the idea of need that underpins professional practice and service provision in the welfare state:

> Needs are not physical things out there waiting to be identified by a competent observer but are intimately related to plans and purposes, and these are subjectively chosen ... the claim that needs are objective and distinct from intensively felt wants sounds paternalistic, as much of the welfare state's activity technically is. (Barry, 1999, p 124)

O'Brien and Penna (1998), reviewing the ideas and values underpinning the Conservative governments' social policy, explain that their commitment to a residual model of welfare reflected both an assumption that welfare is the primary responsibility of the family and community and a belief that when the state steps in it should provide only the basic minimum, because welfare provided by the state is oppressive, inefficient and debilitating. Neo-liberal thinkers, such as Hayek and Friedman, argued that the lack of sensitivity to cost and absence of responsiveness to consumers in public services required the injection of market discipline to create efficiency, innovation and effective services. Further, the state's reliance on professionals and bureaucrats to decide what people need and to apportion support involves both a mistaken faith in professional expertise and an intolerable exercise of power over citizens (George and Wilding, 1994).

The intrusion of managerialism into two areas of the public sector – health and social services – is closely associated with two reports produced by Sir Roy Griffiths, then the managing director of Sainsburys supermarkets. He was invited by the government to comment on 'manpower' and 'resources' within the NHS and was subsequently asked to review community care services and make recommendations for their development (Timmins, 1995). The first Griffiths report, the *NHS Management Inquiry Report* published in 1983, looked at management systems in the NHS and recommended a move away from the system of consensus management in which clinicians, predominantly doctors, played a powerful role in hospital management alongside administrators (Griffiths, 1983). Griffiths was concerned about the absence of clear lines of responsibility for management decision-making: 'In short if Florence Nightingale were carrying her lamp through the corridors of the NHS today she would almost certainly be searching for the people in charge' (1983, General Observations, sec 5). In place of administrators, Griffiths recommended the establishment of a cadre of general managers – professional managers – with responsibility for budgetary control, monitoring performance and quality of service. The government's response to the report was positive and resulted in the recruitment of managers – from within and outside the NHS – to replace administrators; and the introduction of management budgets and clear lines of financial accountability. Managers''... salaries and contracts were linked to performance; if they did not deliver the goods, they risked not having their contracts renewed' (Klein, 1989, p 210).

The second Griffiths report, *Community Care: Agenda for Action*, considered the options for the delivery of community care services. The report and its subsequent acceptance by the government was largely driven by a concern to control rising central government expenditure on residential care through the benefits system (Timmins, 1995). Griffiths recommended that government spending on residential care should be transferred to local authorities, which should assess people to decide whether they needed public funding. The report's approach was antithetical to the idea of social care as a universal service provided by the public sector. Social services were cast in the role of the last port of call, which should only step in when the family or community were unable to provide support. The role of social services was to manage the market of care by coordinating services – strategically and, in the shape of care management, on an individual basis – and limit provision within available resources. The report concluded that local authorities should 'act for these purposes as the designers, organisers and purchasers of non-health care services, and not primarily as direct providers, making the best possible use of voluntary and private bodies to widen consumer choice, stimulate innovation and encourage efficiency' (Griffiths, 1988, p 1).

The Griffiths reports were pivotal points in the advance of managerialism within health and social services and, taken together, suggest some important points about any critical analysis of managers and managerialism. Managerialism is not uniform. It takes different forms in different settings (Harris, 2007; White and Harris, 2007). The first Griffiths report entailed the promotion of general management in the efficient running of the health service, but in the second report the focus was on structural change, in terms of residualising public responsibility for social care. Understanding managerialism entails looking beyond its common forms and recognising how these are motivated by underlying principles. Phenomena associated with managerialism in one setting may not be underpinned by these managerialist principles in another. We need to understand managerialism as the relationship between organisational forms and a particular framework of values and principles. Accordingly, managerialism is not only a set of technical prescriptions about how to run an organisation but is also a broader set of assumptions about the relationship between the state and citizens/customers, the respective roles of the public and private sectors, and the virtues of the market. Finally, managerialism elides a desire for well-run public services with a neo-liberal antipathy to the nature and role of public provision of welfare. However, this combination of commitment and belief is not inevitable. Managerialism is not alone in its commitment to well-managed public services or in expressing concern about professionalism when it becomes 'a conspiracy against the laity'. The dispute that critics have with managerialism is the assumption that well-managed public services must act and look like businesses.

Analysing managerialism in social services

As we have seen, the approach of managerialism in different areas of public service has entailed different forms, reflecting the historical and organisational contexts of each service area. The NHS and social services have presented very different organisational contexts and challenges to managerialism, not the least of which have been the very different nature and role of managers in these services. Health and social services have both been targets for managerial reform because of the powerful role of professionals in these organisations – they have been seen as sites in which professionals have captured public organisations (Alaszewski and Manthorpe, 1990; Harris, this volume, Chapter Four). However, the historic relationship between managers and practitioners in these two organisations has been very different. For instance, in the NHS managers – and administrators before them – constitute a distinct professional group, differentiated from the clinicians they manage (Cox, 1991) and largely recruited from the beginning into the administrator/manager role. By contrast, managers within social services have, since the establishment of social services departments, been appointed from among the ranks of the professionals they manage (Brown, 1975; Laffin and Young, 1990; Harris, 1998a; 1998b). Following on from the different nature of managers in the two organisations, managers in the NHS have had extremely limited ingress into clinical decision making, whereas social service managers have historically had a strong role in case decision making. The point here is that while 'managers' may be similar in some ways, they may also be quite different in different contexts. While managerialism is animated by a set of common basic concerns, assumptions and ideas, its focus, impact and strategies have to be understood within these specific contexts of operation.

The impact of managerialism in social services is usually understood against the backdrop of bureau-professionalism (Harris, 2003, ch 3). Bureau-professionalism refers to the combination of the organising principles of bureaucracy and professionalism in social services departments during the first decade following their establishment in the wake of the Seebohm Report (1968). Social services, while located within the bureaucratic structure of local authorities, were strongly influenced by professional principles of organisation, casting professional supervisors as supportive colleagues, rather than as directive managers, and emphasising a significant degree of discretion in the work of professional staff, trusted by fellow professionals who occupied the significant hierarchical posts within social services departments (Stevenson, 1978; Parry and Parry, 1979; Clarke, 1996; Harris, 1998a; 1998b; 2003; this volume, Chapter Four; Payne, 2005b).

In this context managers were seen as being committed to the idea of professional social work, and advancement in the organisation was based as much on professional standing as on managerial authority (Harris, 1998a). Social work's commitment to 'human rights and social justice' (International Federation of Social Work, undated) involves complex ideas and their interpretations are subject to dispute, but they provide the fundamental matrix within which the 'value talk' of social work is generated and maintained. Within the context of bureau-professionalism, social work and social services expressed these commitments in terms of ideas such as Marshall's notion of social citizenship; in order to realise full and equal participation in society, all its members have 'the right to share to the full in the social heritage and to live the life of a civilised being according to the standards prevailing in the society' (Marshall, 1963, p 74). Further, to realise this goal within the welfare state, professionals should have sufficient discretion not simply to implement policy but also to develop it, translating general welfare rights into particular provision (Marshall and Rees, 1985).

In summary, the advance of managerialism within social services, promoted by successive governments since the early 1980s, has entailed significant changes in the distribution of power and influence within organisations, and has sought to displace traditional professional concern with need and social citizenship and has emphasised business concerns through economy and efficiency in service delivery (Lapsley and Llewellyn, 1998; Harris, 2003).

In this context, there are two broad strands in the literature that analyses the impact of managerialism on social services (Evans, forthcoming). The first strand, referred to here as the 'domination perspective', presents managers and professionals as distinct occupational groups: practitioners are workers within the organisation, which is run by managers whose primary commitment is to the organisation's goals. This literature emphasises the increased power of managers as a class within social services and characterises managers as creatures of the organisation and as antithetical towards practitioners' professional concerns. Managers' authority is based on their hierarchical position and is enforced by means of coercive strategies of control. Practitioners are seen as self-interested workers who must be directed and monitored. From this perspective, managers in social services are engaged in a constant struggle with practitioners and use a range of techniques, such as procedures, performance measures, budgets and eligibility criteria, to exert control and achieve organisational goals (Howe, 1986; 1991a; 1991b; 1996; Hadley and Clough, 1996; Jones, 1999; 2001). These changes are seen as permeating management. Since the mid 1980s, for instance, researchers have identified significant changes in the behaviour and orientation of local managers, reflected in a tendency for managers to exercise increasing control over professional practice and to focus on the enforcement of corporate concerns, particularly rationing resources (Howe, 1986; Nixon, 1993; Pahl, 1994). The community care reforms in the early 1990s are widely seen as a pivotal point in the shift of power and control to social services managers:

> As well as a more prescribed and rigid role for front-line workers, a more prominent part was expected of their superiors. It had been recognized that front-line managers offered an opportunity to complete such roles as regulating the duties of subordinates, survey the stricter eligibility (for services) criteria applied to clients during assessment, and also guard finite resources against claims for assistance from outside. (Carey, 2003, p 122)

The second strand of analysis, designated the 'discursive' strand, does not see a clean break from bureau-professional to managerialist social services. Rather, it sees the continuation, alongside an increasingly powerful managerialist discourse, of professional concerns and practices – a bureau-professional discourse – in which, for instance, elements of management may retain professional concerns. It emphasises the fragmentary and dispersed nature of power within social services, seeing the idea of domination as problematic and techniques of control as more openly textured and ambiguous than does the domination perspective. It is sceptical of the rhetoric of management power and critical of approaches that 'treat such strategies [of control] as though they worked rather than as attempts to achieve their desired results' (Clarke and Newman, 1997, p 31). From this perspective, managers are not inevitably engaged with and committed to the managerial discourse (neither are practitioners necessarily its passive subjects nor immune from it). Managers and practitioners are not two distinct and homogeneous groups; they are actors who operate within fields of cross-cutting forces. Accordingly, managerialism has not replaced bureau-professionalism, but is another organisational stratum laid upon it. It may be thick or thin, robust or subject to extensive erosion in particular circumstances. The discursive approach, then, locates actors within fields of tension – sites within which organisational and management practices can reflect professional strategies and concerns alongside increasingly influential managerialist ideas and concerns, to 'produce new focal points of resistance, compromise and accommodation' (Clarke and Newman, 1997, p 76).

Both perspectives accept that managerialism has an influence within social services. However, they disagree about what this entails – whether managerialism is a conclusion, a fait accompli, or whether it is a process of continuing struggle. From the domination perspective, managerialism is equated with managers as a class apart; managers have separated themselves from their professional history and from the professional workers they manage (Howe, 1991a). Further, this management cadre has commitments that are inimical to professionalism and professional commitments within social services (Jones, 1999). Managers now have power, and practitioners do not (Howe, 1991a; Jones 1999). This is power as domination, radically asymmetrical and irrevocable. In short, from the domination perspective, professionalism is no longer a significant factor in social services; managerialism has caused a seismic shift across social services, resulting in managers attaining control.

In contrast, the discursive perspective does not see the influence of managerialism as predetermined and dominant. Its influence within an organisation and on organisational actors must be understood with reference to the particular field of forces in operation at that time. Organisations operate in the context of cross-cutting discourses which generate sites of dispute and conflict and opportunities for manoeuvre; in a particular context managers, for instance, may or may not subscribe to managerialism, they may or may not go along with management principles; they may or may not retain a commitment to the profession from which they came (Evans, forthcoming). Managerialism is not hegemonic but it 'has shifted the terms of reference on which conflicts and tensions around social welfare are fought out both within and beyond organisations' (Clarke and Newman, 1997, pp 76–7).

Managerialism in social services: the evidence

There are good reasons for questioning the rather overwrought picture of the triumph and potency of managerialism presented by the domination perspective. The key claims of the domination perspective relevant here are that in modernised social work practitioners are subjected to the effective and minute control and direction of their managers and that managers are a group distinct from practitioners in terms of their commitments and interests.

Many studies confirm a significant increase in the proceduralism of practice, and support the idea that practitioners are now subject to increasing and intensive scrutiny (Hadley and Clough, 1996; Harris, 1998a; 1998b; Jones, 2001; Carey, 2003). However, it is a matter of interpretation whether proceduralism and supervision reflect business principles or the development of professional tools, ensuring good practice and supporting expertise (Lewis and Glennerster, 1996; Baldwin, 2000; Kirkpatrick, 2002; Robinson, 2003). Robinson (2003), for instance, looked at the implementation of a risk-assessment instrument in a probation service and found that, despite trepidation about its introduction in terms of undermining professional discretion, the instrument was welcomed by many practitioners and managers as a useful tool in helping them assess and manage complex situations and as a spur to greater consistency, transparency and equity in assessment practice. Further, even if policies and procedures within social work are purely aimed at management control, the idea that they constitute an iron cage, severely limiting practitioner discretion, is also problematic. Rules and procedures need interpretation and require the application of background knowledge. The application of any procedure requires the use of judgement and expert knowledge to make it sensible and usable (Munro, 1998). Any body of rules builds up into a complex interrelated body of knowledge that requires judgement in order for it to be interpreted, negotiated and prioritised (Evans and Harris, 2004; Evans, forthcoming). At the very least, it is likely that procedures and supervision entail elements of managerialism and professionalism and that those subject to procedures have some discretion in understanding and applying them. Consideration of eligibility criteria in supervision, for instance, could be narrowly interpreted as a means of restricting access to services or used with professional discretion to recognise need and advocate service provision.

The other set of questions that it is necessary to consider are: do managers now occupy a different conceptual world from that of the professional staff they manage? Have they sought to shed their professional identity and associations? Have they become more business-like, going on high-powered training courses and becoming saturated with business wisdom? Are social services managers now simply concerned with personal advancement and committed to the imposition of market principles in social services?

Overall, the evidence suggests a more complex picture. Research identifies the continuing emphasis on professional skills in the recruitment of managers (Henderson and Seden, 2003), but also finds that managers in post are encouraged to develop business skills (Harris, 1998a; 1998b). There is strong evidence to question the domination perspective view of aggressively managerialist ex-practitioners who are now managers. In a major study of the implementation of the community care reforms, Lewis and Glennerster question the suggestion that 'managers who have wanted to shed their professional association with social work have had reason to welcome the changes' (1996, p 205). Their findings suggest a range of attitudes to the professional culture of social work within social services. Some managers express impatience with this professional culture, while others – including some who were not themselves social workers – remained committed to it.

The national study of the social care workforce undertaken by the National Institute for Social Work (NISW) found that the preparation of practitioners for management roles and managers' commitment to the organisation's goals were patchy. Many managers felt insufficiently trained and ill-prepared for their role (Balloch et al, 1995, p iv). Fewer than half the managers interviewed received support from experienced managers when they became managers, and only a third received any initial training (Balloch et al, 1995, p 53); further, only a quarter of the managers had or were studying for a management qualification (Balloch, 1999, p 152). The NISW study also found significant ambivalence among many managers about their organisations: two-thirds expressed frustration about services' failures to meet service users' needs (McLean, 1999, p 68). Over a third of managers felt their values to be different from those of the organisation – only a slightly lower percentage than for field social workers (Balloch et al, 1995, p 87).

There is evidence to support the notion of increasingly powerful management and managers and of some managers and practitioners who are committed to organisational values. However, the evidence also suggests that there are managers who retain a strong commitment to professional social work and to its values and there is good reason to be sceptical of the assumption that procedures are necessarily antithetical to professionalism and professional values. Further, evidence casts some doubt on the claim that management controls and directs street-level practice. The evidence lends support to the discursive, rather than the domination analysis. The discursive perspective shares with the domination analysis a recognition of the powerful and influential role managerialism can play, but it does not prejudge this; rather, as the evidence suggests, it recognises that managerialism needs to be considered alongside other factors, primarily professionalism, in the analysis of the structuring of street-level practice within social services.

The next section draws on a small-scale study of a local authority older persons social work team. The study illustrates a discursive analysis of the complex interplay of practitioners, local managers and senior managers within a local authority. It also explores the concerns and motivations that underpin the relationship between practitioners and local managers as a way of understanding and explaining resistance to managerialism.

The study

The study examines the experiences of practitioners and their immediate managers – a team manager and two assistant managers – in an older persons social work team in an English local authority. The authority had, for some time, been strongly influenced by managerialism. Historically the authority had been firmly committed to the introduction of the community care reforms in the early 1990s and had organised its adult services using a purchaser/provider split within the department in order to promote a more business-like approach. The older persons team's social workers had a primarily 'purchaser' role, acting as service brokerage care managers (Huxley, 1993) and using eligibility criteria to determine access to funding for public services.

Fieldwork for the study was carried out before the implementation of *Fair Access to Care Services* (Department of Health, 2003d), the framework for eligibility criteria for adult social care. Data gathered included observational visits and archival material, but the main source was individual interviews with social work practitioners and their local managers – five practitioners and three local managers, all qualified social workers. The practitioners were relatively recently qualified, while the managers had all had substantial experience as practitioners before they moved into management. All but one of the interviewees – a practitioner – were women.

The study focused on the application of eligibility criteria as a phenomenon through which to explore: the effectiveness of management control techniques – such as procedures and resource control; the nature of the relationship between local managers and practitioners; and the use of discretion at street level. Eligibility criteria, which govern service users' access to services, have their origin in the Griffiths reform of community care. The 1990 NHS and Community Care Act identifies a duty on the part of local authorities to assess need for community care services and a much narrower duty to meet those needs assessed as being their own responsibility. This requirement has continued to structure access to services under *Fair Access to Care Services* (Department of Health, 2003d).

Within this local authority, eligibility for service was determined by means of a framework – people sometimes referred to it as 'the matrix' – which took into account two ranges of factors: types of need, from social interaction and engagement to physical health; and severity of need, ranging from quality of life to immediate threat to life and limb. While these two dimensions were represented as separate, a close examination of the framework showed that physical need tended to be equated with higher levels of need, while social need was seen as less pressing. When the framework was first introduced this problem was implicitly recognised by the council, which earmarked a small budget for preventive work. However, the main thrust of the eligibility criteria framework was concerned with restricting service provision to people with more severe physical needs. This was underlined by the eventual ending of the budget for preventive work and the narrowing of eligibility for service provision, in the words of one interviewee, to areas of "physical safety, that would include self-neglect, at risk of not feeding themselves, not washing themselves, all those things".

The increasingly restrictive nature of the criteria was just one aspect of the constraints on service provision. The decision to provide services for people whose needs had been assessed had moved up the organisational hierarchy, further away from teams. Local managers now had to present cases at service-wide meetings, which decided whether to release funds to pay for care.

Evaluating the organisation

Managers

In contrast to the picture of managerial solidarity identified in the 'domination' literature, local managers were highly critical of what they saw as under-funding of the service and erosion of local decision making. Their account of their relationship to senior managers within the organisation seemed, in fact, to bear a stronger resemblance to the idea of a 'Berlin Wall', a fundamental fissure in the management hierarchy between senior and local managers (Parsloe, 1981), seen as characteristic of bureau-professional organisations (Harris, 1998b). The context in which local managers were expressing these views was that the social services department had overspent its budget, and the strategy to bring spending back in line with budgetary constraints focused on cutting expenditure on older people's services. Local managers felt that this policy took advantage of older people's services to cut overspend in other areas. In doing this, the authority imposed a requirement – called 'two out, one in' – that for every new unit of service provided, two existing units of service had to be freed up. Local managers were concerned about the legality of this move: "It's not a legal policy, so it's almost like – if somebody ultimately does go to a judicial review about it, [the Council] will almost certainly lose the case ... I think most of us would be quite comfortable for something to go to a judicial review ...".

These managers were critical of the approach of senior managers who were cutting budgets and tightening rationing of services to meet targets, but they also felt that they had to play 'the numbers game' in order to get the best for service users and their teams by being careful to record activity: "They're [senior managers] obsessed with having good percentages. Good places in league tables. Maybe we all know deep down it's a load of rubbish, but you can't avoid playing the game. So if you've got to play the game, get ahead of it".

Practitioners

Practitioners shared the concerns of local managers. They talked about feeling demoralised by the limitations on what they could do: "It's all to do with money, really. As social workers, it's not a very nice position to be in ... You can assess people and you can identify needs, but you are not obliged to provide a service." Across the board, practitioners felt they were not able to do their job as they would like:

> "I think they [senior managers] see social workers as there to, yes, assess the needs, because that's what we're obliged to do; but then as much as possible to limit, to ration what we can do to meet that need as cheaply as possible, as quickly as possible and as long as we get the paperwork done then they're happy ..."

Practitioners were frustrated that the tightening of eligibility criteria was limiting their ability to intervene and do preventive work before a crisis arose. Increasingly they also felt that they were having to compromise professional commitments:

> "I saw [social work] in terms of empowering people and facilitating and advocating for people ... And I still see those roles as being relevant. But ... as you qualify and get into it you realise that there's a political element to your work that you're kind of ... that you're working within certain frameworks and that you're limited in some

things you can do, so you become a bit more of a sort of agent of social control, in a way."

Resistance

This picture of local managers and practitioners united in their criticism of 'the council' and its senior managers leads on to the question of whether practitioners and managers sought to resist these challenges to their fundamental professional concerns. One very interesting incident points to the way in which procedures and rules can be used by practitioners to challenge authority as they manipulate strategies that are often presented as restricting professional practice, in order to advance their professional concerns. Several practitioners referred to a problem in the use of eligibility criteria over the preceding year. Alongside the published eligibility criteria, instructions had come down by word of mouth from 'the council' that the eligibility criteria should be applied in a tighter and narrower manner than was officially acknowledged: "we had a verbal directive. We had no written statement to support that ... there wasn't anything that [the Council] owned, because it wasn't on a piece of paper."

Practitioners were concerned about their position with regard to those people seeking help who met the formal criteria but who were below the line set by the informal 'directive'. Interestingly, they objected to the local authority's failure to acknowledge its tighter criteria publicly and to its use of practitioners to mask a political problem. The practitioners as a group (with the tacit support of the local managers) wrote to senior managers to register their disquiet and demand acknowledgement of the tighter criteria. The authority eventually published the tighter criteria and cases were reassessed against them. Here, overt resistance focused on the use of procedures to re-establish official transparency and political accountability for resource rationing. However, overt professional action to challenge resource constraints was noticeable by its absence. A practitioner explained that the priority was to cope with the day-to-day pressures. One of the managers commented:

> "I find it disappointing how little resistance there is to a lot of things. Why aren't you saying to me 'You can't tell me to do that'? There doesn't seem to be any sort of groundswell. Professionally ... it seems to me that part of our role is to be advising the authority as social workers about things and saying: 'you're employing us as professionals, not as dogsbodies'."

This manager's comments perhaps suggest a successful managerialist strategy to control practice. The policies of senior managers were not popular, but senior managers were still able to control practitioners and ensure that their policies were implemented. Or, perhaps, the practitioners were reflecting a managerial world-view, taking the idea of residual and limited public services as inevitable, even 'natural', and recasting practice as a limited, apolitical, technical task.

However, the latter interpretation would need to indicate more than a lack of overt resistance; it would also need to show the absence of covert modes of resistance, such as those identified, for instance, in street-level bureaucracy analysis (Lipsky, 1980; Ellis et al, 1999; Baldwin, 2000; Evans and Harris, 2004). Could the absence of overt resistance to managerial control suggest a strategic shift to resistance by other means? Local managers, for instance, talking about their own approach to policy and to senior managers, pointed out that: "While we could protest in the '70s, we now have to play another game." This game entailed finding discretionary space and adapting the system to be more responsive to professional concerns about meeting service users' needs (White, this volume, Chapter Seven).

Covert action: finding freedom

In this context, local managers used the freedom they could find within the organisation to create more flexibility in using resources to respond to service users' needs. The local managers, for instance, had been asked by senior managers to set up a budget-monitoring system to manage funding reduction. However, they designed into the monitoring system enough flexibility to allow them to mitigate the impact of the cuts, "using the temporary budget to cover more than temporary items. The rehabilitation budget (a provision for six weeks' funding for rehabilitation, which should then be transferred to the ordinary budget) was used to hold some cases until core funding could be freed up."

This approach was part of a broader culture of flexibility within the team, particularly in the application of eligibility criteria. Eligibility criteria constrained practice but did not eliminate local managers' and practitioners' ability to use discretion. The local managers worked with practitioners to encourage the use of discretion. There were three factors that contributed to this space for discretionary action.

The first factor was recognising that eligibility criteria were, like any text, open to a range of interpretations: "there's still, I think, scope for interpretation ... it's like with anything that's written down ... but I think it's like with anything, it's a substantial amount of care, but what do you mean by that word 'substantial', or 'imminent'?" Second, and related to this, the criteria had to be applied to the complex nature of potential service users' needs, especially as services were increasingly focused on 'vulnerable' older people:

> It's particularly noticeable where there is mental frailty and the element of risk is much harder to control ... when you must say that this person is not safe to be left in their own home, even though they're adamant that that's where they want to be – it's a very difficult one to quantify.

Third, the criteria required practitioners to employ professional expertise and judgement. The local authority and senior managers did not define key terms in the criteria, such as 'risk' and 'need'. These politically and ethically contentious terms were left to professionals to interpret.

Most practitioners were comfortable with employing discretion. One practitioner, for instance, said: "If we as the care managers strongly feel that a particular client needs our service, we would give them a 2 and make them eligible ... it is actually working at the moment ... our managers are agreeing with who we're classifying as 1s and 2s." Another said: "we're allowed to operate a bit of discretion there, and I think our supervisors ... probably, will go along with that quite happily ... I suppose it relies a bit on the supervisor's discretion." Underpinning this: "there's a kind of shared sense of it [eligibility] that's built up ... we'd all probably reach fairly similar decisions about whether they were matrix 1, 2 or below; but we'd be hard put to explain exactly why to someone else."

However, one practitioner was uncomfortable with the use of this locally crafted discretion. Quoting a manager who had told her that "it's like adopting a pragmatic approach", she commented, "I like to think that it's a level playing field, personally, but there we go ... It doesn't rest that easily, but ... I'm not going to beat myself up over it." A point that it is necessary to consider here is whether the acceptance of discretion by practitioners was simply a more successful strategy of managerial control; that local managers, rather than opposing the managerialist stance of senior management, were, in fact, very subtle exponents of managerialism. Leonard (1997), for instance, identifies disciplining through language and ideas as important strategies of managerialist control. Control does not have to be overt: it can also be exercised indirectly, by managing the way in which people understand and think about a situation. Establishing certain ideas as 'sensible', 'acceptable' or 'appropriate' is a common disciplinary practice. Professionals may be said to exercise discretion when they can use their judgement, for instance, in characterising 'need'. However, the organisation assumes and expects need to be equated with immediate physical danger. Any professional who talks or writes about need in wider terms is likely to be challenged and required to explain and justify 'an aberrant view' – to the point of losing heart and eventually accepting the 'naturalness' of dominant ideas. However, Leonard continues, actors are not simply passive; many will continue to resist, challenge and subvert dominant ideas; the lesson they learn may be about doing this more subtly (1997, p 92). The evidence above, of practitioners' and local managers' criticism of the policy context within which they were working, suggests that the exercise of discretion constituted resistance rather than compliance. However, this interpretation, in turn, gives rise to another problem: discretion is neither a good nor a bad thing as such; its merit, or otherwise, lies in how it is used.

The purpose of resistance

One possible explanation for the cooperation of practitioners and local managers in applying discretion to eligibility criteria is that it allowed managers to get the work done, while giving practitioners some control over the choice of whom to help. This view would imply that practitioners and their managers were simply acting as self-interested agents (Lipsky, 1980). An alternative explanation would see this as a form of 'covert resistance' (Leonard, 1997, p 94); in the absence of open opportunities to challenge policy, practitioners and their managers had been driven to find alternative ways of promoting professional concerns. A useful way of considering these alternative explanations of resistance is to examine the values of the practitioners and managers that are embedded in their day-to-day practices (Thompson, 1991; Randall and Charlesworth, 2000).

Local managers and practitioners share a concern about under-funding and attempts by senior managers to control decision making about service provision. There was some evidence of overt resistance to organisational policy when practitioners employed bureau-professional ideas of procedural propriety and clarity to resist attempts by senior managers and politicians to avoid strategic accountability for the rationing of resources. However, resistance to organisational policy was more evident in the covert and cooperative strategies of local managers and practitioners to craft discretionary spaces and use discretion. Two themes were particularly strong when practitioners and local managers described how they sought to use their discretion: extending service provision and supporting service users' autonomy.

Extending service provision

At the team level, the approach to interpreting eligibility criteria was to make them as inclusive as possible. This was achieved by combining interpretation of criteria with the flexibility that local managers had built into the budget monitoring system. One example, provided by a practitioner, is the approach taken to 'urgent' cases:

> "What happens in this team for home care is, if it's urgent it will be agreed on a temporary basis and it will carry on being temporary until they've got sufficient hours to make it permanent. So in a sense they give you the package when you need it … It's just a way of working the system, which I respect. I think it's very sensible."

A different practitioner talked about the value of this approach in terms of seeking fairer results: "I can see that if we don't do something about this we're going to have a problem, you know. Or that client will continue to deteriorate, or the carer will … there may be the straw that breaks the camel's back.…" Another approach was to use professional judgement to reframe the situation to which the criteria were applied. In this regard, one method outlined by another practitioner was to focus on the needs of users, taking carers out of the equation in order to get a service in:

> "And the assistant team manager said, well, what would he be like if his wife wasn't around? Once you start taking his wife out of the equation, we're probably faced with someone who would never go out, who probably wouldn't go out to get any shopping, who probably would only just about … wouldn't maintain the household or the bills or anything like that. So looking at it in terms of him as an individual, once you start taking key people or key support networks out of it, then the eligibility criteria look different."

In seeking to make the criteria inclusive, practitioners and local managers were conscious that they were responsible not only to existing clients but also to potential service users. One manager noted that making all service users eligible might

> "make your life easier because you won't have to take her services away, or you can give her what she wants and she won't have a go at you. But then you've got Mrs Y, the next person you come across. You've got to tackle the problem at some point … that you haven't got enough resources for all the people. The problem would stay there."

Risk and autonomy

Risk, and how to manage it, was a concern for team members and there was a sense in which, working together, they were able to approach risk positively so as to support service users' autonomy. Practitioners were aware of the 'subjectivity' (their word) of their judgements and were anxious about the basis on which they could question and challenge defensive practice:

> "I think clients who are deemed at risk in their homes are probably comfortable with those risks, because with those risks come certain freedoms. But the people who do feel uncomfortable, perhaps care managers – myself to some extent, I'm worried that if I've got a client who's particularly vulnerable that they're found dead one morning and the carer hasn't been in to them because they've been refusing it. There might be some kind of responsibility on myself."

Local managers worked with practitioners to use the eligibility criteria to support service user autonomy, especially in inter-professional work:

> "there is this sort of welfare tendency in older people's services to look after people, do things for people, and to one extent it [the matrix]

challenges that. It does force people to think, well, does this person want to take this risk? Are they capable of making up their minds in order to take that risk? And being quite firm with other professionals and saying, no – this person, yes, there is a risk, but it's one that they want to take."

One practitioner, for instance, described the management of anxiety about risk through discussion and shared responsibility, with local managers: "you've got your supervision, and it's important to discuss those risks with your supervisor and see how they feel about it".

Practitioners and local managers employed discretion to promote their professional commitments. They sought to mitigate the effects of resource rationing on service users and carers. They also sought, in a context where they felt they were being undermined as professionals, to defend the autonomy of service users by resisting defensive practice (Harris, 1987), which might restrict service users' freedom. One element is a use of discretion to subvert organisational policy; the other is an example of a more positive expression of professional social work values. The study reminds us that, in considering resistance in modernised social work, we should be careful to look beyond exceptional and dramatic acts (White, this volume, Chapter Seven). 'rather than see the activist as someone who stands outside the system and speaks the truth to it, activists are recognized as being embedded in the systems which both constrain and enable them to achieve progressive change' (Healy, 2000, p 137).

Conclusion

The beginning of the chapter set out the influential picture of a fractured relationship between social workers and their managers, as a reflection of the impact of managerialism on public services in terms of the intensive regulation of workers by managers in organisations pervaded with a business ethos. Managerialism is increasingly powerful in the modernised public sector, but its impact across public services has varied in different contexts. In social work a particularly important factor in understanding managerialism's role in the relationships between practitioners and their managers is their shared professional heritage and related traditional practices embodied in the notion of bureau–professionalism.

Within the critical literature examining the impact of managerialism on social services, managers and practitioners, it is possible to identify two distinct approaches. First, the domination approach sees managerialism as a clear break with bureau–professionalism. Managers are in control, having separate and different commitments from their former professional selves and the practitioners they manage. Proceduralism undermines professionalism and represents an intensification of control, which is used to impose a business orientation on practice, to the detriment of professional commitments. Second, the discursive viewpoint does not equate the ideas of managerialism with the practices of all managers. New policies and practices interpenetrate existing organisational practices, which embody earlier organisational commitments, such as professionalism. The result is a dynamic conjunction, or field, of forces, giving rise to both control and resistance. This field of forces can be understood by: examining the practices of managers and practitioners; considering how actors can employ organisational techniques to restrain or promote professionalism and managerialism; and identifying the statuses and relationships of actors. While the domination analysis has the strength of clarity and force, it is limited in its ability to capture the complex and dynamic situation that is suggested by the research evidence. The discursive perspective, on the other hand, provides not only a more nuanced theoretical analysis but also an analytic approach that can reflect the interplay of factors suggested by empirical research.

Findings from the small-scale empirical study presented above provide an example of discursive analysis that looks at the conjunction of 'contexts, circumstances and statuses of practitioners and how these factors shape the specific form of street-level practice that operates in particular settings' (Evans and Harris, 2006). The study analyses the field of forces that operate within a particular setting, how this field provides resources for control and resistance and how these resources have been employed by actors to further their concerns. In presenting this study, the aim has not been to make any claims for the generalisability of the substantive findings; the discursive perspective suggests that the situation will be different in particular sites. Rather, it has been to show the value of an approach to the analysis of managerialism that recognises the complex interaction of managerialism and professionalism within modernised social work and can tease out managerialism's impact on the relationships between practitioners and their managers.

This approach provides a way to theorise the impact of managerialism within practice settings and to identify opportunities for professional resistance. The discursive approach acknowledges, and helps to clarify, the extent and limits of control and the resources for resistance in a particular situation and could contribute to individual and collective professional resistance to managerialism. In contrast to this, the domination approach risks casting professional workers as passive victims, subjected to the overwhelming and irresistible domination of managerial control.

Another advantage of the discursive approach is its identification of key areas for further examination. The concern of this chapter has been the relationship between local managers and practitioners. However, the preceding discussion suggests that, while this relationship may be fractured in terms of managers as managerialists and practitioners as professionals, this may not be the case in some settings. Further, there may be other ways in which managerialism and professionalism interact within social services, giving rise to a range of potential conflicts and possible alliances between managers and practitioners. Examples here would be conflict relationships, where managers are committed to professionalism and practitioners are committed to managerialism, and alliance relationships, where both managers and practitioners espouse managerialism. The purpose of further research would be not only to identify and describe these different forms of manager–practitioner relationship, but also to examine how these different configurations might relate to the field of forces within which they operate.

Intensification, individualisation, inconvenience, interpellation

John Harris and Vicky White

The chapters in this volume have examined specific dimensions of what modernising social work involves, some of which have attracted little attention to date. In doing so, all of us as contributors might be criticised for having sidestepped the most significant question: how should modernisation be defined? Our sidestepping of this issue has simply followed that of New Labour itself. The term has many different meanings and no generally accepted definition and describes a vast array of activities, including the "reform of client-facing, service-orientated parts of government" (Powell, 2008a, pp 3, 5, and see Newman, 2005) with which this book has been concerned. This lack of definition has been extremely useful to New Labour. For example, Baldwin argues that in services for adults, New Labour's modernising approach has not been modern, either in the sense of being new and improved or in terms of representing a paradigmatic shift in policy values; any changes have been within the broad framework drawn up by the previous Conservative governments (Baldwin, 2008, p 84). The vagueness of the terminology has meant that New Labour has not had to produce a detailed rationale for modernisation, nor has it had to present it as a steady, even process. Rather, it is a loose dynamic that lives and breathes change, as and where it will. Anything New Labour considers to be dysfunctional needs to be modernised. Anything that needs to be done involves modernisation. If services require changes to their policies and practices they need to be achieved through modernising processes. Almost anything can be justified in the name of modernisation and what right-thinking person, it is implied or explicitly stated, can be opposed to the drive for continuous improvement of the out-of-date?

The dimensions of modernising social work that we have considered are located within neo-liberalism; modernisation is, at base, a strategy for installing forms of policy and practice that are aligned with neo-liberalism's tenets and stems from New Labour's 'neo-liberal hard edge' (Powell, 2008b, p 263; and see other contributions to the same volume). Given that neo-liberalism is the hegemonic framework within which all of the major political parties now operate (at least, at Westminster; there are counter-tendencies in the devolved jurisdictions), rather than seeing modernisation as a specific, time-bound, Third Way-inspired, social democratic project (Blair, 1998), we can anticipate that some variant of modernisation is likely to endure, regardless of any future government's political complexion. For example, the commitment to the supremacy of individual choice, one of the strongest strands of modernisation (see Chapter Four), is favoured by New Labour, the Conservatives and the Liberal Democrats (Needham, 2008, p 272). Future variants may well ditch the term 'modernisation' itself, as one of the tendencies of neo-liberal processes is that they have to be relabelled in order for them to be presented as dynamic and relevant to meeting the ever-changing requirements of globalisation. It is unacceptable within a neo-liberal framework for any government to be simply content to administer what exists. There is a driving requirement for the delivery of constant *improvement*. Given the likely staying power of neo-liberalism as a political ideology for the foreseeable future, here we seek to draw out themes from the preceding chapters that are likely to signify the terrain on which ongoing issues in the modernisation of social work will be played out. These themes do not attempt to explore modernisation in a comprehensive way. (Others have attempted that. See, for example, 6 and Peck, 2004). For example, there is no mention of *integration*, a key theme in terms of how services and professionals are meant to fit together. Instead, the themes identified are those that draw most directly on the chapters in the book and are those to which the chapters have made the most significant contributions.

Intensification of work

As we saw in Chapter One, modernisation has required ever more detailed stipulations concerning the content and process of social workers' practice through performance management. Performance indicators, and measurement of outcomes against them, often seem to dominate the experience of contemporary social work. If performance management has been one of the key means of modernising social work, the ends to which it has been directed have been derived from neo-liberalism, such as installing market mechanisms, making public services as much like the private sector as possible and turning their users into customer-citizens (see Chapter Four). Both the ends and the means of modernisation promote a vision of social work that seeks to massage away the tensions and dilemmas raised in day-to-day social work by difficult political and ethical questions with the balm of 'technical', 'objective', 'neutral' managerialism.

This 'managerial cybernetics' approach (see Chapter One) has resulted in the *intensification* of work processes. Management is no longer seen as a distinct task and function within social work organisations (including many in the voluntary sector, see Poole, 2007). It has become the lightning conductor for neo-liberalism, running through organisations, seeking to manage anything and everything, cajoling and coercing social workers to perform to externally set targets. In the pursuit of targets, social workers are expected to process as much work as possible in the shortest possible time. A recent example, relayed to us by social workers, is the installation of instant messaging on a local authority's computer system so that social workers can multi-task: dealing with phone calls at the same time as attending to different matters through instant messaging, while writing up assessments and care plans. The paradox is that intensification overwhelmingly stresses the quantitative aspects of social work, while at its heart are a series of small-scale, qualitative interpersonal encounters between social workers and service users. This stress on the quantitative has produced forms of practice that are increasingly *instrumental* in their focus on procedures, form-filling and budgets, particularly as the environments in which social workers operate become more complex, resource constrained and subject to reorganisations and new legislation. Such intensified and instrumental social work exerts powerful pressure in the direction of divorcing social workers from the lived experience of service users, ironically at a time when that lived experience is supposed to be at the centre of policy and practice (see Chapter Four). However, there are indications that social workers strive to hang on to the importance of the qualitative aspect of their work and seek to maintain their commitment to advancing service users' interests (see Chapters Seven and Eight).

The instrumentalism of social work is epitomised by the convergence of neo-liberal managerialism and modernisation in the introduction of call centres into social work (see Chapter Two). This is an example of an approach to structuring work processes that was developed in the private sector being applied directly to social work. The roles and identities of social workers in this context have changed and have become more instrumental. For example, the ability to be aware of and to use local networks and resources has traditionally been important in forms of social work practice that were rooted in particular geographical locations. In the anonymity of call-centre social work, this ability disappears. Ironically, such is the pressure of other forms of social work that the social workers who worked in the call centre experienced it as a less intensive environment than that in which they had worked previously (see Chapters Seven and Eight), whereas the bulk of research on private sector call centres identifies work intensification, in 'electronic sweatshops', as the dominant experience. This explains one social worker's suggestion of using the call centre as a convalescent home for burnt-out social workers! (See Chapter Two.)

The increasingly instrumental nature of social work suggests a climate that is not conducive to high staff satisfaction and retention, and in this context, perhaps not surprisingly, a further aspect of modernising social work is the rise of agency working (see Chapter Three). However, the beguiling blandishments of 'portfolio careers' lose their lustre in the face of evidence of agency social workers feeling deskilled by work intensification in the form of treadmill-like, repetitive tasks, with the rapid processing of service users fitting well in workplaces increasingly dominated by the target-driven culture of performance management (see Chapter One). The prevalent view in the literature has been to see agency working as consistent with neo-liberal managerialism, stressing its capacity for work intensification, its contribution to instrumental perspectives and practices and the facility it offers to hire and fire agency workers. Against this dominant perspective, agency working may represent a form of individual resistance for some social workers (see Chapters Two, Seven and Eight) in search of a way to maintain their professional standards.

Intensification has been a key theme in modernising social work. It has installed a neo-liberal workplace culture that has stressed performance to targets. However, intertwined with the theme of intensification have been calls for forms of practice shaped by individualised responses to service users, which are at odds with social workers' dominant experiences of instrumentalism.

 ## Individualisation of service users

Individualisation has been an increasingly prominent motif in policy portrayals of the way social work services are meant to be. As we saw in Chapter Four, it is an approach to individualising service provision that is rooted in consumerism as being key to the modernisation of what are depicted as rigid and uniform social work approaches, dominated by professionals, in which service users are passive recipients. The form and content of this depiction of social work is contrasted with an idealised view of consumer culture in the wider society, seen as being attuned to what each individual wants. That consumer culture is seen as having produced customer-citizens who have high expectations that are carried over into social work, with a keen desire for participation and making active choices about the services received. Accordingly, social work is seen as needing to be modernised so that it can be aligned with the changed nature of the people it serves. As Chapter Four demonstrated, the way in which the users of social work are portrayed in the modernisation agenda and are meant to conceive of themselves (as customer-citizens) has important implications for them and for social work. Modernising discourses emphasise that service users are or, if they are not, should henceforth see themselves as, competent economic and social actors, capable of pursuing their own best interests. Just as intensification represents the installation of neo-liberal tenets in work organisation and processes, customer-citizenship promotes a mode of individual engagement with services that accords roles and behaviours to service users that chime with neo-liberalism.

As a component of individualisation, *involvement* is expressed in terms of partnership and participation. Chapter Five indicated that these concepts faced a tough challenge in child protection work with parents. The chapter suggested that a careful reading of the policy documents questioned whether parents are envisaged as active participants, despite the official promotion of a policy of partnership and parental participation. Even though it is widely used, the terminology of 'working in partnership' has limited value in characterising the nature of parents' involvement in child protection. For example, the rhetoric of choice in individualised services is so at odds with the reality of child protection practice that it can mean little more than social workers making sure that the parents understand the consequences if they decide not to comply with the intervention. As such, the concept of choice, rooted in consumerism, offers parents little potential for involvement.

In services for adults, individualisation has found expression in a stated concern with improving the quality of service users' lives, as distinct from improving the quality of services as an end in itself (see Chapter Six), through person-centred, independence-promoting forms of social work that put the service user in control. Hence there is a clear preference for direct payments and individual budgets, in which the model of individualised consumerism is most clearly defined. Chapter Six indicated the conflicts between this modernising vision of personalised social work services and modernisation's neo-liberal managerialism and the ways in which the latter obstructs the emergence of more user-centred practice. As we have already noted, the concern with individualisation is closely affiliated, in policy and practice, with neo-liberal notions of self-responsibility and this chapter shows how such notions are antithetical to the meanings and preferences of older service users. The pressure towards instrumentalism in current social work, noted in the previous section, was shown to have undermined relationship-based components of the social work role, yet exploring sensitive and complex areas of someone's life is likely to depend to a significant extent on the formation of a conducive relationship. While some adult service users may be able to exercise the role envisaged for them as customer–citizens, those who are less physically and socially advantaged are likely to struggle to do likewise. Among older people, for example, it is the latter who are most likely to be encountered by social workers.

Inconvenience of discretion

While it might be tempting to conclude that social workers have been turned by neo-liberal managerialism from reflective practitioners into unreflective people-processors, Chapter Seven considered the 'discretionary space' available to social workers, notwithstanding the constraints and constrictions involved in modernising social work. As state-mediated professionals, social workers were seen as having opportunities for resistance, mainly expressed through 'quiet challenges' as they go about their day-to-day work, seeking to assist service users. The chapter stresses the value of such challenges in a neo-liberal context that has been widely considered as having robbed social work of its radical potential by expropriating its goals. One aspect of neo-liberal managerialism that has been often asserted is the fractured nature of the relationship between social workers and their managers, who are regarded as no longer sharing the professional concerns and commitments of the practitioners they manage. Chapter Eight questions this view and stresses that, although managerialism is increasingly powerful, its impact has varied in different contexts. In social work a particularly important factor in understanding managerialism's role in the relationships between practitioners and their managers is their shared professional heritage and related practices, embodied in the notion of bureau-professionalism. Modernising policies and practices encounter existing practices, which embody earlier organisational commitments, such as the role accorded to professional discretion. This field of forces results in dynamic and complex interactions between managerialism and professionalism in social worker–manager relationships and provides resources for both control and resistance.

Inscription or interpellation?

One reading of this book's consideration of the dimensions of modernising social work and the themes that have emerged from it might be to suggest that neo-liberalism is now indelibly *inscribed* on the consciousness of service users, social workers and managers, with social workers

> more or less reduced to a walking and breathing embodiment of state structures ... [and] the political framework of the market penetrating the mind of the care manager, student, carer, client etc., at both a conscious and subconscious level, to the point where it can become the only type or form of 'social work' from which to choose or identify with and understand. (Carey, 2008b, pp 353, 357)

An alternative is to see service users, social workers and managers as *interpellated* by the neo-liberal agenda, being called to its modernising discourse and to the adoption of specific identities within it. However, social workers, and others, may be called by the neo-liberal agenda but may not respond to the call, or may respond to it in ways that are not anticipated (see Chapters Seven and Eight). They may be *subjected to* the modernisation discourse but not *subjected by* it. The *intentions* of modernising social work should not be mistaken for unequivocal *accomplishments*. This gap between intention and accomplishment does not mean that we should anticipate immediate far-reaching changes in current forms of social work policy, organisation and practice. The historic moments at which such changes have occurred have been linked to the wider social and economic context and the politics of social movements (Harris, 2008). We have only to think of the impact made on social work in the 1970s and 1980s by, for example, the disabled people's movement, feminism, trade unionism, black perspectives and anti-racism to appreciate the ways in which wider debates and struggles can permeate and influence social work.

Some writers see the need for contemporary social work to be connected to the anti-capitalist movement in order to initiate a similar era of social work being informed by critical perspectives (see, for example, Lavalette, 2007; Ferguson, 2008). In parallel with alliances with wider forces for change, resistance to neo-liberal modernisation will also be conducted within its constraints and is likely to be predominantly at the level of the individual or based on local alliances (see Chapters Seven and Eight). Such resistance suggests that modernising social work is, and will remain, a complex and contested discourse. Rather than representing neo-liberalism's complete and unambiguous triumph it can be regarded as producing a series of temporary 'settlements', which comprise equilibria of varying degrees of stability that at times are capable of being disturbed. The tensions, dilemmas and contradictions raised for the modernising discourse (or whatever neo-liberal variant follows it) by the *intensification* of work, the *individualisation* of service users and the *inconvenience* of discretion will stubbornly refuse to go away.

References

6, P. and Peck, E. (2004) 'Modernisation: the ten commitments of New Labour's approach to public management', *International Public Management Journal*, vol 7, no 1, pp 1–18.

Ackroyd, S., Kirkpatrick, I. and Walker, R.M. (2007) 'Public management reform in the UK and its consequences for professional organization: a comparative analysis', *Public Administration*, vol 85, no 1, pp 9–26.

Alaszewski, A. and Manthorpe, J. (1990) 'Literature review: the new right and the professions', *British Journal of Social Work*, vol 20, no 3, pp 237–51.

Aldgate, J. and Statham, J. (2001) *The Children Act Now – Messages from Research*, London: Department of Health.

Aldridge, M. (1996) 'Dragged to market; being a profession in the postmodern world', *British Journal of Social Work*, vol 26, no 2, pp 177–94.

Alford, J. (2004) 'Dienstleistungsqualität in Australien: Kontrakualismus versus Partnerschaft', in C. Beckmann, H.-U. Otto, M. Richter and M. Scrödter (eds) *Qualität in der Sozialen Arbeit: Zwischen Nutzerinteresse und Kostenkontrolle*, Wiesbaden: Leske und Budrich.

Andrew, T. and McLean, J. (1995) 'Current working patterns in the personal social services', in S. Balloch, T. Andrew, J. Ginn, J. McLean, J. Pahl and J. Williams (eds) *Working in the Personal Social Services*, London: National Institute of Social Work.

Anleu, S.L. (1992) 'The professionalisation of social work? A case study of three organisational settings', *Sociology*, vol 26, no 1, pp 23–43.

Arksey, H. and Glendinning, C. (2007) 'Choice in the context of informal care-giving', *Health and Social Care in the Community*, vol 15, no 2, pp 165–75.

Arnstein, S.R. (1969) 'A ladder of citizen participation', *Journal of the American Planning Association*, vol 35, no 4, pp 216–24.

Aronson, J. (2002) 'Elderly people's accounts of home care rationing: missing voices in long-term care policy debates', *Ageing and Society*, vol 22, no 4, pp 399–418.

Association of Directors of Social Services (2003) *All Our Tomorrows: Inverting the Triangle of Care*, London: Association of Directors of Social Services/Local Government Association.

Audit Commission (1983) *Performance Review in Local Government: A Handbook for Auditors and Local Authorities*, London: Audit Commission.

Audit Commission (1989) *Managing Services Effectively – Performance Review*, Management Paper 5, London: Audit Commission.

Audit Commission (1992) *Citizen's Charter Performance Indicators: Charting a Course*, London: Audit Commission.

Audit Commission (1999) *Best Value and the Audit Commission in England*, London: Audit Commission.

Audit Commission (2000) *Aiming to Improve: The Principles of Performance Measurement*, London: Audit Commission.

Audit Commission (2001) *Brief Encounters: Getting the Best from Temporary Nursing Staff*, London: Audit Commission.

Bain, P., Taylor, P. and Dutton, E. (2005) 'The thin front line: call handling in police control rooms', paper given at the 23rd International Labour Process Conference, Glasgow: University of Strathclyde.

Bain, P., Watson, A., Mulvey, G., Taylor, P. and Gall, G. (2002) 'Taylorism, targets and the pursuit of quantity and quality by call centre management', *New Technology, Work and Employment*, vol 17, no 3, pp 170–85.

Baldock, J. (2003) 'On being a welfare consumer in a consumer society', *Social Policy and Society*, vol 2, no 1, pp 65–71.

Baldock, J. and Hadlow, J. (2002) 'Self-talk versus needs-talk: an exploration of the priorities of housebound older people', *Quality in Ageing – Policy, Practice and Research*, vol 3, no 1, pp 42–8.

Baldock, J. and Ungerson, C. (1994) *Becoming Consumers of Community Care: Households within the Mixed Economy of Welfare*, York: Joseph Rowntree Foundation.

Baldwin, M. (1998) 'The positive use of discretion in social work practice: developing practice through co-operative inquiry', *Issues in Social Work Education*, vol 18, no 42, pp 42–8.

Baldwin, M. (2000) *Care Management and Community Care: Social Work Discretion and the Construction of Policy*, Aldershot: Ashgate.

Baldwin, M. (2004) 'Critical reflection: opportunities and threats to professional learning and service development in social work organisations', in N. Gould and M. Baldwin (eds) *Social Work, Critical Reflection and the Learning Organisation*, Aldershot: Ashgate.

Baldwin, M. (2008) 'Social care under Blair: are social care services more modern?', in M. Powell (ed) *Modernising the Welfare State*, Bristol: The Policy Press.

Ball, K. and Wilson, D. (2000) 'Power, control and computer-based performance monitoring: repertoires, resistance and subjectivities', *Organizational Studies*, vol 21, no 3, pp 539–65.

Balloch, S. (1999) 'Education and training in social work and social care', in S. Balloch, I. McLean and M. Fisher (eds) *Social Services: Working Under Pressure*, Bristol: The Policy Press.

Balloch, S., Andrew, T., Ginn, J., McLean, J., Pahl, J. and Williams, J. (1995) *Working in the Social Services*, London: National Institute for Social Work.

Baltes, M. and Carstensen, L. (1996) 'The process of successful ageing', *Ageing and Society*, vol 16, no 4, pp 397–422.

Banks, S. (2006) *Ethics and Values in Social Work* (3rd edn), Basingstoke: Palgrave Macmillan.

Barlow, J. and Hainsworth, J. (2001) 'Volunteerism among older people with arthritis', *Ageing and Society*, vol 21, no 2, pp 203–17.

Barnes, M. (1997) *Care, Communities and Citizens*, Harlow: Addison Wesley Longman.

Barnes, M. (1998) 'Whose needs, whose resources?', in M. Langan (ed) *Welfare: Needs, Rights and Risks*, London: Routledge.

Barnes, M. and Prior, D. (1995) 'Spoilt for choice? How consumerism can disempower service users', *Public Money and Management*, July–September, pp 53–9.

Barnes, M. and Prior, D. (2000) *Private Lives as Public Policy*, Birmingham:Venture Press.

Barnes, M. and Shaw, S. (2000) 'Older people, citizenship and collective action', in A.Warnes, L.Warren and M. Nolan (eds) *Care Services for Later Life:Transformations and Critiques*, London: Jessica Kingsley.

Barns, I., Dudley, J., Harris, P. and Petersen, A. (1999) 'Introduction: themes, context and perspectives', in A. Petersen, I. Barns, J. Dudley and P. Harris (eds) *Poststructuralism, Citizenship and Social Policy*, London: Routledge.

Barry, N. (1999) *Welfare*, Buckingham: Open University Press.

Batt, R. and Moynihan, L. (2002) 'The viability of alternative call centre production models', *Human Resource Management Journal*, vol 12, no 4, pp 14–34.

Bauman, Z. (1992) *Intimations of Postmodernity*, London: Routledge.

BBC News (1999) 'Mentally ill denied quality care', 13 October, http://news.bbc.co.uk1/hi/health/292823.stm

Beaumont, J. and Kenealy, P. (2004) 'Quality of life perceptions and social comparisons in healthy old age', *Ageing and Society*, vol 24, no 5, pp 755–69.

Bchan, D. (2006) 'Why Commissioning is the Key to Delivering Personalised Care', transcript of speech delivered at West Midlands Conference for Health and Social Care Commissioners, 26 May.

Beresford, P. (2003) *It's Our Lives: A Short Theory of Knowledge, Distance and Experience*, London: Citizen Press.

Beresford, P. (2005) 'The adult social care Green Paper', *The Guardian*, 23 May, reproduced at www.shapingourlives.org.uk/guardian230305.html

Beresford, P. (2007) *'The Changing Roles and Tasks of Social Work from Service Users' Perspectives: A Literature Informed Discussion Paper*, London: Shaping Our Lives National User Network.

Beresford, P. and Branfield, F. (2006) 'Developing inclusive partnerships: user-defined outcomes, networking and knowledge: a case study', *Health and Social Care in the Community*, vol 14, no 5, pp 436–44.

Beresford, P. and Croft, S. (1993) *Citizen Involvement. A Practical Guide for Change*, Houndsmill: Macmillan.

Bergstrom, O. and Storrie, D. (eds) (2003) *Contingent Employment in Europe and the United States*, Cheltenham: Edward Elgar .

Biggs, S. (2000) 'User voice, interprofessionalism and postmodernity', in C. Davies, L. Finlay and A. Bullman (eds), *Changing Practice in Health and Social Care*, London: Sage.

Black, N. (2006) 'Temporary agency workers; what are their rights and what are yours?', *Engineering Management*, vol 16, no 1, pp 32–3.

Blair, T. (1998) *The Third Way: New Politics for the New Century*, London: The Fabian Society.

Blair, T. (2003) *A Future Fair for All: The Big Conversation*, London: Cabinet Office.

Blair, T. (2004), quoted in *The Guardian*, 24 June, p 1.

Blau, R. (2003) 'Public sector, private skills', *People Management*, April, pp 19–20.

Bloomfield, B. and Hayes, N. (2004) 'Modernisation and the joining-up of local government services in the UK: boundaries, knowledge and technology', paper presented at conference on Information, Knowledge and Management: Reassessing the Role of ICTs in Public and Private Organizations, 3–5 March, Bologna: Superior School of Public Administration.

Bolton, S. and Houlihan, M. (2005) 'The (mis)representation of customer service', *Work Employment and Society*, vol 19, no 4, pp 685–703.

Booth, A., Francesconi, M. and Frank, J. (2002) 'Temporary jobs; stepping stones or dead-ends?', *Economic Journal*, vol 112, no 480, pp 189–213.

Bovens, M. and Zouridis, S. (2002) 'From street-level to system-level bureaucracies: how information and communication technology is transforming administrative discretion and constitutional control', *Public Administration Review*, vol 62, no 2, pp 174–84.

Bowling, A. and Gabriel, Z. (2007) 'Lay theories of quality of life in older age', *Ageing and Society*, vol 27, no 6, pp 827–48.

Bradley, G. and Manthorpe, G. (2000) *Working on the Fault Line*, Birmingham: Venture Press.

Braverman, H. (1974) *Labor and Monopoly Capital*, New York: Monthly Review Press.

Brignall, S. and Modell, S. (2002) 'An institutional perspective on performance and management in the "new public sector"', *Management Accounting Research*, vol 11, no 3, pp 281–306.

Bronstein, A. (1991) 'Temporary work in Western Europe: threat or complement to permanent employment', *International Labour Review*, vol 130, no 3, pp 291–310.

Brown, R. (1975) *The Management of Welfare*, London: Martin Robertson.

Bryman, A. (2004) *The Disneyization of Society*, London: Sage.

Burgess, J., Rasmussen, E. and Connell, J. (2003) 'Temporary agency work and precarious employment: a review of the current situation in Australia and New Zealand', *Management Review*, vol 16, no 3, pp 351–69.

Burns, D., Hambleton, R. and Hoggett, P. (1994) *The Politics of Decentralisation*, Basingstoke: Macmillan.

Butcher, T. (1995) *Delivering Welfare. The Governance of the Social Services in the 1990s*, Buckingham: Open University Press.

Butler, I. and Drakeford, M. (2002) '"Which Blair project?" Communitarianism, social authoritarianism and social work', *Journal of Social Work*, vol 1, no 1, pp 7–19.

Butt, J., Bignall, T. and Stone, E. (eds) (2000) *Directing Support: Report from a Workshop on Direct Payments and Black and Minority Ethnic Disabled People*, York: Joseph Rowntree Foundation.

Cabinet Office (1998) *Service First: The New Charter Programme*, London: The Stationery Office.

Cabinet Office (1999) *Modernising Government* (Cm 4310), London: Cabinet Office.

Cabinet Office (2000a) *E-government: A Strategic Framework for Public Services in the Information Age*, London: Cabinet Office.

Cabinet Office (2000b) *Delivery of Public Services, 24 Hours a Day, Seven Days a Week (24x7): People's Panel Wave 4*, London: Cabinet Office.

Cabinet Office (2000c) *The People's Panel: The First Year Evaluation*, London: Cabinet Office; available online at http://archive.cabinetoffice.gov.uk/servicefirst/2000/panel/wave4/reportquant.pdf [accessed 2 January 2008].

Cabinet Office (2005) *Transformational Government: Enabled by Technology*, London: Cabinet Office.

Caldock, K. (1994) 'Policy and practice: fundamental contradictions in the conceptualization of community care for elderly people?', *Health and Social Care*, vol 2, no 3, pp 133–41.

Callaghan, G. and Thompson, P. (2001) 'Edwards revisited: technical control and call centres', *Economic and Industrial Democracy*, vol 22, no 1, pp 13–27.

Campbell, J. and Oliver, M. (1996) *Disability Politics: Understanding Our Past, Changing Our Future*, London: Routledge.

Care Services Improvement Partnership (2007a) *More About POPP: Introduction to the Framework*, London: Health and Social Care Change Agent Team, Department of Health.

Care Services Improvement Partnership (2007b) *National Evaluation of Partnership for Older People Projects: Interim Report of Progress*, London: Health and Social Care Change Agent Team, Department of Health.

Carey, M. (2003) 'Anatomy of a care manager', *Work, Employment and Society*, vol 17, no 1, pp 121–35.

Carey, M. (2006) 'Everything must go? The privatisation of state social work', *British Journal of Social Work*, advance access doi:10.1093/bjsw/bcl373

Carey, M. (2007) 'White-collar proletariat? Braverman, the deskilling/upskilling of social work and the paradoxical life of the agency care manager', *Journal of Social Work*, vol 7, no1, pp 93–114.

Carey, M. (2008a) 'The order of chaos: exploring agency care managers' construction of social order within fragmented worlds of state social work', *British Journal of Social Work*, advance access doi:10.1093/bjsw/bcm143

Carey, M. (2008b) 'The quasi-market revolution in the head: ideology, discourse, care management', *Journal of Social Work*, vol 8, no 4, pp 341–62.

Carter, N., Klein, R. and Day, P. (1992) *How Organisations Measure Success: The Use of Performance Indicators in Government*, London: Routledge.

Caulkin, S. (2003) *People and Public Services; Why Central Targets Miss the Mark*, CIPD, www.cipd.co.uk/subjects/corpstrgy/general/pandpserv.htm?IsSrchRes=1

Causer, G. and Exworthy, M. (1999) 'Professionals as managers across the public sector', in M. Exworthy and S. Halford (eds) *Professionals and the New Managerialism in the Public Sector*, Buckingham: Open University Press.

Challis, L. (1990) *Organising Public Social Services*, London: Longman.

Chevannes, M. (2002) 'Social construction of the managerialism of needs assessment by health and social care professionals', *Health and Social Care in the Community*, vol 10, no 3, pp 168–78.

Clark, H., Dyer, S. and Horwood, J. (1998) *That Bit of Help: The High Value of Low Level Preventative Services for Older People*, Bristol: The Policy Press.

Clark, H., Gough, H. and Macfarlane, A. (2004) *'It pays dividends': Direct Payments and Older People*, Bristol: The Policy Press.

Clarke, A. and Warren, L. (2007) 'Hopes, fears and expectations about the future: what do older people's stories tell us about active ageing?', *Ageing and Society*, vol 27, no 4, pp 465–88.

Clarke, J. (1996) 'After social work', in N. Parton (ed) *Social Theory, Social Change and Social Work*, London: Routledge.

Clarke, J. (2000) 'A world of difference? Globalization and the study of social policy', in G. Lewis, S. Gerwitz and J. Clarke (eds) *Rethinking Social Policy*, London: Sage.

Clarke, J. (2004) *Changing Welfare, Changing States: New Directions in Social Policy*, London: Sage.

Clarke, J. and Newman, J. (1997) *The Managerial State*, London: Sage.

Clarke, J., Gewirtz, S. and McLaughlin, E. (2000a) 'Reinventing the welfare state', in J. Clarke, S. Gewirtz and E. McLaughlin (eds) *New Managerialism, New Welfare?* London: Sage.

Clarke, J., Gewirtz, S., Hughes, G. and Humphrey, J. (2000b) 'Guarding the public interest? Auditing public services', in J. Clarke, S. Gewirtz and E. McLaughlin (eds) *New Managerialism, New Welfare?*, London: Sage.

Clarke, J., Newman, J., Smith, N., Vidler, E. and Westmarland, L. (2007) *Creating Citizen-consumers: Changing Publics and Changing Public Services*, London: Sage.

Clements, L. (2004) *Community Care and the Law* (3rd edn), London: Legal Action Group.

Cliggett, L. (2005) *Grains from Grass: Ageing, Gender and Famine in Rural Africa*, London: Cornell University Press.

Cochrane, A. (1994) 'Restructuring the local welfare state', in R. Burrows and B. Loader (eds) *Towards a Post-Fordist Welfare State?*, London: Routledge.

Coleman, N. (2007) 'Slowing down or seizing up? Social work practice in a call centre environment', *The International Journal of Technology, Knowledge and Society*, vol 3, no 5, pp 1–10.

Coleman, N. and Harris, J. (2008) 'Calling social work', *British Journal of Social Work*, vol 38, no 3, pp 580–99.

Collin-Jacques, C. (2004) 'Professionals at work: a study of autonomy and skill utilization in nurse call centres in England and Canada', in S. Deery and N. Kinnie (eds) *Call Centres and Human Resource Management*, Basingstoke: Palgrave Macmillan.

Collin-Jacques, C. and Smith, C. (2005) 'Nursing on the line: experiences from England and Quebec (Canada)', *Human Relations*, vol 58, no 1, pp 5–32.

Collins, S. (2007) 'Social workers, resilience, positive emotions and optimism', *Practice*, vol 19, no 4, pp 254–69.

Collinson, D. (1994) 'Strategies of resistance: power, knowledge and subjectivity in the workplace', in M. Jermier, D. Knights and W. Nord (eds) *Resistance and Power in Organisations*, London: Routledge.

Commission for Social Care Inspection (2004a) *Leaving Hospital: The Price of Delays*, London: Commission for Social Care Inspection.

Commission for Social Care Inspection (2004b) *Direct Payments: What are the Barriers?*, London: Commission for Social Care Inspection.

Commission for Social Care Inspection (2005a) *Making Every Child Matter. Messages from Inspections of Children's Social Services*, London: Commission for Social Care Inspection.

Commission for Social Care Inspection (2005b) *The State of Social Care in England 2004–05*, London: Commission for Social Care Inspection.

Commission for Social Care Inspection (2006) *Time to Care: An Overview of Home Care Services for Older People in England*, London: Commission for Social Care Inspection.

Commission for Social Care Inspection (2008a) *Star Ratings*, www.csci.org.uk/care_provider/councils/star_ratings.aspx#2

Commission for Social Care Inspection (2008b) *The State of Social Care in England 2006–07*, London: Commission for Social Care Inspection.

Commission for Social Care Inspection and National Statistics Office (2005) *Social Services Performance Assessment Framework Indicators 2004–2005*, London: Commission for Social Care Inspection and National Statistics Office.

Community Care (2000) News pages, 7 December, pp 20–1.

Community Care (undated) 'Stand up for social work', www.communitycare.co.uk/Onlineteam/Standup/Home

Coombs, R. (2005) 'Authorities grow their own social workers', *The Guardian*, 18 May, p 6.

Corby, B., Millar, M. and Young, L. (1996) 'Parental participation in child protection work: rethinking the rhetoric', *British Journal of Social Work*, vol 26, no 4, pp 475–92.

Cousins, C. (1987) *Controlling Social Welfare*, Brighton: Wheatsheaf.

Cox, D. (1991) 'Health service management – a sociological view: Griffiths and the non-negotiated order of the hospital', in J. Gabe, M. Calnan and M. Bury (eds) *The Sociology of the Health Service*, London: Routledge.

Cree, V.E. and Davis, A. (2007) *Social Work: Voices from the Inside*, London: Routledge.

Croft, S. and Beresford, P. (2002) 'Service users' perspectives', in M. Davies (ed), *The Blackwell Companion to Social Work*, Oxford: Blackwell.

Cutler, T. and Waine, B. (1994) *Managing the Welfare State. The Politics of Public Sector Management*, Oxford: Berg.

Daniel, L. (2006) 'Using temps in HR', Society for Human Resource Management, *HR Magazine*, vol 52, no 2, www.shrm.org/hrmagazine/articles/0206/0206daniel.asp

Davies, A. and Thomas, R. (2000) 'Researching public sector change: the argument for a gender-inclusive framework', *Public Management*, vol 2, no 4, pp 547–54.

Davies, A. and Thomas, R. (2002) 'Gendering and gender in public service organizations: changing professional identities under new public management', *Public Management Review*, vol 4, no 4, pp 461–84.

Davies, L. and Leonard, P. (2004) *Social Work in a Corporate Era: Practices of Power and Resistance*, Aldershot: Ashgate.

Davis, A., Ellis, K. and Rummery, K. (1997) *Access to Assessment: Perspectives of Practitioners, Disabled People and Carers*, Bristol: The Policy Press.

Davis, H., Martin, S. and Downe, J. (2001) *The Impact of External Inspection on Local Government*, www.jrf.org.uk/knowledge/findings/government/921.asp

Day, P. and Klein, N. (1990) *Inspecting the Inspectorates*, Bath: University of Bath, Centre for Analysis of Social Policy.

Deacon, B., Hulse, M. and Stubbs, P. (1997) *Global Social Policy. International Organizations and the Future of Welfare*, London: Sage.

Deery, S. and Kinnie, N. (2002) 'Call centres and beyond: a thematic evaluation', *Human Resource Management Journal*, vol 12, no 4, pp 3–14.

Deery, S., Iverson, R. and Walsh, J. (2002) 'Work relationships in telephone call centres: understanding emotional exhaustion and employee withdrawal', *Journal of Management Studies*, vol 39, no 4, pp 471–96.

Department for Education and Skills (2003) *Every Child Matters* (Cm 5860), London: Department for Education and Skills.

Department for Education and Skills, Department of Health and Home Office (2003) *Keeping Children Safe. The Government's Response to the Victoria Climbié Inquiry Report and Joint Chief Inspector's Report Safeguarding Children* (Cm 5861), London: Department for Education and Skills, Department of Health and Home Office.

Department of the Environment, Transport and the Regions (1998) *Modern Local Government: In Touch with the People*, London: Department of the Environment, Transport and the Regions.

Department of Health (1991) *The Children Act 1989: Guidance and Regulations Volume 2. Family Support, Day Care and Educational Provision for Young Children*, London: Department of Health.

Department of Health (1997) *The New NHS Modern, Dependable*, London: Department of Health.

Department of Health (1998) *Modernising Social Services* (Cm 4169), London: Department of Health.

Department of Health (1999) *Working Together to Safeguard Children* (updated edn 2000), London: Department of Health.

Department of Health (2000a) *A Quality Strategy for Social Care*, London: Department of Health.

Department of Health (2000b) *The NHS Improvement Plan*, London: Department of Health.

Department of Health (2000c) *Framework for the Assessment of Children in Need and their Families*, London: Department of Health.

Department of Health (2001a) *National Service Framework for Older People*, London: Department of Health.

Department of Health (2001b) *The Children Act Report 2000*, London: Department of Health.

Department of Health (2002a) *Requirements for Social Work Training*, London: The Stationery Office.

Department of Health (2002b) *Improving Older People's Services – Policy into Practice: The Second Phase of Inspections into Older People's Services*, London: Department of Health.

Department of Health (2002c) *The Single Assessment Process*, London: Department of Health.

Department of Health (2003a) *Every Child Matters*, London: Department of Health.

Department of Health (2003b) *What to do if You're Worried a Child is Being Abused. Children's Services Guidance*, London: Department of Health.

Department of Health (2003c) *The Children Act Report 2002*, London: Department of Health.

Department of Health (2003d) *Fair Access to Care Services*, London: Department of Health.

Department of Health (2005) *Independence, Well-being and Choice: Our Vision For the Future of Social Care for Adults in England and Wales* (Cm 6499), London: Department of Health.

Department of Health (2006) *Our Health, Our Care, Our Say: A New Direction for Community Services* (Cm 6737), London: Department of Health.

Department of Health (2007a) *Social Services Performance Assessment Framework Indicators: Annex C: New Adult PIs*, London: Department of Health.

Department of Health (2007b) *Putting People First: A Shared Vision and Commitment to the Transformation of Adult Social Care*, London: Department of Health; www.dh.gov.uk/en/Publicationsandstatistics/Publications/PublicationsPolicyAndGuidance/DH_081118

Department of Health and Social Services Inspectorate (2003) *Modern Social Services, A Commitment to the Future. The 12th Annual Report of the Chief Inspector of Social Services. 2002–2003*, London: Department of Health and Social Services Inspectorate.

Department of Social Security (1998) *New Ambitions for our Country: A New Contract for Welfare* (Cm 3805), London: Department of Social Security.

Department for Work and Pensions (2005) *Opportunity Age – Opportunity and Security Throughout Life*, London: Department for Work and Pensions.

Derber, C. (1982) 'Managing professionals: ideological proletarianization and mental labor', in C. Derber (ed) *Professionals as Workers. Mental Labor in Advanced Capitalism*, Boston: G.K. Hall.

Derber, C. (1983) 'Managing professionals: ideological proletarianization and post-industrial labor', *Theory and Society*, vol 12, no 3, pp 309–41.

Director of Social Services (2000) *Corporate Management Team "Northshire Connect" Centralised Contact Centre*. Report of the Director of Social Services, Northshire: Northshire County Council.

Dominelli, L. (2004) *Social Work: Theory and Practice for a Changing Profession*, Cambridge: Polity Press.

Dominelli, L. and Hoogvelt, A. (1996) 'Globalization and technocratization of social work', *Critical Social Policy*, vol 16, no 2, pp 45–62.

Drakeford, M. (2000) *Privatisation and Social Policy*, Harlow: Pearson.

Drakeford, M. (2006) 'Ownership, regulation and the public interest: the case of residential care for older people', *Critical Social Policy*, vol 26, no 4, pp 932–4.

Dransfield, R. (2000) *Human Resource Management*, Oxford: Heinemann.

Druker, J. and Stanworth, C. (1999) 'Brief encounters', *People Management*, September, pp 51–3.

Dunleavy, P., Margetts, H., Bastow, S. and Tinkler, J. (2006) 'New public management is dead: long live digital-era governance', *Journal of Public Administration Research and Theory*, vol 16, no 3, pp 467–94.

Dustin, D. (2007) *The McDonaldization of Social Work*, Aldershot: Ashgate.

Dwyer, P. (2000) *Welfare Rights and Responsibilities. Contesting social citizenship*, Bristol: The Policy Press.

Edwards, T. (2000) *Contradictions of Consumption: Concepts, Practices and Politics in Consumer Society*, London: Sage.

Ellis, K. (1993) *Squaring the Circle: User and Carer Participation in Needs Assessment and Community Care*, York: Joseph Rowntree Foundation.

Ellis, K. (2007) 'Direct payments and social work practice: the significance of "street-level bureaucracy" in determining eligibility', *British Journal of Social Work*, vol 37, no 3, pp 405–22.

Ellis, K., Davis, A. and Rummery, K. (1999) 'Needs assessment, street-level bureaucracy and the new community care', *Social Policy and Administration*, vol 33, no 3, pp 262–80.

Engellandt, A. and Riphahn, R. (2003) *Temporary contracts and employee effort*, Discussion Paper Series, London: Centre for Economic Policy Research.

Evans, A. (2006) 'Discretion and Street-level Bureaucracy Theory: A Case Study of Local Authority Social Work', Coventry: University of Warwick, unpublished PhD thesis.

Evans, T. (forthcoming) *Professional Discretion in Modern Social Services*, Aldershot: Ashgate.

Evans, T. and Harris, J. (2004) 'Street-level bureaucracy, social work and the (exaggerated) death of discretion', *British Journal of Social Work*, vol 34, no 6, pp 871–95.

Evans, T. and Harris, J. (2006) 'A case of mistaken identity? Debating the dilemmas of street-level bureaucracy with Musil et al', *European Journal of Social Work*, vol 9, no 6, pp 445–59.

Exworthy, M. and Halford, S. (1999) 'Professionals and managers in a changing public sector: conflict, compromise and collaboration?', in M. Exworthy and S. Halford (eds) *Professionals and the New Managerialism in the Public Sector*, Buckingham: Open University Press.

Farnham, D. and Horton, S. (1993) 'Public service managerialism: a review and evaluation', in D. Farnham and S. Horton (eds) *Managing the New Public Services* (2nd edn), Basingstoke: Macmillan.

Farnsworth, K. (2006) 'Capital to the rescue? New Labour's business solutions to old welfare problems', *Critical Social Policy*, vol 26, no 4, pp. 817–42.

Faulkner, A. (1997) *Knowing Our Own Minds*, London: Mental Health Foundation.

Featherstone, M. (1991) *Consumer Culture and Postmodernism*, London: Sage.

Ferguson, I. (2007) 'Increasing user choice or privatising risk? The antinomies of personalization', *British Journal of Social Work*, vol 37, no 3, pp 387 403.

Ferguson, I. (2008) *Reclaiming Social Work: Challenging Neo-liberalism and Promoting Social Justice*, London: Sage.

Ferguson, I. and Lavalette, M. (2005) '"Another world is possible": social work and the struggle for social justice', in I. Ferguson, M. Lavalette and E. Whitmore (eds) *Globalisation, Global Justice and Social Work*, London: Routledge.

Fernie, S. and Metcalf, D. (eds) (1999) *Not Hanging on the Telephone: Payment Systems in the New Sweatshops*, London: JAI Press.

Figes, O. (2007) *The Whisperers: Private Life in Stalin's Russia*, London: Allen Lane.

Fish, D. and Coles, C. (2000) 'Seeing anew: understanding professional practice as artistry', in C. Davies, C. Finlay and A. Bullman (eds) *Changing Practice in Health and Social Care*, London: Sage.

Fisher, M. (2004) 'The crisis of civil service trade unionism: a case study of call centre development in a civil service agency', *Work, Employment and Society*, vol 18, no 1, pp 157 77.

Fleming, G. and Taylor, B. (2007) 'Battle on the home care front: perceptions of home care workers of factors influencing staff retention in Northern Ireland', *Health and Social Care in the Community*, vol 15, no 1, 67–76.

Fleming, P. and Spicer, A. (2003) 'Working at a cynical distance: implications for power, subjectivity and resistance', *Organization*, vol 10, no 1, pp 157–79.

Flynn, N. (2007) *Public Sector Management* (5th edn), London: Sage.

Forbes, J. and Sashidharan, S.P. (1997) 'User involvement in services: incorporation or challenge', *British Journal of Social Work*, vol 27, no 4, pp 481–98.

Forde, C. (2001) 'Temporary arrangements, the activities of employment agencies in the UK', *Work, Employment and Society*, vol 15, no 4, pp 631–44.

Forde, C. and Slater, G. (2005) 'Agency working in Britain: character, consequences and regulation', *British Journal of Industrial Relations*, vol 43, no 2, pp 249–71.

Forster, N. (2005) *Maximum Performance: A Practical Guide to Leading and Managing People at Work*, Cheltenham: Edward Elgar.

Foster, M., Harris, J., Jackson, K., Morgan, H. and Glendinning, C. (2006) 'Personalised social care for adults with disabilities: a problematic concept for frontline practice', *Health and Social Care in the Community*, vol 14, no 2, pp 125–35.

Foster, P. and Wilding, P. (2000) 'Whither welfare professionalism?', *Social Policy and Administration*, vol 34, no 2, pp 143–59.

Fraser, J. and Gold, M. (2001) 'Portfolio workers' autonomy and control among freelance translators', *Work, Employment and Society*, vol 15, no 4, pp 679–97.

Frenkel, S.J., Tam, M., Korczynski, M. and Shire, K. (1998) 'Beyond bureaucracy? Work organization in call centres', *International Journal of Human Resource Management*, vol 9, no 6, pp 957–79.

Froggett, L. (2000) 'Care and commodity aesthetics: fetishism and transformation in social welfare', in I. Paylor, L. Froggett and J. Harris (eds) *Reclaiming Social Work: The Southport Papers Volume Two*, Birmingham: Venture Press.

Garrett, P.M. (2003) *Remaking Social Work with Children and Families*, London: Routledge.

Garrett, P.M. (2005) 'Social work's "electronic turn": notes on the deployment of information and communication technologies in social work with children and families', *Critical Social Policy*, vol 25, no 4, pp 529–53.

Garrett, P.M. (2008) 'How to be modern: New Labour's neoliberal modernity and the "Change for Children" programme', *British Journal of Social Work*, vol 38, no 2, pp 270–89.

General Social Care Council (2002) *Codes of Practice for Social Care Workers and Employers*, London: General Social Care Council.

George, V. (1998) 'Political ideology, globalisation and welfare futures in Europe', *Journal of Social Policy*, vol 27, no 1, pp 17–36.

George, V. and Wilding, P. (1994) *Welfare and Ideology*, Hemel Hempstead: Harvester-Wheatsheaf.

Ghobadian, A. and Ashworth, J. (1994) 'Performance measurement in local government? Concept and practice', *International Journal of Operations & Production Management*, vol 14, no 5, pp 35–51.

Giddens, A. (1998) *The Third Way and the Renewal of Social Democracy*, Cambridge: Polity Press.

Giddens, A. (2003) 'Introduction – neoprogressivism: a new agenda for social democracy', in A. Giddens (ed) *The Progressive Manifesto*, Cambridge: Polity Press.

Gilliatt, S., Fenwick, J. and Alford, D. (2000) 'Public services and the consumer: empowerment or control?', *Social Policy & Administration*, vol 34, no 3, pp 333–49.

Glasby, J. and Henwood, M. (2007) 'Part of the problem or part of the solution? The role of care homes in tackling delayed hospital discharges', *British Journal of Social Work*, vol 37, pp 299–312.

Glendinning, C., Clarke, S., Hare, P., Kotchetkova, I., Maddison, J. and Newbronner, L. (2006) *Outcomes-focused Services for Older People*, University of York: Social Care Institute for Excellence.

Glucksmann, M.A. (2004) 'Call configurations: varieties of call centre and divisions of labour', *Work Employment and Society*, vol 18, no 4, pp 795–811.

Godfrey, M. (2001) 'Prevention: developing a framework for conceptualizing and evaluating outcomes of preventive services for older people', *Health and Social Care in the Community*, vol 9, no 2, pp 89–99.

Godfrey, M., Townsend, J. and Denby, T. (2004) *Building a Good Life for Older People in Local Communities: The Experience of Ageing in Time and Place*, York: Joseph Rowntree Foundation.

Gott, M., Barnes, S., Payne, S., Parker, C., Seamark, D., Gariballa, S. and Small, N. (2007) 'Patient views of social service provision for older people with advanced heart failure', *Health and Social Care in the Community*, vol 15, no 4, pp 333–42.

Gottfried, H. (1994) 'Learning the score: the duality of control and everyday resistance in the temporary-help service industry', in J. Jermier, D. Knights and W. Nord (eds) (1994) *Resistance and Power in Organisations*, London: Routledge.

Greatbatch, D., Hanlon, G., Goode, J., O'Caithain, A., Strangleman, T. and Luff, D. (2005) 'Telephone triage, expert systems and clinical expertise', *Sociology of Health and Illness*, vol 27, no 6, pp 802–30.

Grenier, A. (2007) 'Constructions of frailty in the English language, care practice and the lived experience', *Ageing and Society*, vol 27, no 3, pp 425–45.

Grewal, I., Nazroo, J., Bajekal, M., Blane, D. and Lewis, J. (2004) 'Influences on quality of life: a qualitative investigation of ethnic differences among older people in England', *Journal of Ethnic and Migration Studies*, vol 30, no 4, pp 737–61.

Griffiths, R. (1983) *NHS Management Inquiry*, London: Department of Health.

Griffiths, R. (1988) *Community Care Agenda for Action*, London: Department of Health.

Grimshaw, D., Earnshaw, J. and Hebson, G. (2003) 'Private sector provision of supply teachers: a case of legal swings and roundabouts', *Journal of Education Policy*, vol 18, no 3, pp 267–88.

Grundy, E. (2006) 'Ageing and vulnerable elderly people: European perspectives', *Ageing and Society*, vol 26, no 1, pp 105–34.

Gupta, A. and Blewett, J. (2007) 'Change for children? The challenges and opportunities for children's social work workforce', *Child and Family Social Work*, vol 12, no 2, pp 172–81.

Hadley, R. and Clough, R. (1996) *Care in Chaos: Frustration and Challenge in Community Care*, London: Cassell.

Hall, C. and Slembrouck, S. (2001) 'Parent participation in social work meetings: the case of child protection conferences', *European Journal of Social Work*, vol 4, no 2, pp 143–60.

Hall, S. (1998) 'The great moving nowhere show', *Marxism Today*, November/December, pp 9–14.

Hall, S. (2003) 'New Labour's double shuffle', *Soundings*, issue 24, pp 10–24.

Hancock, P. and Tyler, M. (2008) 'Beyond the confines: management, colonization and the everyday', *Critical Sociology*, vol 34, no 1, pp 29–49.

Handy, C. (1994) *The Empty Raincoat; Making Sense of the Future*, London: Hutchinson.

Harding, T. and Beresford, P. (1996) *The Standards We Expect: What Service Users and Carers Want from Social Services Workers*, London: National Institute for Social Work.

Hardy, B., Young, R. and Wistow, G. (1999) 'Dimensions of choice in the assessment and care management process: the views of older people, carers and care managers', *Health and Social Care in the Community*, vol 7, no 6, pp 483–91.

Harlow, E. (2003) 'Information and communication technologies in the welfare services: wired wonderland or hypertext hell?', in E. Harlow and S. Webb (eds) *Information and Communication Technologies in the Welfare Services*, London: Jessica Kingsley.

Harlow, E. and Webb, S. (eds) (2003) *Information and Communication Technologies in the Welfare Services*, London: Jessica Kingsley.

Harris, J. (1998a) *Managing State Social Work. Frontline Management and the Labour Process Perspective*, Aldershot: Ashgate.

Harris, J. (1998b) 'Scientific management, bureau-professionalism, new managerialism: the labour process of state social work', *British Journal of Social Work*, vol 28, no 6, pp 839–62.

Harris, J. (1999) 'Social work sent to market', in B. Lesnick (ed), *Social Work and the State: International Perspectives in Social Work*, London: Pavilion, pp 99–108.

Harris, J. (2003) *The Social Work Business*, London: Routledge.

Harris, J. (2007) 'Looking backward, looking forward: current trends in human services management', in J. Aldgate, L. Healy, B. Malcolm, B. Pine, W. Rose and J. Seden (eds) *Enhancing Social Work Management: Theory and Best Practice from the UK and USA*, London: Jessica Kingsley.

Harris, J. (2008) 'State social work: constructing the present from moments in the past', *British Journal of Social Work*, vol 38, no 4, pp 662–79.

Harris, N. (1987) 'Defensive social work', *British Journal of Social Work*, vol 17, no 1, pp 61–71.

Haubrich, D. and McLean, I. (2006) 'Evaluating the performance of local government: a comparison of the assessment regimes in England, Scotland and Wales', *Policy Studies*, vol 27, no 4, pp 271–93.

Healthcare Commission (2005) *Ward Staffing*, www.healthcarecommission.org. uk/_db/_documents/ 04018124.pdf

Healthcare Commission, Commission for Social Care Inspection and Audit Commission (2006) *Living Well in Later Life: A Review of Progress against the National Service Framework for Older People, Summary Report*, London: Commission for Healthcare Audit and Inspection.

Healy, K. (2000) *Social Work Practices: Contemporary Perspectives on Change*, London: Sage.

Healy, K. (2005) *Social Work Theories in Context: Creating Frameworks for Practice*, Basingstoke: Palgrave Macmillan.

Healy, K. and Meagher, G. (2004) 'The reprofessionalisation of social work; collaborative approaches for achieving professional recognition', *British Journal of Social Work*, vol 34, no 2, pp 243–60.

Heffernan, K. (2006) 'Social work, new public management and the language of "service user"', *British Journal of Social Work*, vol 36, no 1, pp 139–47.

Henderson, J. and Forbat, L. (2002) 'Relationship-based social policy: personal and policy constructions of "care"', *Critical Social Policy*, vol 22, no 4, pp 669–87.

Henderson, J. and Seden, J. (2003) 'What do we want from social care managers? Aspirations and realities', in J. Reynolds, J. Henderson, J. Seden, J. Charlesworth and A. Bullman (eds) *The Managing Care Reader*, London: Routledge.

Henwood, M. (2006) 'Effective partnership working: a case study of hospital discharge', *Health and Social Care in the Community*, vol 14, no 5, pp 400–7.

Hey, V. (1999) 'Frail elderly people: difficult questions and awkward answers', in S. Hood, B. Mayall and S. Oliver (eds) *Critical Issues in Social Research: Power and Prejudice*, Buckingham: Open University Press.

Higgs, P. (1997) 'Citizenship theory and old age: from social rights to surveillance', in A. Jamieson, S. Harper and C. Victor (eds) *Critical Approaches to Ageing and Later Life*, Buckingham: Open University Press.

Hill, M. (1997) *The Policy Process in the Modern State*, Hemel Hempstead: Harvester-Wheatsheaf.

Hill, M. (2000) 'The personal social services', in M. Hill (ed) *Understanding Social Policy*, Oxford: Blackwell, pp. 160–85.

Hoggett, P. (1991) 'A new management in the public sector?' *Policy & Politics*, vol 19, no 4, pp 243–56.

Hoggett, P. (2000) 'Social policy and the emotions', in G. Lewis, S. Gewirtz and J. Clarke (eds) *Rethinking Social Policy*, London: Sage.

Holland, C., Kellaher, L., Peace, S., Scharf, T., Breeze, E., Gow, J. and Gilhooly, M. (2005) 'Getting out and about', in A. Walker (ed) *Understanding Quality of Life in Old Age*, Maidenhead: Open University Press, pp 49–63.

Hollis, F. (1972) *Social Work: A Psycho-social Therapy* (2nd edn), New York: Random House.

Holman, D. (2004) 'Employee well-being in call centres', in S. Deery and N. Kinnie (eds) *Call Centres and Human Resource Management*, Basingstoke: Palgrave Macmillan.

Hood, C. (1998) *The Art of the State*, Oxford: Oxford University Press.

Houlihan, M. (2002) 'Tensions and variations in call centre management strategies', *Human Resource Management Journal*, vol 12, no 4, pp 67–85.

House of Commons Committee of Public Accounts (2007) *Department of Health: Improving the Use of Temporary Nursing Staff in NHS Acute and Foundation Trusts, Twenty-ninth Report of Session 2006–07, Report, together with Formal Minutes, Oral and Written Evidence*, www.publications.parliament.uk/pa/cm200607/cmselect/cmpublic/142/142.pdf

House of Commons Health Committee (1999) *Future NHS Staffing Requirements*, www.publications.parliament.uk/pa/cm199899/cmselect/38/3807/htm

Howe, D. (1986) *Social Workers and their Practice in Welfare Bureaucracies*, Aldershot: Gower.

Howe, D. (1991a) 'Knowledge, power and the shape of social work practice', in M. Davies (ed) *The Sociology of Social Work*, London: Routledge.

Howe, D. (1991b) 'The family and the therapist', in M. Davies (ed) *The Sociology of Social Work*, London: Routledge.

Howe, D. (1996) 'Surface and depth in social work practice', in N. Parton (ed) *Social Theory, Social Change and Social Work*, London: Routledge.

Hudson, B. (1989) 'Michael Lipsky and street-level bureaucracy: a neglected perspective', in L. Barton (ed) *Disability and Dependency*, Brighton: Falmer Press.

Hudson, B., Dearey, M. and Glendinning, C. (2005) *A New Vision for Adult Social Care: Scoping Service Users' Views*, York: Social Policy Research Unit.

Hughes, J. (2005) 'Bringing emotion to work: emotional intelligence, employee resistance and the reinvention of character', *Work, Employment and Society*, vol 19, no 3, pp 603–25.

Hughes, M. and Wearing, M. (2007) *Organisations and Management in Social Work*, London: Sage.

Hugman, R. (1991) 'Organization and professionalism: the social work agenda in the 1990s', *British Journal of Social Work*, vol 21, no 3, pp 199–216.

Hugman, R. (2001) 'Post welfare social work? Reconsidering post-modernism, post-Fordism and social work education', *Social Work Education*, vol 20, no 3, pp 321–33.

Humphrey, J. (2002) 'Joint reviews; retracing the trajectory, decoding the terms', *British Journal of Social Work*, vol 32, no 4, pp 463–76.

Humphrey, J. (2003a) 'Joint reviews: the methodology in action', *British Journal of Social Work*, vol 33, no 2, pp 177–90.

Humphrey, J. (2003b) 'Joint reviews: judgement day and beyond', *British Journal of Social Work*, vol 33, no 6, pp 727–38.

Hunt, G. and Campbell, D. (1998) 'Social workers speak out', in G. Hunt (ed) *Whistleblowing in the Social Services: Public Accountability and Professional Practice*, London: Edward Arnold.

Hutton, J. (2005) 'Making public services serve the public', Speech to the Social Market Foundation, 24 August.

Huxley, P. (1993) 'Case management, care management and community care', *British Journal of Social Work*, vol 23, no 4, pp 366–81.

IDeA (Improvement Development Agency) and the Employers' Association (2004) *Draft Final Report – Evaluation of [Northshire County Contact Centre]*, London: Improvement Development Agency and Employers' Association.

Individual Budgets Evaluation Network (IBSEN) (2007) *Individual Budgets Evaluation: A Summary of Early Findings*, York: Individual Budgets Evaluation Network.

International Federation of Social Workers (undated) 'Definition of Social Work', www.ifsw.org/en/p38000208.html

International Federation of Social Workers (2001) *Ethics in Social Work, Statement of Principles*, Bern, Switzerland: International Federation of Social Workers.

Jermier, J., Knights, D. and Nord, W. (eds) (1994) *Resistance and Power in Organisations*, London: Routledge.

Jessop, B. (2002) *The Future of the Capitalist State*, Cambridge: Polity Press.

Johnsen, Å. (2005) 'What does 25 years of experience tell us about the state of performance measurement in public policy and management?' *Public Money and Management*, vol 25, no 1, pp 9–17.

Johnson, C. and Barer, B. (1997) *Life Beyond 85 Years: The Aura of Survivorship*, New York: Springer Publishing.

Johnson, T.J. (1972) *Professions and Power*, London: Macmillan.

Jones, C. (1999) 'Social work: regulation and managerialism', in M. Exworthy and S. Halford (eds) *Professionals and the New Managerialism in the Public Sector*, Buckingham: Open University Press.

Jones, C. (2001) 'Voices from the front line: state social workers and New Labour', *British Journal of Social Work*, vol 31, no 4, pp 547–62.

Jones, C. (2005) 'The neo-liberal assault: voices from the front line of British state social work', in I. Ferguson, M. Lavalette and E. Whitmore (eds) *Globalisation, Global Justice and Social Work*, London: Routledge.

Jones, C. and Novak, T. (1993) 'Social work today', *British Journal of Social Work*, vol 23, no 3, pp 195–212.

Jones, C., Ferguson, M., Lavalette, M. and Penketh, L. (2004) 'Social work and social justice: a manifesto for a new engaged practice', www.liv.ac.uk/sspsw/manifesto

Jordan, B. (2004) 'Emancipatory social work? Opportunity or oxymoron', *British Journal of Social Work*, vol 34, no 1, pp 5–19.

Jordan, B. (2007) *Social Work and Well-being*, Lyme Regis: Russell House.

Jordan, B. and Jordan, C. (2000) *Social Work and the Third Way: Tough Love as Social Policy*, London: Sage.

Joseph Rowntree Foundation (Task Group) (2004) *From Welfare to Well-being: Planning for an Ageing Society. Summary Conclusions of Joseph Rowntree Foundation Task Group on Housing, Money and Care for Older People*, York: Joseph Rowntree Foundation, www.jrf.org.uk/knowledge/findings/foundations/pdf/034.pdf

Keane, J. (1988) *Democracy and Civil Society*, London: Verso.

Keat, R., Whitely, N. and Abercrombie, N. (eds) (1994) *The Authority of the Customer*, London: Routledge.

Kent County Council on-Line (2008) *Self Assessment*, www.kent.gov.uk/SocialCare/adults-and-older-people/self-assessment/

King, D.S. (1987) *The New Right: Politics, Markets and Citizenship*, Basingstoke: Macmillan.

Kinnie, N., Hutchinson, S. and Purcell, J. (2000) 'Fun and surveillance: the paradox of high commitment management in call centres', *International Journal of Human Resource Management*, vol 11, no 5, pp 967–85.

Kirkpatrick, I. (2002) 'A jungle of competing requirements: management "reform" in the organisational field of UK social services', *Social Work and Social Sciences Review*, vol 10, no 3, pp 24–7.

Kirkpatrick, I. (2007) 'Taking stock of the new managerialism in English social services', *Social Work and Society*, vol 5, no 2, www.socwork.net/2006/1/series/professionalism/kirkpatrick

Kirkpatrick, I. and Hoque, K. (2006) 'A retreat from permanent employment? Accounting for the rise in professional agency work in UK public services', *Work, Employment and Society*, vol 20, no 4, pp 649–66.

Kirkpatrick, I., Ackroyd, S. and Walker, R. (2005) *New Managerialism and Public Service Professions: Change in Health, Social Services and Housing*, Basingstoke: Palgrave Macmillan.

Klein, R. (1989) *The Politics of the National Health Service*, London: Longman.

Kloot, L. and Martin, J. (2000) 'Strategic performance management: a balanced approach to performance management issues in local government', *Management Accounting Research*, vol 11, no 2, pp 231–51.

Korczynski, M. (2002) *Human Resource Management in Service Work*, London: Palgrave Macmillan.

Labour Party (1991) *Citizen's Charter: Labour's Better Deal for Consumers and Citizens*, London: The Labour Party.

Laffin, M. and Young, K. (1990) *Professionalism in Local Government*, Harlow: Longman.

Laming, H. (2003) *The Victoria Climbié Inquiry. Summary and Recommendations*, London: Department of Health.

Langan, M. (2000) 'Social services: managing the Third Way', in J. Clarke, S. Gewirtz and E. McLaughlin (eds) *New Managerialism, New Welfare?*, London: Sage.

LaNuez, D. and Jermier, J. (1994) 'Sabotage by managers and technocrats: neglected patterns of resistance at work', in J. Jermier, J. Knights and W. Nord (eds) (1994) *Resistance and Power in Organisations*, London: Routledge.

Lapierre, S. (2008) 'Taking the Blame? Women's Experiences of Mothering in the Context of Domestic Violence', Coventry: University of Warwick, unpublished PhD thesis.

Lapierre, S. and Bain, K. (2008) 'Parental responsibility and partnership: citizenship and gender in British children and families social services', in E.H. Oleksy, A. Petö and B. Waaldijk (eds) *Gender and Citizenship in a Multicultural Context*, Frankfurt am Main: Peter Lang, pp 77–92.

Lapsley, I. and Llewellyn, S. (1998) 'Markets, hierarchies and choices in social care', in W. Bartlett, J. Roberts, and J. Le Grand (eds) *A Revolution in Social Policy*, Bristol: The Policy Press.

Larsson, K. (2006) 'Care needs and home-help services for older people in Sweden: does improved functioning account for the reduction in public care?', *Ageing and Society*, vol 26, no 3, pp 413–29.

Lavalette, M. (2007) 'Social work today: a profession worth fighting for?', in G. Mooney and A. Law (eds) *New Labour/Hard Labour? Restructuring and Resistance inside the Welfare Industry*, Bristol: The Policy Press.

Lawler, J. (2007) 'Leadership in social work: a case of caveat emptor?', *British Journal of Social Work*, vol 37, no 1, pp 123–41.

Leece, J. (2007) 'Direct payments and user-controlled support: the challenges for social care commissioning', *Practice*, vol 19, no 3, pp 185–98.

Lefebvre, H. (2000) *Everyday Life in the Modern World*, London: Athlone.

Le Grand, J. and Bartlett, W. (2003) *Quasi-markets and Social Policy: The Way Forward?*, Basingstoke: Macmillan.

Leonard, P. (1997) *Postmodern Welfare: Reconstructing the Emancipatory Project*, London: Sage.

Lewis, J. and Glennerster, H. (1996) *Implementing the New Community Care*, Buckingham: Open University Press.

Lipsky, M. (1980) *Street-level Bureaucracy: The Dilemmas of Individuals in Public Service*, New York: Russell Sage Foundation.

London Edinburgh Weekend Return Group (1979) *In and Against the State*, London: Pluto Press.

Loney, M. (1986) *The Politics of Greed: The New Right and the Welfare State*, London: Pluto Press.

Loughlin, M. (1994) 'The constitutional status of local government', London: Commission for Local Democracy.

Lymbery, M. (2000) 'The retreat from professionalism: from social worker to care manager', in N. Malin (ed) *Professionalism, Boundaries and the Workplace*, London: Routledge.

Lymbery, M. (2001) 'Social work at the crossroads', *British Journal of Social Work*, vol 31, no 3, pp 369–84.

Lymbery, M. and Butler, S. (2004) 'Social work ideals and practice realities: an introduction', in M. Lymbery and S. Butler (eds) *Social Work Ideals and Practice Realities*, Basingstoke: Palgrave Macmillan.

Lymbery, M., Lawson, J., MacCallum, H., McCoy, P., Pidgeon, J. and Ward, K. (2007) 'The social work role with older people', *Practice*, vol 19, no 2, pp 97–113.

Lyons, K. (2007) 'Work in progress: social work, the state and Europe', *Social Work and Society*, vol 5, no 2, www.socwork.net/2007/festschrift/esw/lyons/index_html

Lyons, K., Manion, K. and Carlsen, M. (2006) *International Perspectives on Social Work: Global Conditions and Local Practice*, Basingstoke: Palgrave Macmillan.

McDonald, A. (2006) *Understanding Community Care; A Guide for Social Workers* (2nd edn), Basingstoke: Palgrave Macmillan.

McDonald, C. (2006) *Challenging Social Work: The Institutional Context of Practice*, Basingstoke: Palgrave Macmillan.

McLaughlin, H. (2008) 'What's in a name: "client", "patient", "customer", "consumer", "expert by experience", "service user" – what's next?' *British Journal of Social Work*, advance access doi:10.1093/bjsw/bcm155

McLean, J. (1999) 'Satisfaction, stress and control over work', in S. Balloch, I. McLean and M. Fisher (eds) (1999) *Social Services: Working Under Pressure*, Bristol: The Policy Press.

McNally, S. (2000) 'Professionalism and user advocacy', in N. Malin (ed) *Professionalism, Boundaries and the Workplace*, London: Routledge.

Manias, J., Aitken, R., Peerson, A., Parker, J. and Wong, K. (2003), 'Agency nursing work in acute care settings; perceptions of hospital nursing managers and agency nurse providers', *Journal of Clinical Nursing*, vol 12, no 4, pp 457–66.

Marquand, D. (1988) *The Unprincipled Society*, London: Fontana.

Marshall, T. and Rees, A. (1985) *Social Policy*, London: Hutchinson.

Marshall, T.H. (1963) 'Citizenship and social class', in *Sociology at the Crossroads*, London: Heinemann.

Marshall, T.H. (1975) *Social Policy in the Twentieth Century*, London: Hutchinson.

Marshall, T.H. (1981) *The Right to Welfare and Other Essays*, London: Heinemann.

Mashaw, J.L. (1983) *Bureaucratic Justice*, New Haven: Yale University Press.

Mason, D., Button, G. and Lankshear, G. (2002) 'Getting real about surveillance and privacy at work', in S. Woolgar (ed) *Virtual Society? Technology, Cyberbole, Reality*, Oxford: Oxford University Press.

Matosevic, T., Knapp, M., Kendall, J., Henderson, C. and Luis-Fernandez, J. (2007) 'Care-home providers as professionals: understanding the motivations of care-home providers in England', *Ageing and Society*, vol 27, no 1, pp 103–26.

May, M. (2001) 'Protecting the "vulnerable": welfare and consumer protection', in M. May, R. Page and E. Brunsdon (eds) *Understanding Social Problems: Issues in Social Policy*, Oxford: Blackwell.

Meagher, G. and Healy, K. (2003) 'Caring, controlling, contracting and counting: government and non-profits in community services', *Australian Journal of Public Administration*, vol 62, no 3, pp 40–51.

Means, R., Richards, S. and Smith, R. (2003) *Community Care. Policy and Practice* (2nd edn), Basingstoke: Palgrave Macmillan.

Midgley, J. and Jones, C. (1994) 'Social work and the radical right: the impact of developments in Britain and the United States', *International Social Work*, vol 37, no 2, pp 115–26.

Milner, E. and Joyce, P. (2005) *Lessons in Leadership: Meeting the Challenges of Public Services Management*, London: Routledge.

Mishra, R. (1999) *Globalization and the Welfare State*, Cheltenham: Edward Elgar.

Moriarty, P. and Kennedy, D. (2002) 'Performance measurement in public sector services: problems and potential', in A. Neely, A. Walters and R. Austin (eds) *Performance Measurement and Management: Research and Action*, Cranfield: Cranfield School of Management.

Moss, G. and O'Loughlin, B. (2005) 'New Labour's information age policy programme: an ideology analysis', *Journal of Political Ideologies*, vol 10, no 2, pp 165–83.

Mouffe, C. (2000) 'For an agonistic model of democracy', in N. O'Sullivan (ed) *Political Theory in Transition*, London: Routledge.

Muetzelfeldt, M. (1994) 'Contracts, politics and society', in J. Alford and D. O'Neill (eds) *The Contract State: Public Management and the Kennett Government*, Melbourne: Deakin University Press.

Munro, E. (1998) 'Improving social workers' knowledge base in child protection', *British Journal of Social Work*, vol 28, no 1, pp 101–2.

National Audit Office (2002) *Better Public Services through E-government*, London: The Stationery Office.

Nazroo, J., Bajekal, M., Blane, D. and Grewal, I. (2004) 'Ethnic inequalities', in A. Walker and C. Hagan Hennessy (eds) *Growing Older: Quality of Life in Old Age*, Maidenhead: Open University Press.

Needham, C. (2006) 'Customer care and the public service ethos', *Public Administration*, vol 84, no 4, pp 845–60.

Needham, C. (2008) 'Choice in public services: "No choice but to choose!"', in M. Powell (ed) *Modernising the Welfare State*, Bristol: The Policy Press.

Newman, J. (2000) 'Beyond the new public management? Modernizing public services', in J. Clarke, S. Gewirtz and E. McLaughlin (eds) *New Managerialism, New Welfare?* London: Sage.

Newman, J. (2003) 'The new public management, modernization and institutional change: disruptions, disjunctures and dilemmas', in K. McLaughlin, S.P. Osbourne and E. Ferlie (eds) *New Public Management: Current Trends and Future Prospects*, London: Routledge.

Newman, J. (2005) *Modernising Governance. New Labour, Policy and Society*, London: Sage.

Nixon, J. (1993) 'Implementation in the hands of senior managers: community care in Britain', in M. Hill (ed) *New Agendas in the Study of the Policy Process*, London: Harvester-Wheatsheaf.

Northshire Social Services (2001) *Centralised Contact Centre Business/Service Plan*, Northshire: Northshire County Council.

O'Brien, M. and Penna, S. (1998) *Theorising Welfare*, London: Sage.

Office of Public Services Reform (2002) *Reforming our Services: Principles into Practice*, London: Office of Public Services Reform.

Office of Public Services Reform (2005) *Choice and Voice in the Reform of Public Services. Government Responses to the PASC Report – Choice, Voice and Public Services* (Cm 6630), London: Office of Public Services Reform.

Office of the Deputy Prime Minister (2002) *E-Gov@Local: Towards a National Strategy for Local E-government: Consultation*, London: Office of the Deputy Prime Minister.

Office of the Deputy Prime Minister (2006) *A Sure Start to Later Life: Ending Inequalities for Older People*, London: Office of the Deputy Prime Minister.

OFSTED (2007) *Joint Area Review of Children's Services*, London: OFSTED.

Oldman, C. (2002) 'The importance of housing and home', in B. Bytheway, V. Bacigalupo, J. Bornat, J. Johnson and S. Spurr (eds) *Understanding Care, Welfare and Community: A Reader*, London: Routledge.

O'Sullivan, N. (2000) 'Introduction', in N. O'Sullivan (ed) *Political Theory in Transition*, London: Routledge.

Page, R.M. (2007) *Revisiting the Welfare State*, Maidenhead: McGraw Hill/Open University Press.

Pahl, J. (1994) 'Like the job but hate the organisation: social workers and managers in social services', in R. Page and J. Baldock (eds) *Social Policy Review 6*, University of Kent at Canterbury: Social Policy Association.

Parker, S. (2002) 'One in ten social work vacancies unfilled', *The Guardian*, 11 September, www.guardian.co.uk/society/2002/sep/11/uknews1

Parry, N. and Parry, J. (1979) 'Social work professionalism and the state', in N. Parry, M. Rustin and C. Satyamurti (eds) *Social Work, Welfare and the State*, London: Edward Arnold.

Parsloe, P. (1981) *Social Services Area Teams*, London: George Allen and Unwin.

Parton, N. (2008) 'Changes in the form of knowledge in social work: from the "social" to the "informational"?', *British Journal of Social Work*, vol 38, no 2, pp 253–69.

Patmore, C. (2001) 'Improving home care quality: an individual–centred approach', *Quality in Ageing*, vol 2, no 3, pp 15–24.

Payne, M. (2005a) *Modern Social Work Theory* (3rd edn), Basingstoke: Palgrave.

Payne, M. (2005b) *The Origins of Social Work*, Basingstoke: Palgrave Macmillan.

Pearson, C. (2000) 'Money talks? Competing discourses in the implementation of direct payments', *Critical Social Policy*, vol 20, no 4, pp 459–77.

Phillips, J., Bernard, M., Phillipson, C. and Ogg, J. (2000) 'Social support in later life: a study of three areas', *British Journal of Social Work*, vol 30, no 6, pp 837–53.

Pierson, C. (1994) 'Continuity and discontinuity in the emergence of the post-Fordist welfare state', in R. Burrows and B. Loader (eds) *Towards a Post-Fordist Welfare State?* London: Routledge.

Pierson, C. (1998) *Beyond the Welfare State: The New Political Economy of Welfare* (2nd edn), Cambridge: Polity Press.

Pierson, J. and Thomas, M. (2002) *Collins Dictionary of Social Work* (2nd edn), Glasgow: Harper Collins.

Pithouse, A. (1987) *Social Work: The Social Organisation of an Invisible Trade*, Aldershot: Gower.

Pithouse, A. (1991) 'Guardians of autonomy: work orientations in a social work office', in P. Carter, T. Jeffs and S. Smith (eds) *Social Work and Social Welfare Yearbook 2*, Buckingham: Open University Press.

Plant, R. (1992) 'Citizenship, rights and welfare', in A. Coote (ed) *The Welfare of Citizens*, London: Rivers Oram Press.

Platman, K. (2004) '"Portfolio careers" and the search for flexibility in later life', *Work, Employment and Society*, vol 18, no 3, pp 573–9.

Platt, D. (2005) 'The future of children's services', Keynote speech at the Making Research Count national conference, www.uea.ac.uk/swk/research/mrc/futureofchildrensservices.pdf

Policy Commission on Public Services (2004) *Making Public Services Personal: A New Compact for Public Services. Report to the National Consumer Council*, London: Policy Commission on Public Services.

Pollitt, C. (1990) *Managerialism in the Public Sector: The Anglo-American Experience*, Oxford: Blackwell.

Pollitt, C. (1993) *Managerialism and the Public Services*, Oxford: Blackwell.

Pollitt, C. (1994) 'The Citizen's Charter: a preliminary analysis', *Public Money and Management*, April–June, pp 9–14.

Pollitt, C. (2003) *The Essential Public Manager*, Buckingham: Open University Press.

Poole, L. (2007) 'Working in the non-profit welfare sector: contract culture, partnership, compacts and the "shadow state"', in G. Mooney and A. Law (eds) *New Labour/Hard Labour? Restructuring and Resistance inside the Welfare Industry*, Bristol: The Policy Press.

Postle, K. (2001) 'The social work side is disappearing. I guess it started with us being called care managers', *Practice*, vol 13, no 1, pp 13 26.

Postle, K. (2002) 'Working "between the idea and the reality": ambiguities and tensions in care managers' work', *British Journal of Social Work*, vol 32, no 3, pp 335–51.

Powell, F. (1997) 'The new Poor Law', in M. Mullard and S. Lee (eds) *The Politics of Social Policy in Europe*, Cheltenham: Edward Elgar.

Powell, F. (2001) *The Politics of Social Work*, London: Sage.

Powell, J., Robinson, J., Roberts, H. and Thomas, G. (2007) 'The single assessment process in primary care: older people's accounts of the process', *British Journal of Social Work*, vol 37, no 6, pp 1043–58.

Powell, M. (2008a) 'Introduction: modernising the welfare state', in M. Powell (ed) *Modernising the Welfare State*, Bristol: The Policy Press.

Powell, M. (2008b) 'Conclusion: the Blair legacy', in M. Powell (ed) *Modernising the Welfare State*, Bristol: The Policy Press.

Priestley, M. (1999) *Disability Politics and Community Care*, London: Jessica Kingsley.

Prime Minister (1991) *The Citizen's Charter: Raising the Standard*, London: Cabinet Office.

Purcell, J., Purcell, K. and Tailby, S. (2004) 'Temporary work agencies; here today, gone tomorrow?', *British Journal of Industrial Relations*, vol 42, no 4, pp 705–25.

Quinton, D. (2004) *Supporting Parents. Messages from Research*, London: Jessica Kingsley.

Qureshi, H. and Henwood, M. (2000) *Older People's Definitions of Quality Services*, York: Joseph Rowntree Foundation.

Radnor, Z. and McGuire, M. (2004) 'Performance management in the public sector', International Journal of Productivity and Performance Management, vol 53, no 3, pp 245–60.

Randall, A. and Charlesworth, A. (2000) 'The moral economy: riot, markets and social conflict', in A. Randall and A. Charlesworth (eds) *Moral Economy and Popular Protest*, Basingstoke, Macmillan.

Ranson, S. and Stewart, J. (1994) *Management for the Public Domain*, Basingstoke: Macmillan.

Reder, P., Duncan, S. and Gray, M. (1993) *Beyond Blame: Child Abuse Tragedies Revisited*, Hove: Brunner-Routledge.

Revans, L. (2007) 'Finding the time', *Community Care*, 26 April, pp 18–19.

Richards, S. (2000) 'Bridging the divide: elders and the assessment process', *British Journal of Social Work*, vol 30, no 1, pp 37–49.

Richter, J., Cornford, J. and McLoughlin, I. (2005) 'The e-citizen as talk, as text and as technology: CRM and e-government' *Electronic Journal of E-government*, vol 3, no 1, www.ejeg.com

Rickford, F. (2001) 'Going through the motions?', *Community Care*, 20 September, pp 18–19.

Ritzer, G. (2000) *The McDonaldization of Society* (New Century edn), Thousand Oaks: Pine Forge Press.

Robinson, G. (2003) 'Technicality and indeterminacy in probation practice: a case study', *British Journal of Social Work*, vol 33, no 5, pp 593–610.

Roche, M. (1987) 'Citizenship, social theory and social change', *Theory and Society*, vol 16, no 3, pp 363–99.

Rogowski, S. (2001) 'Where has all the idealism gone?' *Community Care*, 18 January.

Russell, C. and Schofield, T. (1999) 'Social isolation in old age: a qualitative exploration of service providers' perceptions', *Ageing and Society*, vol 19, no 1, pp 69–91.

Salaman, G. (1979) *Work Organizations: Resistance and Control*, London: Longman.

Sale, A.U. (2007) 'Here today, gone tomorrow?', *Community Care*, 22 March, pp 26–7.

Sanderson, I. (1992) 'Defining quality in local government', in I. Sanderson (ed) *Management of Quality in Local Government*, Harlow: Longman.

Sanderson, I. (2001) 'Performance management, evaluation and learning in "modern" local government', *Public Administration*, vol 79, no 2, pp 297–313.

Sanderson, I., Bovaird, T., Davis, P., Martin, S. and Foreman, A. (1998) *Made to Measure: Evaluation in Practice in Local Government*, London: Local Government Management Board.

Sargent, P., Pickard, S., Sheaff, R., and Boaden, R. (2007) 'Patient and carer perceptions of case management for long-term conditions', *Health and Social Care in the Community*, vol 15, no 6, pp 511–19.

Schaarschuch, A. and Schnurr, S. (2004) 'Konflikte um Qualität: Zur theoretischen Grundlegung eines relationen Qualitätsbegriffs', in C. Beckmann, H.-U. Otto, M. Richter and M. Schrödter (eds) *Qualität in der Sozialen Arbeit: Zwischen Nutzerinteresse und Kostenkontrolle*, Wiesbaden: Leske und Budrich.

Scourfield, J. (2003) *Gender and Child Protection*, Basingstoke: Palgrave Macmillan.

Scourfield, P. (2006) '"What matters is what works"? How discourses of modernisation have both silenced and limited debate on domiciliary care for older people', *Critical Social Policy*, vol 26, no 1, pp 5–30.

Scourfield, P. (2007) 'Social care and the modern citizen: client, consumer, service user, manager and entrepreneur', *British Journal of Social Work*, vol 37, no 1, pp 107–22.

Secker, J., Hill, R., Villeneau, L. and Parkman, S. (2003) 'Promoting independence: but promoting what and how?', *Ageing and Society*, vol 23, no 3, pp 375–91.

Seebohm Report (1968) *Report of the Committee on Local Authority and Allied Personal Social Services* (Cmnd 3703), London: HMSO.

Sharkey, P. (2007) *The Essentials of Community Care* (2nd edn), Basingstoke: Palgrave Macmillan.

Sibeon, R. (1991) *Towards a New Sociology of Social Work*, Aldershot: Avebury.

Silcock, R. (2001) 'What is e-government?' *Parliamentary Affairs*, vol 54, no 1, pp 88–101.

Sinclair, R. and Grimshaw, R. (1997) 'Partnership with parents in planning the care of their children', *Children and Society*, vol 11, no 4, pp 231–41.

Smale, G., Tuson, G. and Statham, D. (2000) *Social Work and Social Problems: Working Towards Social Inclusion and Social Change*, Basingstoke: Macmillan.

Smith, P. (1995) 'On the unintended consequences of publishing performance data in the public sector', *International Journal of Public Administration*, vol 18, nos 2 and 3, pp 277–310.

Smith, R. (2005) *Values and Practices in Children's Services*, Basingstoke: Palgrave Macmillan.

Social Services Inspectorate (1991a) *Care Management and Assessment: Practitioners' Guide*, London: Department of Health.

Social Services Inspectorate (1991b) *Care Management and Assessment: Managers' Guide*, London: Department of Health.

Stanley, N. (1999) 'User-practitioner transactions in the new culture of community care', *British Journal of Social Work*, vol 29, no 3, pp 417–35.

Stevenson, O. (1978) 'Practice: an overview' in Department of Health and Social Security, *Social Services Teams: The Practitioners' View*, London: HMSO.

Steverink, N., Lindenberg, S. and Ormel, J. (1998) 'Towards understanding successful ageing: patterned change in resources and goals', *Ageing and Society*, vol 18, no 4, pp 441–67.

Stewart, J. and Walsh, K. (1992) 'Change in the management of public services', *Public Administration*, vol 70, no 4, pp 499–518.

Steyaert, J. and Gould, N. (1999) 'Social services, social work, and information management: some European perspectives', *European Journal of Social Work*, vol 2, no 11, pp 165–75.

Suomi, R. and Tähkäpää, J. (2003) 'Establishing a contact centre for public health care', paper presented at the 36th International Conference on System Sciences, Hawaii.

Tanner, D. (2001a) 'Partnership in prevention: messages from older people', in V. White and J. Harris (eds) *Developing Good Practice in Community Care: Partnership and Participation*, London: Jessica Kingsley.

Tanner, D. (2001b) 'Sustaining the self in later life: implications for community-based support', *Ageing and Society*, vol 21, no 3, pp 255–78.

Tanner, D. (2007) 'Starting with lives: supporting older people's strategies and ways of coping', *Journal of Social Work*, vol 7, no 1, pp. 7–30.

Tanner, D. and Harris, J. (2008) *Working with Older People*, Abingdon: Routledge.

Taylor, A. (2007) 'The war on the wards', *Community Care*, 13 December, pp 19–20.

Taylor, H. (2005) *Assessing the Nursing and Care Needs of Older Adults. A Patient-centred Approach*, Abingdon: Radcliffe.

Taylor, J., Williams, V., Johnson, R., Hiscutt, I. and Brennan, M. (2007) *We Are Not Stupid*, London: Shaping Our Lives and People First Lambeth.

Taylor, P. and Bain, P. (1999) 'An assembly line in the head: work and employee relations in the call centre', *Industrial Relations Journal*, vol 30, no 2, pp 101–17.

Taylor, P. and Bain, P. (2005) 'India calling to the far away towns: the call centre labour process and globalization', *Work Employment and Society*, vol 19, no 2, pp 261–82.

Taylor, P., Baldry, C., Bain, P. and Ellis, V. (2003) 'A unique working environment: health, sickness and absence management in UK call centres', *Work Employment & Society*, vol 17, no 3, pp 435–58.

Taylor-Gooby, P. and Lawson, R. (1993) 'Introduction', in P. Taylor-Gooby and R. Lawson (eds) *Markets and Managers: New Issues in the Delivery of Welfare*, Buckingham: Open University Press.

Tester, S., Hubbard, G., Downs, M., MacDonald, C. and Murphy, J. (2004) 'Frailty and institutional life', in A. Walker and C. Hagan Hennessy (eds) *Growing Older: Quality of Life in Old Age*, Maidenhead: Open University Press.

Thomas, R. and Davies, A. (2005) 'What have the feminists done for us? Feminist theory and organisational resistance', *Organization*, vol 12, no 5, pp 711–40.

Thompson, C. and Postle, K. (2007) 'The use of local community resources to facilitate a preventative approach to the care of older people: an examination in a rural context', *Practice*, vol 19, no 3, pp 211–26.

Thompson, E.P. (1991) *Customs in Common*, Harmondsworth: Penguin.

Thompson, N. (2005) *Understanding Social Work* (2nd edn), Basingstoke: Palgrave Macmillan.

Timmins, N. (1995) *The Five Giants: A Biography of the Welfare State*, London: HarperCollins.

Timonen, V., Convery, J. and Cahill, S. (2006) 'Care revolutions in the making? A comparison of cash-for-care programmes in four European countries', *Ageing and Society*, vol 26, no 3, pp 455–74.

Townsend, J., Godfrey, M. and Denby, T. (2006) 'Heroines, villains and victims: older people's perceptions of others', *Ageing and Society*, vol 26, no 6, pp 883–900.

Union of Shop, Distributive and Allied Workers (2006) *Agency and Migrant Workers*, Manchester: USDAW.

van den Broek, D. (2003) 'Selling human services: public sector rationalisation and the call centre labour process', *Australian Bulletin of Labour*, vol 29, no 3, pp 236–52.

Waine, B. (2000) 'Managing performance through pay', in J. Clarke, S. Gewirtz and E. McLaughlin (eds) *New Managerialism, New Welfare?* London: Sage.

Wallace, C.M. (1999) 'The sacrificial strategy', Paper presented at a workshop at the Centre for Economic Performance, London: London School of Economics and Political Science.

Warburton, R.W. (1988) *Key Indicators of Local Authority Social Services: A Demonstration Package*, London: Social Services Inspectorate.

Warde, A. (1994) 'Consumers, consumption and post-Fordism', in R. Burrows and D. Loader (eds) *Towards a Post-Fordist Welfare State?*, London: Routledge.

Ware, T., Matosevic, T., Hardy, B., Knapp, M., Kendall, J. and Farder, J. (2003) 'Commissioning care services for older people in England and Wales: the view from care managers, users and carers', *Ageing and Society*, vol 23, no 4, pp 411–28.

Watson, D. and West, J. (2006) *Social Work Process and Practice. Approaches, Knowledge and Skills*, Basingstoke: Palgrave Macmillan.

Webb, D. (1996) 'Regulations for radicals. The state, CCETSW and the academy', in N. Parton (ed) *Social Theory, Social Change and Social Work*, London: Routledge.

Westhues, A., LaFrance, J. and Schmidt, G. (2001) 'A SWOT analysis of social work education in Canada', *Social Work Education*, vol 20, no 1, pp 35–56.

White, V. (1991) 'Being a feminist in statutory social work: prescriptions and practice', Coventry: University of Warwick, unpublished MA dissertation.

White, V. (2006) *The State of Feminist Social Work*, London: Routledge

White, V. and Harris, J. (1999) 'Social Europe, social citizenship and social work', *European Journal of Social Work*, vol 2, no 1, pp 3–14.

White, V. and Harris, J. (2001) *Developing Good Practice in Community Care: Partnership and Participation*, London: Jessica Kingsley.

White, V. and Harris, J. (2004) *Developing Good Practice in Children's Services*, London: Jessica Kingsley.

White, V. and Harris, J. (2007) 'Management', in M. Lymbery and K. Postle (eds) *Social Work: A Companion to Learning*, London: Sage.

Wilding, P. (1992) 'The British welfare state: Thatcherism's enduring legacy', *Policy and Politics*, vol 20, no 3, pp 201–12.

Williams, F. (1994) 'Social relations, welfare and the post-Fordist debate', in R. Burrows and B. Loader (eds) *Towards a Post-Fordist Welfare State*, London: Routledge.

Wistow, G., Waddington, E. and Godfrey, M. (2003) *Living Well in Later Life: From Prevention to Promotion*, Leeds: Nuffield Institute for Health.

Woolas, P. (2006) 'Driving improvement: beyond CPA', Speech to the Local Government Association conference, 28 February, www.odpm.gov.uk/index.asp?id=1163896

Young, J. and Stevenson, J. (2006) 'Intermediate care in England: where next?', *Age and Ageing*, vol 35, no 4, pp 339–41.

Index